Finishes and Finishing
Techniques

Finishes and Finishing Techniques

The Best Of Fine WoodWorking

The Taunton Press

Cover photo by Tsuyoshi Ito

TAUNTON
BOOKS & VIDEOS

...by fellow enthusiasts

©1991 by The Taunton Press, Inc.
All rights reserved

First printing: July 1991

A FINE WOODWORKING Book

FINE WOODWORKING® is a trademark of The Taunton Press, Inc.,
registered in the U.S. Patent and Trademark Office.

The Taunton Press, Inc.
63 South Main Street
Box 5506
Newtown, Connecticut 06470-5506

Library of Congress Cataloging-in-Publication Data

The Best of fine woodworking. Finishes and finishing techniques :
    40 articles / selected by the editors of Fine woodworking
    magazine.
      p. cm.
     "A Fine woodworking book"—T.p. verso.
     Includes index.
     ISBN 1-56158-003-1
     1. Wood finishing.   I. Fine woodworking.
     II. Title: Finishes and finishing techniques.
TT325.B564   1991   91-17308
684.1'043–dc20   CIP

Contents

Introduction

Shortly after I realized it would take a lifetime to master woodworking, I discovered that another lifetime would be required to learn what I needed to know about finishing. Wood finishing is an alchemical combination of science, craft and art, and as such, is often a source of confusion for the average woodworker.

If the truth be told, most of us don't worry about finishing until it's time to do it—and then we have plenty to worry about, such as which finish to use, how to apply it and what effect it will have on the project that's taken countless hours to build. Unfortunately, there are no easy answers to these questions. Each type of finish has certain advantages and disadvantages, and to choose the right one for a given project you need the experience of someone who has done more than just read the manufacturer's instructions on the can.

The 40 articles in this book, collected from back issues of *Fine Woodworking* magazine, were written by people who understand finishing. They know about the tools and methods for applying the finish; the relative strengths and weaknesses of various compounds, including their hazards; how to prepare the wood for finishing; how to handle tints, dyes and stains to achieve special effects; and how to rub out the finish to the luster that's right for your prized project.

It might be too late for you and me to devote our lives to mastering the art of finishing, but it's not too late to learn from those who have.

—Jim Boesel, executive editor

The "Best of *Fine Woodworking*" series spans issues 46 through 80 of *Fine Woodworking* magazine, originally published between mid-1984 and the end of 1989. *(Finishes and Finishing Techniques* contains five articles from later issues.) There is no duplication between these books and the popular *"Fine Woodworking* on..." series. A footnote with each article gives the date of first publication; product availability, suppliers' addresses and prices may have changed since then.

Chemical Hazards of Woodworking

What you don't know can hurt you

by Theodore J. Fink, M.D.

These products, representative of those found in many woodworkers' shops, all contain hazardous substances. While they all have warning labels of potential dangers, many reveal the contents only as petroleum distillates, which can include a number of dangerous solvents.

All too often woodworkers are needlessly exposed to toxic levels of various chemicals. Sometimes this happens because workers ignore warning labels, but frequently it's because they just don't know enough about the chemical products they use to appreciate the risks involved and take adequate precautions. Toxic chemicals are found in a variety of woodshop supplies, including adhesives, paints and varnishes. By presenting an overview of the basic principles of chemical toxicity, I hope to drive home the single most important lesson for woodworkers: protect yourself—it is infinitely better to prevent an illness or injury than it is to treat it after it occurs.

The chart in figure 1 on pp. 10-11 should help you identify the products containing potentially harmful chemicals, clarify the risks associated with the most common toxins and choose safer alternatives. The following discussion of chemical hazards and how toxins are absorbed into the body will also help you understand the information presented in the chart.

Hazards of organic solvents—Toxicity refers to a chemical's, or solvent's, ability to produce a harmful effect on a biological system, in this case, your body. These harmful chemicals, called toxins, often target specific tissues. Benzene, for example, attacks the blood-forming elements in bone marrow. Any chemical can produce a toxic effect. Some do so with a single, brief contact, often called an acute exposure; others require chronic exposure: repeated or prolonged contact. The crucial point is that there are no harmless chemicals, only relatively safe ways of using them.

All chemicals can produce both acute and chronic effects. Acute effects generally happen quickly and the illness lasts only a short time. If exposure is low enough, the effects are reversible. More intense acute exposures can cause permanent damage, even death. Chronic effects, on the other hand, may not be apparent until after weeks, months or even years of repeated exposures, and they are usually permanent and irreversible. Some people do not realize that they are being harmed because early symptoms of these effects can vary greatly depending on the type of substance, exposure level and individual sensitivity.

Both acute and chronic effects may be localized or affect the entire system. A local reaction would be something like redness or blistering of the skin at the point of contact. A systemic reaction occurs when the chemical is absorbed into the bloodstream. Harmful effects may occur anywhere in the body, but the toxins in solvents most often affect the central nervous system (CNS). Generally, the chemicals depress the CNS, but some substances, like xylene, may produce agitated hyperactive behavior. Symptoms of depression of the CNS can include dizziness, headache, nausea, confusion, sleepiness, incoordination or irrational behavior.

In the workshop, these symptoms not only decrease productivity, but also lead to higher injury rates. However, the damage can be more far-reaching. The brain has very limited regenerative capacity, so once any neurologic deficit is established, it usually becomes permanent. Very high chronic exposure to solvents can cause dementia, resulting in impairments of judgment, insight, orientation and memory. This raises a question that is currently being studied: Can repetitive, low-level exposures cause premature aging and reduce mental and physical abilities? Until there is an answer, it is wise to minimize exposure to solvents.

How chemicals get into the body—Chemical toxins can be absorbed into the blood system through the respiratory and digestive tracts as well as through the skin. Many solvents are very volatile and quickly transform into vapors, so inhalation is the main method of absorption. The lung tissue exposed to vapors during inhalation is enormous, totaling about two acres of surface area in the lungs' air sacs. Relative volatility of various solvents, determined by measuring the vapor pressure (VP) of the evaporating liquid in millimeters of mercury (mm Hg), is shown in the chart on the following two pages. The more volatile a solvent, the higher the VP, and the more quickly it will fill a room with vapors. Bear in mind that the VP measurements shown were made at 68°F; any increase in temperature will also increase the volatility.

On the body, a thick outer layer of skin generally forms an effective barrier to most materials. Despite this, many of the organic solvents in wood finishing products, such as methylene chloride or isopropyl alcohol, can penetrate the skin and cause dermatitis and exacerbate the absorption. Also, chemicals are absorbed quickly through cuts and abrasions or areas inflamed by eczema or psoriasis.

Workshop chemicals, like those shown in the photo on the facing page, gain entry to the digestive system in two ways. Consumption of food, drink or cigarettes brought into the shop and contaminated by chemicals is the most common process. A not-so-obvious method involves the lungs. The inner walls of the respiratory tract are protected by a thin fluid layer, which is moved upward by small, constantly moving hairs (cilia). Once the inhaled particles reach the throat, they are swallowed, and then any chemicals in the particles are absorbed by the stomach and intestines. This situation can easily develop when you don't wear a dust mask while sanding out finishes.

Chemical classifications – Organic solvents can be combined into groups of similar chemical structures and solvent characteristics, which simply means you can generally use a solvent within a group as a substitute for another solvent from that same group. The groups of solvents that woodworkers encounter most frequently include aliphatic hydrocarbons, chlorinated hydrocarbons, aromatic hydrocarbons, alcohols and ketones, as outlined in figure 1.

Aliphatic hydrocarbons are often petroleum derivatives, such as naphthas, paraffins, mineral spirits, n-hexane and kerosene. From the chart, you can see that n-hexane, found in adhesives, varnishes and seed-oil extracts, is not only extremely flammable, but can cause peripheral nerve damage resulting in weakness of hands and feet. One of the safest solvents for woodworkers is odorless paint thinner, which is mineral spirits or VM&P (varnish maker's and painter's) naphtha with the aromatic hydrocarbons removed.

Chlorinated hydrocarbons are identified by the "chloro" or "chloride" in their names. These are good solvents for many paints and varnishes because they are nonflammable, but most are now known to be very toxic, cause damage to the liver and contain carcinogens. For example, methylene chloride, a common ingredient in paint strippers, forms carbon monoxide in the body and has been shown to cause cancer in laboratory animals. The government has banned its use in cosmetics and further restrictions are expected soon.

Aromatic hydrocarbons show up in a variety of products, from lacquer thinners and strippers to adhesives and tung oils, and present special hazards as a class. The most toxic, benzene, causes destruction of the blood-forming elements and may wipe out these cells, causing aplastic anemia (bone marrow destruction), or result in leukemia. You are not likely to encounter benzene due to current governmental restrictions; however, some of the older products on the back of your shelf may contain this solvent, and these should be disposed of properly through your local environmental agencies. Toluene and xylene have been widely used as benzene substitutes, and although not as hazardous as benzene, they can still cause serious toxic effects, as shown in the chart.

Among the safest and most important classes of solvents are alcohols, which are found in many types of finishes and other products. Methanol or wood alcohol, which is by far the most toxic of this group, can damage the optic nerve and cause blind-

Further reading

Artist Beware by Michael McCann. Watson-Guptil Publications, New York, NY; 1979.

A large variety of good information is available from the Center for Safety in the Arts, 5 Beekman St., New York, NY 10038.

Chemical Hazards of the Workplace by Nick Proctor and James Hughes. J. B. Lippincott Co., Philadelphia, PA; 1978.

Handbook of Organic Industrial Solvents (LC-TG-07-683) by Alliance of American Insurers, 1501 Woodfield Rd., Suite 400 W., Schaumburg, IL 60173; 1987.

Industrial Toxicology by Phillip Williams and James Burson. Van Nostrand Reinhold Co., New York, NY; 1985.

"A Distinct Pattern of Personality Disturbance Following Exposure to Mixtures of Organic Solvents," *Journal of Occupational Medicine,* Vol. 31, No. 9, (Sept. 1989), by Lisa Morrow, Ph.D., et al.

"Neurobehavioral Effects of Solvents," *Journal of Occupational Medicine,* Vol. 30, No. 2, (Feb. 1988), by Edward L. Baker, M.D., et al.

Occupational Diseases by U.S. Department of Health, Education and Welfare, U.S. Government Printing Office, Washington, DC; 1977.

Organic Solvent Neurotoxicity (Publication No. 87-104); March 31, 1987 and *Pocket Guide to Chemical Hazards* (Publication No. 85-114); September, 1985, by U.S. Department of Health and Human Services, National Institute for Occupational Safety and Health (NIOSH), 4676 Columbia Parkway, Cincinnati, OH 45226.

Solvents in Museum Conservation Labs by Center for Safety in the Arts, 5 Beekman St., New York, NY 10038; 1985.

Threshold Limit Values and Biological Exposure Indices for 1987-88 by American Conference of Governmental Industrial Hygienists (AC-GIH), 6500 Glenway Ave., Building D-7, Cincinnati, OH 45211; 1987.

ness. Ethanol, or grain alcohol, is the least toxic alcohol and has about half the depressant effect on the brain and spinal cord as isopropanol (isopropyl or rubbing alcohol).

Ketones are commonly used in quick-drying finishes and have become more widespread with the increased popularity of vinyl resin finishes. Of the many ketones, three commonly cited on labels are acetone, methyl ethyl ketone and methyl isobutyl ketone. Methyl n-butyl ketone, which you might find in an old product, has generally been banned because it can cause severe nerve damage, the symptoms of which appear gradually over weeks or months and consist of numbness, tingling and weakness in hands and feet. The safest solvent of the ketone group is acetone; however, it is extremely flammable and a real fire or explosion hazard.

Other hazardous materials – Adhesives represent another large group of potentially hazardous materials, as illustrated in figure 2 on p. 12, and should be treated with caution. Some are dangerous because of the flammability of their solvents, such as nitro cellulose cement with 39% acetone and contact cements with various volatile hydrocarbons. Other common adhesives that have lower toxicity are white glue, also known as polyvinyl acetate (PVA), yellow glue (modified PVA/aliphatic resins), hide glue, hot-melt glue (hydrocarbon resin: 50%, ethylene vinyl or acetate copolymer: 45%, wax: 5%) and wet casein glue. These may, however, cause skin irritation or skin allergies. And casein dust, from mixing dry powders, may irritate the upper respiratory tract.

Limiting toxic exposure – Always choose the least-toxic solvent that will get the job done, and always follow the manufacturer's recommendations for safe use. Product labels are now more detailed than ever and should always be your first source of toxicity information. All warnings on labels, such as "use in well-ventilated

(continued on p. 12)

FIG. 1: HAZARDOUS CHEMICALS USED IN WOODWORKING

Solvent (synonym)	Where Used	Toxicity [1] * TLV (Threshold Limit Value) in PPM	Flammability [2] * Combustability FP (Flash Point) in Degrees F	Volatility * Vapor Pressure in mm Hg
Aliphatic Hydrocarbons				
n-Hexane (Skellysolve-B)	Spray adhesives and fixatives, fast-drying cements, rubber and contact cements, inks, varnishes, seed-oil extracts, diluent	50	-7	124
Petroleum naphtha	Plastic wood filler, wax, lacquer thinner, petroleum distillates	100	-50	40
VM&P naphtha (varnish maker's and painter's)	Quick-drying thinner, degreaser, varnish, lacquer thinner, petroleum distillates	300	20-55	2-20
Mineral spirits	General-purpose thinner, degreaser, brush cleaner, petroleum distillates, plastic wood filler, varnish, tung oils	200	86-105	0.8
Kerosene	Petroleum distillates, solvents, thinners	None	100-165	Varies
Chlorinated Hydrocarbons				
Methylene chloride (dichloromethane, methylene dichloride)	Paint and varnish removers, furniture refinishers, contact cement, aerosols, urethane foam, adhesives, paint	50**	None [3]	350
Aromatic Hydrocarbons				
Benzene (benzol, cyclohexatriene)	Paint stripper, petroleum distillates, lacquer thinner	10	12	75
Toluene (toluol, methyl benzene)	Petroleum distillates, polyurethane lacquer thinners, inks, adhesives, spray products, modified tung oil, furniture refinishers, strippers, plastic wood putty	100	40	22
Xylene (xylol, dimethyl-benzene)	Petroleum distillates, dewaxer, degreaser, substitute for benzene	100	81	9
Alcohols				
Ethanol (denatured, ethyl or grain alcohol)	Shellac, spirit stain, resorcinol	1000	55	43
Methanol (wood or methyl alcohol, wood spirit)	Paints, varnishes, lacquers, dyes, furniture refinishers, strippers, wood hardener	200	52	97
Isopropanol (isopropyl or rubbing alcohol)	Plastic wood fillers, lacquer thinner, surface cleaner	400	53	33
Ketones				
Acetone (dimethyl ketone, 2-propanone, ketone propane)	Strippers, wood fillers, lacquer thinner, wood hardener, diluent for epoxy and polyester resins and plastic cements, cleaner	750	1.4	266
Methyl ethyl ketone (MEK, 2-butanone)	Lacquer thinner, plastic wood filler, plastic cements, spray can products	200	21	70
Methyl n-butyl ketone (MBK, 2-hexanone)	Fast-drying finishes, plastic wood fillers, aerosols, lacquers, nitrocellulose, resins, oils, waxes, varnish and lacquer removers	5	77	3
Methyl isobutyl ketone (MIBK, hexone)	Plastic wood fillers, spray can products, plastic cements	50	73	15
Others				
Gum turpentine/wood turpentine	Waxes, finishes, tung oils, general-purpose thinner, brush cleaner, degreaser	100	95	5
Methyl cellosolve*** (Glycol ether, 2-methoxy ethanol, many others)	Degreasers, cleaners (water based), lacquer thinners, dyestuffs, some latex paints, spray products, epoxies	5	107	6
Diglycidyl ether*** (DGE, 2-epoxypropyl ether)	Epoxies (especially liquid), some other plastic resin systems	0.1	147	.09

1. Toxicity—highly toxic: less than 101 PPM; moderately toxic: 101 to 500 PPM; slightly toxic: more than 500 PPM
2. Flammability—extremely flammable: less than 21°F; flammable: 21°F to 99°F; combustible: 100°F to 150°F
3. No FP, but flammable when vapors reach 14% to 22% by volume of air at 77°F.

*See further discussion of these values in the sidebar on p. 13.
**Indicated for change based on its cancer status.
***First in a large class of chemicals that have similar uses and hazards.

Usual Route of Absorption L=Lung S=Skin	Comments	Organs Affected	Symptoms
L, S	Can damage PNS and cause CNS depression.	Skin, URT, CNS, PNS	Irr., peripheral neuropathy, numbness and weakness of hands and feet, headache, nausea, loss of balance, weight loss, fatigue
L, S	Mixture of aliphatic hydrocarbons may contain benzene.	Eyes, skin, URT, CNS, lungs	Irr., narcosis, derm.
L, S	One of the least toxic.	Skin, CNS, lungs	Irr., derm., narcosis
L, S	Try to use odorless paint thinner or mineral spirits with reduced aromatics.	Skin, CNS, lungs, eyes	Irr., derm., narcosis
S	—	Skin, lungs, URT, CNS	Irr., narcosis, lung hemorrhage, chemical pneumonia
L, S	Try to avoid as a class. May produce phosgene gas and other toxins when heated or exposed to ultraviolet radiation. Most are suspected carcinogens. Forms carbon monoxide in blood and stresses heart. Reaches maximum levels 3 to 4 hours after exposure. Organic vapor cartridge not approved for use with methylene chloride. Suspected carcinogen. Often used with methanol, which increases toxicity.	Skin, URT, CNS, CVS, liver	Irr., narcosis, numbness of limbs, heart palpitations, headache, shortness of breath, angina, heart attack
	Try to avoid as a class.		
L, S	Do not use: Carcinogen, absorbed through skin.	Skin, CNS, blood, chromo-somes, liver, kidneys	Derm., narcosis, leukemia, aplastic anemia
L, S	Recently identified by EPA as top air pollutant and is targeted for regulation.	CNS, liver, URT, kidneys, skin, eyes	Irr., derm., narcosis, muscular weakness, liver and kidney damage
L, S	May cause CNS excitation.	Skin, URT, CNS, liver, GI, blood	Irr., narcosis, derm., stomach pain, incoordination, staggering gait
	One of the safer classes.		
L	Least toxic in class.	Eyes, nose, skin, CNS	Irr., headache, drowsiness, fatigue
L, S	Use ethanol when possible. Toxic effects due to the metabolic products formaldehyde and formic acid, occurring primarily from ingestion or repeated high-level exposure. No approved filtering medium.	Eyes, skin, CNS	Blurred or double vision, loss of peripheral vision, optic nerve damage, blindness, narcosis
L, S	One of least toxic in class.	Eyes, skin, CNS	Irr., headache, drowsiness
L	Least toxic in class. Principal hazard is fire and explosion.	Skin, URT, CNS, eyes	Irr., narcosis, derm.
L	—	Skin, URT, CNS	Irr., narcosis, derm.
L, S	Can cause PNS damage after 4 to 8 weeks' exposure.	Skin, URT, CNS, PNS	Numbness and weakness of hands and feet, narcosis
L	—	Skin, URT, CNS	Irr., narcosis, derm.
L, S	Use mineral spirits or odorless paint thinner when possible.	Skin, eyes, URT, lungs, CNS, kidneys, bladder	Irr., derm., sensitization, pulmonary edema, narcosis, convulsions, kidney and bladder damage, fever
L, S	Do not use: Absorbed rapidly through skin, causes birth defects in animals, penetrates many gloves. Check with manufacturer for appropriate protection.	Skin, eyes, URT, CNS, kidneys, liver, reproductive system, blood	Headache, irr., narcosis, renal failure, pulmonary edema, fatigue, anemia
L, S	Do not use: Absorbed rapidly through skin, causes birth defects in animals, affects bone marrow, penetrates many gloves. Check with manufacturer for appropriate protection.	Skin, eyes, CNS, reproductive system	Irr., allergies

Abbreviations:
CNS—central nervous system
CVS—cardiovascular system
derm.—dermatitis
GI—gastrointestinal system
Irr.—irritating to eyes, skin and/or URT
PNS—peripheral nervous system
URT—upper respiratory tract

FIG. 2: ADHESIVES

	Hazardous Solvents or Materials	Comments	Organs Affected	Symptoms
Nitro cellulose cement	Acetone (39%)	See figure 1.	–	–
Casein (dry powder)	Strong alkalis	Irritating dust possible when mixing powders.	URT, lungs, eyes	Irr.
Plastic resin glues (urea-formaldehyde) and resorcinol	Formaldehyde	Out-gases formaldehyde, a suspected carcinogen. Avoid breathing powder and fumes. Wear appropriate gloves. Fumes may arise from machining plywood. Formaldehyde has a TLV of 1 PPM.	Skin, eyes, URT	Irr., bronchospasm, pulmonary irr., derm., nausea, vomiting
Epoxy hardeners and resins	Aliphatic amine, diglycidyl ethers	Main toxicity is due to extremely alkaline amine curing agents, which are highly caustic. Uncured liquid resins are irritants and sensitizers. See figure 1.	Skin, URT, eyes	Irr., burns, allergies
Instant glues and accelerators	Cyanoacrylate, freon	Bonds skin, which requires solvent (acetone) to separate.	Skin, URT	Irr., pulmonary edema, headaches
Acrylic plastic glues	Methyl methacrylate	TLV is 100 PPM.	Skin, URT, eyes	Irr., mucous membrane irr.
Contact cements	Aliphatic and chlorinated hydrocarbons	All are toxic, solvent based and most are highly flammable. See figure 1. Nonflammable cements contain 1-1-1 trichloroethane (methyl chloroform).	Skin, CNS, CVS, eyes, liver	Headache, irr., derm., CNS depression, narcosis, more. See figure 1.

area," should not be taken lightly. For more detailed information on the safe use and storage of a particular product, request a material safety data sheet (MSDS), which is outlined on the facing page. The new United States and Canadian right-to-know laws require employers make MSDSs available to employees working with potentially hazardous materials. MSDSs are also available from either the product manufacturer or the local distributor.

Since chemical toxicities usually occur through inhalation and skin contact, it is important that such exposures be minimized to prevent injury. Provide adequate ventilation by exhausting fumes away from you to the outdoors with a source of fresh replacement air. This can be facilitated by placing a fan to your side, blowing across the work area toward the means of exhaust. A fan blowing from behind can actually create a low-pressure area directly in front of your body, drawing the toxic fumes toward you.

In addition to ventilation, most manufacturers recommend using a respirator, which is available in a variety of styles from a low-cost disposable mask to a full-coverage self-contained breathing apparatus that has numerous filtering media designed to handle specific toxins and concentrations. Consult the package, MSDS or manufacturer for the protection appropriate for your situation. Many solvents can be effectively filtered through activated charcoal. However, check with manufacturers first, because there are no approved filters or cartridges for certain solvents, such as methanol and methylene chloride. There also aren't any that will protect you from very high concentrations of chemicals, such as from a spill, which cause cartridges to saturate quickly. Even when exposed to low concentrations of contaminants, activated cartridges have a limited life span. Again, consult the manufacturers for the cartridges' life span, keep track of the time you wear them and seal them in a plastic bag when not in use because exposure to air decreases their useful life span.

Effective function of a respirator depends on proper fit, which can be checked by placing your hands over the cartridges, sucking in and holding your breath. If there is an air leak, the mask will return to its original shape. The Occupational Safety and Health Administration (OSHA) requires more formal fit tests and employers should check with their respirator supplier for more details. Because beards prevent masks from sealing tightly to the face, OSHA usually requires bearded employees to wear an "air-powered" respirator, which supplies filtered air under pressure to a mask or hood. Home or self-employed bearded users can try smearing their beards with petroleum jelly for a tighter seal. If the chemical you use is also an eye irritant, use a full-face respirator that covers the eyes.

To prevent direct skin contact, wear gloves specified by the chemical manufacturer. This is important even when using a non-toxic finish because it may require using a solvent, such as mineral spirits, to remove the finish from your hands. Barrier creams, also a skin protection method, are less effective and should only be used to resist occasional splashes rather than direct contact. Try to avoid using solvents to clean your hands and be sure to wash with plenty of soap and water after handling any solvents.

All of these precautions are meant for healthy adults. You may need to take extra precautions if you have heart disease, lung problems, chronic illnesses or disabilities, or take medication. For example, methylene chloride should be particularly avoided by someone with coronary heart disease. Children and the elderly also are at greater risk from solvents and chemicals. Children under 13 should not work with solvent-containing materials. At greatest risk is the fetus. From before conception through cessation of breast feeding, women should avoid exposure to all chemicals. Also, chemical exposures should be avoided by men prior to conception to reduce the risk of genetic abnormalities.

All woodworkers should consult their physicians anytime they experience any of the previously mentioned symptoms. Always be prepared to help physicians make a diagnosis by telling them the chemicals you use and that you are exposed to wood dust. And even if you have no symptoms, have regular checkups. □

Dr. Fink is an internist in Shelburne, Vt., a consulting physician for Digital Equipment Corp. and an amateur woodworker.

Reading a manufacturer's safety sheet

by Charley Robinson

A material safety data sheet (MSDS) provides helpful information for working safely with potentially hazardous chemicals. Employers must have an MSDS for products that contain hazardous ingredients, but you should be able to obtain one from chemical suppliers or a manufacturer's technical or customer service department. Some companies are now including an 800 hot-line number on the product label that you can call for additional information.

All MSDSs must contain certain information. OSHA has suggested a format, as shown below, but many manufacturers develop their own style. Generally, information is organized in sections and is self-explanatory. The following terms and information will help you further understand the MSDS.

Identity: The product trade name, chemical name and usual synonyms.

Section II—Hazardous ingredients: Each hazardous ingredient comprising more than 1% of the total, or more than 0.1% if carcinogenic, must be listed, except those ingredients the manufacturer claims are a trade secret. Any known health hazards of secret ingredients must be disclosed in a later section. Many ingredients, especially trade secrets, have never been studied, so their risks are unknown. Ingredients, such as

formaldehyde, that can produce toxic effects at levels less than 0.1% must be indicated. This section indicates OSHA-permissible exposure levels (PEL) and short-term exposure limits (STEL), which are OSHA-enforced. Also, the threshold limit values (TLVs), updated annually by the American Conference of Governmental Industrial Hygienists (ACGIH), are included. All of these values are expressed in parts per million (PPM). The PEL and TLV numbers indicate the airborne contaminant levels that most healthy, adult workers may be repeatedly exposed to for 8 hours a day, 40 hours a week without adverse effect. The STEL number is the maximum concentration of contaminant that a worker should be exposed to for a specified time, usually 15 minutes.

Section III—Physical data: An essential piece of information is the vapor pressure (VP), which indicates the force exerted by the evaporated vapors on the atmosphere directly above the liquid, usually in millimeters of mercury (mm Hg). The greater the vapor pressure, the more volatile the liquid.

Section IV—Fire and explosion hazards: The flash point (FP) is the lowest temperature at which vapors above a volatile combustible substance ignite in air when exposed to flame. Materials with a FP below 100°F are dangerous because a spark or stat-

ic electricity can cause a fire or explosion. No FP means the material is nonflammable. The appropriate fire extinguisher and special fire hazards, such as spontaneous combustion from linseed oil-soaked rags, should also be specified here.

Section V—Reactivity data: A chemical's stability, its likelihood of reacting with other materials and all special cautions to be taken, as shown on the form, are revealed here. Don't mix chemicals without reading this section.

Section VI—Health hazard data: This section usually specifies how chemicals normally enter the body, the acute effects of exposure, signs and symptoms of exposure, and emergency and first-aid procedures. A manufacturer must identify all ingredients classified as a carcinogen by OSHA, the International Agency for Research on Cancer (IARC) or the National Toxicology Program (NTP).

Section VIII—Control measures: Because of manufacturers' concerns for liability, protective measures are often geared to the worst possible circumstances, such as a large spill. A manufacturer might suggest, for example, using a self-contained breathing apparatus when any approved respirator would suffice for limited exposure. □

Charley Robinson is Assistant Editor at FWW.

Material Safety Data Sheet
May be used to comply with OSHA's Hazard Communication Standard, 29 CFR 1910.1200. Standard must be consulted for specific requirements.

U.S. Department of Labor
Occupational Safety and Health Administration
(Non-Mandatory Form)
Form Approved
OMB No. 1218-0072

IDENTITY (As Used on Label and List)

Note: Blank spaces are not permitted. If any item is not applicable, or no information is available, the space must be marked to indicate that.

Section I

Manufacturer's Name	Emergency Telephone Number
Address (Number, Street, City, State, and ZIP Code)	Telephone Number for Information
	Date Prepared
	Signature of Preparer (optional)

Section II — Hazardous Ingredients/Identity Information

Hazardous Components (Specific Chemical Identity; Common Name(s))	OSHA PEL	ACGIH TLV	Other Limits Recommended	% (optional)

Section III — Physical/Chemical Characteristics

Boiling Point		Specific Gravity (H₂O = 1)	
Vapor Pressure (mm Hg.)		Melting Point	
Vapor Density (AIR = 1)		Evaporation Rate (Butyl Acetate = 1)	
Solubility in Water			
Appearance and Odor			

Section IV — Fire and Explosion Hazard Data

Flash Point (Method Used)		Flammable Limits	LEL	UEL
Extinguishing Media				
Special Fire Fighting Procedures				
Unusual Fire and Explosion Hazards				

(Reproduce locally)

OSHA 174, Sept. 1985

F-5

Section V — Reactivity Data

Stability	Unstable	Conditions to Avoid
	Stable	
Incompatibility (Materials to Avoid)		
Hazardous Decomposition or Byproducts		
Hazardous Polymerization	May Occur	Conditions to Avoid
	Will Not Occur	

Section VI — Health Hazard Data

Route(s) of Entry:	Inhalation?	Skin?	Ingestion?
Health Hazards (Acute and Chronic)			
Carcinogenicity:	NTP?	IARC Monographs?	OSHA Regulated?
Signs and Symptoms of Exposure			
Medical Conditions Generally Aggravated by Exposure			
Emergency and First Aid Procedures			

Section VII — Precautions for Safe Handling and Use

Steps to Be Taken in Case Material Is Released or Spilled
Waste Disposal Method
Precautions to Be Taken in Handling and Storing
Other Precautions

Section VIII — Control Measures

Respiratory Protection (Specify Type)			
Ventilation	Local Exhaust		Special
	Mechanical (General)		Other
Protective Gloves		Eye Protection	
Other Protective Clothing or Equipment			
Work/Hygienic Practices			

Page 2

F-6

Evaluating Wood Finishes
Shop methods for gauging durability

by Tim B. Inman

Comparing wood finishes for durability requires a few simple tools and an objective approach. The 5-in. by 12-in. samples above are prepared with each finish to be tested and then cut into four pieces and labeled 1 through 4 with the finish's name.

How do you compare the protective qualities of one wood finish to another? Do you rely on the manufacturer's literature or advice from sales clerks or company representatives? Reports from independent testing laboratories are often scarce or unavailable, so picking the right product can become a guessing game. But you can evaluate finishes in your own shop with a little knowledge of scientific techniques and simple, inexpensive supplies and equipment. If you can rate products objectively, you can match a finish to a job's requirement.

A wood finish protects by shielding itself as well as the wood from injury. To evaluate these protective qualities, you must develop a battery of tests. Generally, I determine what protective qualities are desired, identify what damages the finish, devise tests to simulate these forces and observe how well the finish stands up. I concentrate on how well a finish adheres, its distortion, abrasion and solvent resistance, and its sensitivity to temperature changes. These factors are reliably and fairly evaluated with the tests I'll describe here. Since evaluating application characteristics and aesthetic qualities often requires subjective responses that are difficult or impossible to test scientifically, I won't cover those subjects here.

Begin testing by carefully preparing identical samples of wood and applying the finishes to be tested. To render objective results, apply each finish in the same environment and with identical tools and methods. Each sample panel should be about 5 in. by 12 in. and from the same area of a board. After finishing the panels with a different product, cut them into four, 3-in. by 5-in. pieces, label each with the name of the finish applied and number them 1, 2, 3 and 4.

In addition to standard shop and home equipment, you'll need a 10-power hand lens, a 1-in. steel ball and sandblasting abrasive. As you perform each of the tests, tally the ratings on a scorecard, like the one I developed on the facing page. Circle the appropriate score (1 to 5) for individual tests and then total them for a category score. If you're testing finishes for general-purpose applications, multiply each category score by one. If you're testing finishes that must perform a specific duty and a category is especially important, as heat sensitivity is for dining-table finishes, weight that category

more by multiplying its score by two. After you total the results, compare one finish's total score to another's. The finish that scores the highest should perform the best. Use one scorecard per finish and be sure to compare equally weighted scorecards only.

Adhesion refers to a film's ability to stick to itself and the wood without peeling or flaking off. Good adhesion is an indication of a film's ability to withstand further damage after an injury, and you won't be able to test other protective qualities if the film won't adhere to the samples.

You can evaluate adhesion with a simple *cross-cut* test. Cut a grid on a 1-in.-square area at one end of the number 1 samples of each product, disrupting film bonding enough to allow the film to flake off of sections with poor adhesion. Using a razor knife and straightedge, cut 11 parallel lines with the grain and 11 more across the grain. Apply uniform pressure with a sharp blade to produce a grid with 100, $\frac{1}{10}$-in. squares, as shown in the top photo on the facing page. The cuts should be just deep enough to go all the way through the finish into the wood.

Now, study the finish in the grid with a hand lens and rate what you see on a 1 (failure) through 5 (successful) scale. Rate 1 if the finish has completely flaked off in many squares; 3 if there's considerable loss at the intersection of the cuts, without the loss of whole squares; and 5 if there was little or no adhesion failure due to the cuts. Next, add extra punishment by scrubbing the grid with a toothbrush, using an equal number of strokes in each direction on each sample. Repeat your observations and again rate the bonding performance on a scale of 1 through 5.

The "acid test" for adhesion is to see if the finish film can be pulled off with adhesive tape. Cover the grid with sticky tape, firmly press it down and then pull it straight up with a slow, steady motion. Again, record the results on a 1 through 5 scale.

Distortion resistance is a finish's ability to move and bend, to resist impacts and gouges that might break its adhesion. Although a harder finish might seem more durable, you'll see that it can be

From *Fine Woodworking* magazine (May 1990) 82:62-64

brittle and break apart when distorted or injured. But if the film is too soft, it offers little protection from scrapes or gouges.

You can evaluate a film's resistance to scratches as well as its hardness with the *pencil-scratch* test: attempting to scratch the finish with pencils of known hardness. Use common drafting pencils because their leads are graded by hardness on a scale from 9H, which is like nails, to 6B, which is as soft as charcoal. Only five leads—6H, 4H, HB, 2B and 5B—are needed for this test. Sharpen all the pencils uniformly and with equal pressure from each pencil, scribe a line on the end of the number 1 samples. Be sure to save the middle of these samples for another test. Use successively harder leads, holding each pencil at the same angle, and then record your observations. Rate hardness according to the hardest pencil that scratches the finish, as shown in the bottom photo. Rate 1 if the 5B scratches through, 2 if the 2B does, 3 for the HB, 4 for the 4H and 5 for the 6H.

The *mandrel-bend* test evaluates a film's ability to flex without breaking. Flexibility enables a finish to withstand normal wood movement due to temperature and humidity fluctuations. The test reveals how a film bends over five wooden dowels (mandrels): 1 in. dia., ¾ in. dia., ½ in. dia., ¼ in. dia. and ⅛ in. dia. In order to bend the film enough to cause it to break, apply the finish to aluminum foil, putting as many coats on the foil as you did on the wood. After cutting the foil into 1-in.-wide strips, begin bending them over the largest, 1-in.-dia. dowel. Continue with each successively smaller dowel, as shown in the left photo on the following page, and use the hand lens to look for cracks or flaking. Rate the sample 1 through 5 according to the smallest dowel the finish can bend around without failure: 1 for the 1-in.-dia. dowel and 5 for the ⅛-in.-dia. dowel.

The *ball-drop* test rates a film's ability to distort, or flex, under sudden shock. Did you play with Silly Putty when you were younger? If so, you may recall that if you pull slowly, you can stretch and pull it into long strings, like bubble gum. When jerked or snapped, it breaks. Finishes are like Silly Putty: they can crack or craze when suddenly hit, even though they may flex slowly without failure.

Drop a 1-in.-dia. steel ball onto the number 2 samples from a height of 36 in. Failures are most notable at the top edge of the resultant dent (shown in the center photo on the following page). Observe the dent with a hand lens and rate the performance with the 1 through 5 scale: 1 if there are several concentric bands of cracking, perhaps with some flaking off; 3 if there's some hairline cracking, but only near the top edge of the dent; and 5 if there is no cracking.

Abrasion resistance goes hand in hand with distortion resistance, and is especially related to a film's hardness. Usually, hard films

---

Protective Performance Finish Scorecard

Finish Type: _____ Date: _____
Manufacturer: _____ Wood: _____

When testing finishes for general purposes, multiply scores by one. When testing finishes that perform a specific duty and a category is especially important, as heat sensitivity is for dining tables, weight that category more by multiplying its score by two. Compare finishes by comparing their total scores.

I. Adhesion Testing
  A. *Cross-cut* test
     1 2 3 4 5
  B. *Cross-cut* test, after brushing
     1 2 3 4 5
  C. *Cross-cut* test, after pulling tape
     1 2 3 4 5
                     Score: _____ × _____ = _____

II. Distortion Resistance
  A. *Pencil-scratch* test
     5B: 1 2B: 2 HB: 3 4H: 4 6H: 5
  B. *Mandrel-bend* test
     1 in.: 1 ¾ in.: 2 ½ in.: 3 ¼ in.: 4 ⅛ in.: 5
  C. *Ball-drop* test
     1 2 3 4 5
                     Score: _____ × _____ = _____

III. Abrasion Resistance
  A. *Sand-drop* test
     1 2 3 4 5
                     Score: _____ × _____ = _____

IV. Heat Sensitivity
  A. *Hot-drink* test
     after 10 seconds: 1 2 3 4 5
     after 1 minute: 1 2 3 4 5
     after 5 minutes: 1 2 3 4 5
  B. *Hot-casserole* test
     after 10 seconds: 1 2 3 4 5
     after 1 minute: 1 2 3 4 5
     after 5 minutes: 1 2 3 4 5
  C. *Cold-check-resistance* test
     1 2 3 4 5
                     Score: _____ × _____ = _____

V. Solvent Resistance
  A. *Solvent-drop* test, rate 1 - 5

	10 seconds	1 minute	5 minutes
1. Tap water	_____	_____	_____
2. TSP + water	_____	_____	_____
3. Vinegar	_____	_____	_____
4. Lacquer thinner	_____	_____	_____
5. Naphtha	_____	_____	_____
6. Denatured alcohol	_____	_____	_____
7. Acetone	_____	_____	_____

  B. *Acetone-rub* test
     fail: 1
     pass: 5
                     Score: _____ × _____ = _____

                     Total Score: _____

Above: Evaluate how well a film adheres to wood with the cross-cut test. Cut a grid with 100, 1/10-in. squares, and rate by counting the number of failed squares: right after making the cut, after trying to brush them off and after trying to pull them off with tape. Only the corners of eight squares have flaked off after pulling the tape on this sample; it is rated high: 4 to 5.

Below: The pencil-scratch test evaluates the film's hardness. The hardest pencil, 6H, scratched clear through the finish, a 4H just broke the surface, and the soft 5B left a mark that could be cleaned off. Rating: 3.

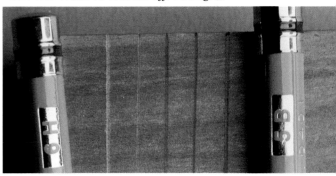

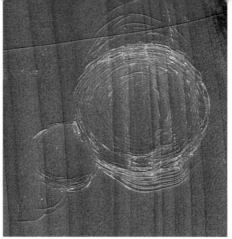

The mandrel-bend test evaluates a film's flexibility. Ratings are based on the smallest dowel that coated foil can be bent over without the film peeling. This film bent over a 1/8-in.-dia. dowel and rated high: 5.

Test distortion resistance after a sudden shock by dropping a 1-in. steel ball from 3 ft. onto a test sample. Base ratings on the amount of cracking at the edge of the resultant crater. This film rated low: 1.

Evaluate abrasion resistance by pouring sandblasting grit through a 3-ft. pipe onto a sample. Rate the finish based on the amount of abrasion. This finish is abraded nearly to the wood. Rating: 2 to 3.

are more susceptible to abrasion than soft films. Consider that people who sandblast letters into granite monuments sometimes mask off their work with rubber templates. Although the hard granite is abraded by the sand, the soft rubber is not. Similarly, soft films usually withstand grit attack better than hard films. But since hard finishes are usually more desirable than soft ones, the perfect finish film is a compromise.

The *sand-drop* test can prove a finish's abrasion resistance. Pour two cups of sandblasting grit through a funnel inserted into the top of a 36-in.-long, 1/2-in.-dia. pipe and onto the middle of the number 1 samples. Secure the pipe so its lower end is 1 in. from the surface of each sample, which should be inclined so the grit hits it at 30° to 40°, as shown in the right photo above. Use a hand lens to make your observations and rate the sample 1 if the finish is abraded away to the wood, 3 if there is superficial marking and 5 if there isn't any noticeable abrasion. Increasing the length of the pipe or using a coarser-grit abrasive will make the results more obvious, but use the same height and grit for each sample.

Heat sensitivity—Dining tables are especially subject to heat damage since they regularly support hot dishes and coffee cups. Sometimes the heat is dry and sometimes it is moist, but it's always potentially damaging. Most films are heat sensitive, so it's important to identify which are most subject to heat distress and at what temperatures they break down. Protect yourself from burns by using pot holders when performing the following tests.

The *hot-drink* test evaluates resistance to moist heat. Heat a small cup of water to about 160°F, spill some on one end of the number 3 samples, and then set the filled cup in the spill. Lift the cup and check the finish after 10 seconds, 1 minute and 5 minutes. In this test, 1 equals failure, showing wet wood beneath the finish film; 3 means there is some blush- or white-ring blemishing; and 5 indicates no obvious damage.

The *hot-casserole* test determines if the finish can stand up to much hotter dry heat. This test will probably ruin most finishes, and the real question is, how badly? Heat an oven-proof glass dish in a 400°F oven for 20 minutes. Then, carefully place the heated dish on the unused end of the number 3 samples. Again, lift the plate to observe and rate the damage, such as melting, at intervals of 10 seconds, 1 minute and 3 minutes; for total failure, such as the finish melting, burning or blistering away to the wood, rate the sample a 1; for some melting or blistering, rate it a 3; and if there is no damage, rate it a 5.

The next test is to see how well the film tolerates the cold. Temperature fluctuations from subfreezing to warm can distort the wood and finish by causing them to move due to temperature changes. *Cold-check resistance* is the American Standard Testing Materials (ASTM) term used to determine a film's ability to resist hairline cracking or checking caused by repeated exposure to cold. Put the number 2 samples in a freezer, where the temperature is minus 10°F or lower, for 30 minutes and then remove them to room temperature for 30 minutes. Continue this and count the cold-to-hot cycles before hairline cracks occur. The samples are rated as follows: 1 if cracks appear after 1 cycle, 3 if cracks appear after less than 5 cycles and 5 if there's no cracking after 10 cycles. Use a hand lens to check only the areas that weren't damaged by the steel ball.

Solvent resistance—Two final tests evaluate another common potential injury: chemical attack. Even the finest furniture comes into contact with several household chemicals and solvents that can be very destructive. Use ordinary home and industrial chemicals, which are found in many cleaners, perfumes and other products, but you should also test finishes with other chemicals you routinely use. I suggest the following: tap water (which can degrade shellac), trisodium phosphate detergent (TSP) and water, vinegar, lacquer thinner, naphtha (varnish maker's and painter's fast-drying thinner), denatured alcohol and acetone. Testing for solvent resistance is simple, but be sure to take precautions prescribed by the material safety data sheet on each of these products. (For more on this, see "Chemical Hazards of Woodworking" on pp. 8-13.) If you use these chemicals as directed, avoid major spills and wear Butyl gloves, goggles and a chemical-cartridge respirator with an organic-vapor cartridge or canister, you should be reasonably protected from hazards due to absorption and inhalation.

For the *solvent-drop* test, put one or two drops of each chemical in three different places on one half of each of the number 4 samples. After 10 seconds, wipe one spot away; after 1 minute, wipe off another; and after 5 minutes, wipe away the last spot. Now rate the results for each interval: 1 if the finish was completely dissolved away to the bare wood, 3 if the finish is softened and 5 if there is no damage. An *acetone-rub* test is the acid test for chemical resistance. Dampen a 0000 steel wool pad with acetone and rub the other half of the number 4 samples with 50 strokes, using uniform pressure on each sample. Rate the finish with a 1 if there is damage and 5 if there isn't damage. □

Tim B. Inman professionally tests finishes and restores furniture in Lake Mills, Wisc.

Protecting Wood from Humidity

Lab tests show which finishes work, which don't

by William Feist and Gary Peterson

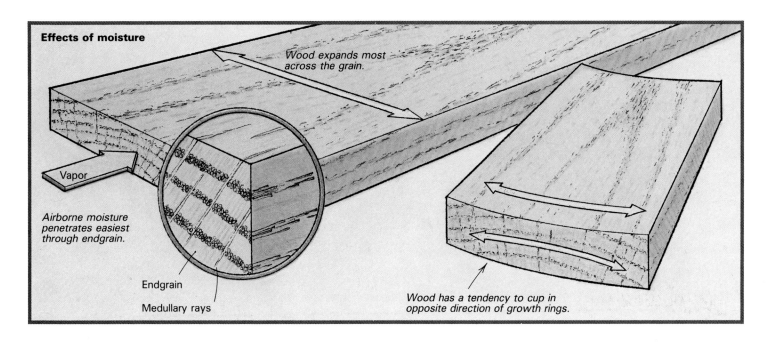

Effects of moisture

Wood expands most across the grain.

Vapor

Airborne moisture penetrates easiest through endgrain.

Endgrain

Medullary rays

Wood has a tendency to cup in opposite direction of growth rings.

W hether indoors and protected from weather, or outdoors and exposed to the elements, wood is always affected by moisture. It swells when it adsorbs liquid from rain, dew or moisture vapor in the air and shrinks as it dries.

Protecting wood from moisture is of no small importance. The more moisture that gets beyond the finish, the more grief you'll have with warped panels, joints that swell and break, drawers that stick and wood that discolors. Of course, the woodworker's dream finish would seal the wood entirely against moisture and protect the surface against dirt and abrasion, all without obscuring the appeal of the grain that makes us appreciate wood in the first place.

About a year and a half ago, the Forest Products Laboratory (FPL) completed a study that examined just how well finishes resist moisture vapor. And, while we didn't necessarily find that ideal finish, we did learn that wood coated with some types of finishes will be less affected than wood left completely unfinished. Our tests of 91 finishes showed that no coating entirely prevents wood from adsorbing moisture. We also found great differences in the effectiveness of many finishes. Some popular ones (linseed oil, tung oil and lacquer, for example) represent hardly any barrier to moisture vapor while other materials that aren't even considered to be finishes—paraffin wax, for instance—sealed the wood almost completely.

The problem with protecting wood from moisture vapor lies in the material itself: it's literally full of holes. In fact, when

seen under magnification, it would not be inaccurate to describe wood as mostly pores surrounded by smaller amounts of organic material. These pores provide lots of entry points for moisture vapor; and even the finish meant to seal them will be somewhat permeable. Ultimately, even the best moisture-resisting finishes only slow, but don't completely stop, the exchange of moisture vapor.

As wood takes on moisture vapor, it expands—which explains why a door that closes just so in the winter sticks annoyingly when humid summer weather arrives. As the drawing above shows, most of the expansion (and when the wood dries, contraction) occurs across a board's width rather than along its length. More shrinking and swelling will take place parallel to the growth rings than perpendicular to them. Thus, a board sawn so its growth rings are parallel to its face (plainsawn) will shrink and swell much more than a board sawn with rings perpendicular to its face (quartersawn).

This bit of wood lore is useful to know for two reasons. First of all, a quartersawn board will be less likely to warp because it expands less across its face. Secondly, to reduce warpage in any wood, moisture exchange must occur evenly on all sides and edges of the board. So, if you coat only one side with a finish, the face you skip will pick up or lose moisture faster than the coated side. This uneven exchange promotes warping. It's imperative, therefore, that the same number of finish coats be applied to both sides of the board. And don't forget the end-grain, either. A great deal of moisture exchange occurs through the exposed pores of the endgrain.

In our tests, we refer to the effectiveness of a finish in terms of moisture-excluding effectiveness (MEE). To make it easier to understand the results, we used a numeric rating for each finish. This is a relative value, based on the number of coats applied to the clear Ponderosa pine samples we used in our tests. To get this rating, we took a piece of smooth pine, cut it in half and completely finished one half while the other half was left uncoated. To establish a reference point, we exposed both samples to 80°F temperatures at 30% humidity until both would adsorb no more water vapor. Then, both samples were exposed for one, seven and 14 days at 80°F and 90% relative humidity. (This exposure to controlled atmospheres of higher humidity imitated a "real world" situation, similar to going from low humidity in the winter to high humidity in the summer.) To arrive at the MEE, we simply weighed the pieces before and after exposing them to the higher humidity.

Perfect protection by the coating—or no gain of water vapor—would be represented by 100% effectiveness; complete lack of protection (as with unfinished wood) by 0%. Most of the coatings were brushed on; a few were dipped. We kept the more moisture-resistant finishes in the test longer (up to 150 days). Also, all test samples were completely coated with the finish.

As the chart shows, most clear and pigmented coatings that form some sort of film and are not latex-based will slow the rate at which water vapor enters wood. In general, solvent-based pigmented coatings, such as paints, are more effective in slowing moisture exchange than clear coatings, such as varnish or shellac, since pigments—the fine solid particles used to color finishes—increase the barrier against moisture

vapor. Within practical limits, the more coats applied, the greater the barrier to moisture vapor penetration and the slower the moisture level will change.

The finishes shown in the chart illustrate the range of our test results. Although not generally considered a finish, paraffin wax still proved to be the most effective, with an MEE rating of 95% after a dip-coated sample was exposed for 14 days. We had good results brushing it on as well: a one-coat, molten paraffin wax brush treatment topped the ratings for one-coat, brush-applied finishes, with an MEE of 69%.

Another unusual finish we tested was a two-part (resin and hardener) epoxy coating. It had a rating of 91% for three coats and 88% for two coats. Conventional two-part epoxy paints, often intended for marine use, were also very effective, especially with three coats.

The degree of moisture vapor protection afforded by a coating or finish depends on several factors. Among these are how thick a film the finish leaves; whether it contains pigments; the type of binder (the non-volatile, solid portion of the finish that holds the pigment particles together after the film is dry); the kind of resin (a film-forming solid or semi-solid organic substance, usually derived from chemical or natural products); and how long the wood is exposed to high or low humidity.

We found the wood samples adsorbed more water vapor as time went on. The longer the finished pieces were exposed to high humidity, the poorer their vapor retardance; eventually, moisture vapor finds its way in.

The chart shows that penetrating finishes like linseed oil, tung oil and furniture polishes are at the bottom of the scale, offering minimal or no protection even after three heavy brush coats. Because penetrating finishes don't form a film, they're usually not effective for controlling water vapor, even though they may be

Naming names

by Roy Berendsohn

Although 91 different finishes were tested by the Forest Products Laboratory (FPL), there wasn't enough space in this article to show the results for all of them. This is a list of some of the more unusual or hard-to-find products shown in the chart; in no way does this list or the chart represent an endorsement. When more than one brand of a type of finish was tested, the chart shows the one with the highest MEE. The FPL was reluctant to provide manufacturers' names and addresses out of concern that the test results are meant to show general characteristics of finishes—not the characteristics of individual brands. Nonetheless, I felt it useful to include this information when it was readily available.

Finishes are listed in the order they appear on the chart. Brand names and manufacturers of general finishes, such as linseed oil, have been excluded. However, we've listed this information for more unusual finishes.

—Two-part epoxy sheathing: Chem-tech Sheathing Epoxy L-26. Chem-Tech, 4669 Lander Rd., Chagrin Falls, Ohio 44022.
—Two-part epoxy polyamide gloss paint: Lindsay Epoxy Kote-Gloss. Lindsay Finishes, Inc. 1898 East Johnson St., Madison, Wisc. 53704.
—Aluminum-pigmented polyurethane gloss varnish: Mautz V-200 and Alcoa aluminum leafing pigment. Mautz Paint Co., Box 7068, Madison, Wisc. 53707.
—Soya-tung alkyd satin enamel: Mautz Deluxe Enamel Satin Finish, No. E-725, White.
—Two-part polyurethane gloss varnish: Brolite Z-spar Lincar Polyurethane, Clear LP-300. Koppers Co., Att. Pam Keeler, 1850 Koppers Bldg., Pittsburgh, Penn. 15219.
—Epoxy gloss varnish: Mautz Deluxe Epon Varnish, V-100.
—Polyurethane gloss varnish: Old Masters Polyurethane, Gloss. Darworth Co. (Product no longer available.)

Also tested were Mautz Exterior/Interior, Gloss V1-Ray Polyurethane, Clear, No. V-200; Flecto Varathane Liquid Plastic, Clear, Gloss; Gloss Zar Polyurethane Coating.)
—Alkyd satin wood finish: Mautz Satin Wood Finish, Clear, V-104.
—Nitrocellulose alkyd lacquer: Zynolyte Spee-E-Lac, Clear No. 0728.
—Phenolic tung floor sealer: Mautz Floor Seal, Tung Oil Base, V-55.
—Soya epoxy gloss and trim sealer: Valspar Val-Speed Epoxy Floor and Trim Sealer/Finish, No. 16, Clear Gloss. The Valspar Corp., 1101 Third St. S., Minneapolis, Minn. 55415.
—Soya alkyd phenolic/tung gloss spar varnish: Mautz Spar Varnish, No. V-11.
—Acrylic gloss latex varnish: Aquakleer, Water-based Clear Finish, Gloss. Benjamin Moore and Co.
—Tung Oil: Hope's Pure Tung Oil. □

Roy Berendsohn is an assistant editor of Fine Woodworking.

good at protecting against liquid water and staining from dirt. Latex- or water-based varnishes are also not very effective (although not shown, neither are latex paints). When these coatings dry, they leave small openings that allow water vapor to penetrate.

While penetrating oils, such as linseed and tung, are not very effective—even when three coats are applied—their effectiveness is greatly increased by blending them with other resins (making varnishes), or by adding both resins and pigments (paints). The more resin or pigment incorporated, within practical limits, the greater the effectiveness. As a rule, oil-based paints are more effective than varnishes; enamels (essentially paints with finer-ground pigments) are even more so.

The use of fillers to "plug" wood pores will indirectly contribute to improving the MEE and will also provide a smooth surface on which to build a uniform top coat. Woods with large pores, such as oak, will be more difficult to coat effectively than, say, cherry. Thinning a finish so it acts as a "sealer" may indirectly help in the same way, but it will probably do more to improve the appearance and durability of the final finish than to enhance the MEE.

The first coat of any finish may "seal" the wood, but it won't provide a totally defect-free, uniform film coating. The second coat usually covers any defects of the first coat and doubles the film thickness. Each succeeding coat will increase the MEE, but when compared to the MEE produced by the first and second coats, the gains will be relatively small—even when up to six coats are applied. This is because the film thickness is doubled for the second coat, but is increased only by a third for the third coat, a fourth for the fourth coat, and so on.

A coating that is effective at keeping water vapor *out* is also effective at keeping it *in*. It took as long—or longer—for a coated specimen to lose water when the humidity was decreased. In fact, it took nearly a year for specimens with the most effective finishes to lose all their moisture after they were exposed at 90% relative humidity for six months.

The information in our studies relates to coatings that are only a few weeks old and not exposed to prolonged aging or severe conditions, such as outdoor weathering (which will quickly damage most coatings, causing them to lose effectiveness).

The moisture resistance of finishes also depends on the type of exposure. For example, water-repellent treatments are quite ineffective against water vapor but—because they cause water to bead on the surface—they're fairly effective against liquid water. So, this type of sealer finish would protect your outdoor wood against rain and dew for some time, but not for very long against humidity.

Most of our studies dealt with brush-applied finishes, although we also compared the effectiveness of dipping. With a conventional finish like gloss polyurethane varnish, we found that one dip coat was equal in moisture-excluding effectiveness to two brush coats. One dip coat of a soya alkyd gloss enamel paint was equal to three brush coats. The better MEE from dipping occurs because more finish is applied over the wood surface and because dipping for some time (we used 30 seconds) increases penetration and provides greater sealing of the endgrain pores, where most moisture enters.

Protecting wood against humidity is important whether the wood will be outdoors or in. The information shown here should help you determine which finish to use. Perhaps, as well, we have dispelled a few old wives' tales on how to control the effect water vapor has on wood. Among them, that penetrating oils are effective in reducing the adsorption of water vapor.

Moisture-excluding effectiveness

This chart shows the moisture-excluding effectiveness (MEE) of a variety of finishes and other materials. Of the 91 finishes tested, these figures are the best for each finish type. The chart is arranged from highest MEE to lowest. Ratings are given for one, two and three coats after 14 days of exposure at 80°F and 90% relative humidity. Negative numbers indicate that the finish itself adsorbed water. (N.A. = not applicable)

	1 Coat	2 Coats	3 Coats
Melted paraffin wax (dip coat) (brush coat)	95 69	N.A. N.A.	N.A. N.A.
Two-part epoxy sheathing	54	88	91
Two-part epoxy polyamide sheathing gloss (paint)	53	82	87
Aluminum-flake-pigmented polyurethane gloss varnish	41	77	84
Soya-tung alkyd satin enamel	50	70	80
Two-part polyurethane gloss varnish	0	46	66
Epoxy gloss varnish	3	34	50
Orange shellac	2	25	46
Polyurethane gloss varnish	11	36	44
Alkyd satin wood finish	8	29	43
Polyurethane satin varnish	8	27	41
Nitrocellulose alkyd lacquer	7	24	40
Phenolic tung floor sealer	-1	18	35
Soya epoxy gloss and trim sealer	1	13	31
Soya alkyd phenolic/tung gloss spar varnish	0	15	30
Acrylic gloss latex varnish	-1	6	10
Tung oil	-1	-1	2
Brazilian carnauba paste wax	0	0	1
Linseed oil	-5	-4	0
Spray furniture polish lemon oil/silicone	0	0	0

Similarly, thinning a finish so the first coat acts as a sealer may help improve the appearance and durability of the final finish, but it won't do much to protect against humidity.

The most important criteria, then, for protecting against humidity are film thickness and impermeability. But no matter how effective your finish, some vapor still gets through and is adsorbed by the wood. Although it happens too slowly to watch, this means your wood (solid wood, anyway) is always on the move. □

William Feist is a wood finish researcher at the Forest Products Laboratory. Gary Peterson was formerly an information specialist at the lab.

Wood Stains
Five ways to add color

by George Mustoe

Woodworkers often dismiss staining as an unpleasant, unskilled task that seldom produces natural-looking colors. That's to be expected. Retailers primarily stock semi-opaque stains, which can smother the wood if they are applied improperly. Manufacturers often encourage applications like "rosewood" stain on fir plywood, as if you could make drab wood exotic by tinting it a lurid shade. All this advertising hype ignores the real value of stains—they let you make a board's heartwood and sapwood a uniform color without fundamentally changing the wood's natural hue. Stains let you make six chairs and a dining table all the same color, without cutting a forest of trees to obtain matching boards.

Five basic groups of coloring agents are commonly called stains. *Semi-opaque stains,* the well-known oil stains sold in every hardware store, are surface finishes made by mixing transparent and opaque pigments with mineral spirits and linseed oil or varnish. *Transparent wood stains,* close chemical cousins of fabric dyes, are relatively color-fast aniline compounds derived from coal tars. The dye powder is dissolved in water or alcohol. These solvents carry the color deep into the wood cells. *Varnish and lacquer stains* are the conventional clear sealer coats tinted with transparent dyes. *Tinted penetrating oils* are billed as a complete finishing system that penetrates deeply into the wood to seal it, and provide a satiny "handrubbed" look. The oils, usually tung or linseed, are colored with dyes or pigments. *Chemical stains* are water-soluble inorganic compounds that react with the wood to create colorfast tints without dyes or pigments.

Transparent dyes are the best choice for hardwoods. More than 70 colors are available, ranging from subtle browns to spectacular bright colors. Their high degree of transparency means you won't hide the beauty of the underlying wood grain. Avoid these dyes on softwoods which absorb the watery solutions so rapidly that it's difficult to get even coloration.

Water-soluble aniline dyes are non-toxic (good for toys if you add a moisture-proof coat of clear varnish), non-flammable and very fade-resistant. Dissolve an ounce of dye powder in a quart of hot water in a glass, plastic or stainless steel container, then saturate a sponge or rag with dye. Wearing rubber gloves, squeeze out enough liquid to prevent dripping and splashing, then wipe on a generous coat parallel to the wood grain. To obtain a lighter shade, water down the dye rather than apply a skimpy coat, or you'll get uneven coloration. After wetting the surface, wipe off excess dye with a squeezed-out sponge or rag. The color will lighten as it dries, so leave the piece overnight before you decide if the shade is right. Apply a second dye coat for more intense color. Since water in the dye also swells the wood fibers, smooth the dried coat with fine 400- to 600-grit paper before adding a top coat of finish. An alternate method is to moisten the wood with water before adding any color, then sand the raised grain before dyeing.

Aniline dyes soluble in methyl (wood) alcohol are called "spirit stains." These are available as powders or pre-mixed liquids (Watco 5-Minute Wood Stain). Although not as fade resistant as water-soluble dyes, they produce sparkling clear colors. You apply them the same way as water-soluble dyes (the alcohol even contains enough water to raise the grain), but the solvent makes them potentially hazardous. Good ventilation is essential because respirators won't completely block out the fumes. Wear rubber gloves to prevent skin contact. These dyes are difficult to apply evenly on large surfaces because they dry so fast, usually within 15 minutes—if one section dries before the adjacent area is covered, you'll get a hard line between the two. The dyes are, however, particularly useful for touch-up work. The alcohol solvent lets them bind to oily woods or surfaces with traces of old finish that would repel water-soluble dyes. Adding a little shellac increases this ability.

You can avoid the grain-raising problems of water- and alcohol-soluble dyes by using NGR (Non-Grain Raising) dyes. You buy these pre-mixed in a water-free hydrocarbon solvent. NGR dyes are lightfast, but their fast drying rate limits them to small surfaces. The vapors are toxic, so good ventilation is essential.

Oil stains have done the most to give staining a bad name, but they can be good for enhancing the not-so-nice softwoods used in much interior carpentry. Go easy, though. The stains' high pigment content makes it easy to produce dingy-looking finishes, and the colors may be way off. "Mahogany" stains can range from red to brown to nearly purple, and maple can be anything from tan to orange. However, you can mix several colors to obtain a more pleasing shade; the formulas are so similar that even different brands can usually be intermixed.

Oil stains should be wiped on in the direction of the grain with a brush or a soft cloth. After waiting a few minutes for the wood to absorb the stain, wipe off the excess. If you want a darker shade, increase the waiting period or apply a second coat of thinned stain. Wiping the surface with mineral spirits will lighten the color. Again, good ventilation is essential because the vapors are flammable and toxic; oily rags are also a fire hazard.

Water-based stains, like those by Deft, are a fairly new product made up of opaque pigments suspended in a vinyl or acrylic base. Generally the colors are less intense than most oil stains,

From *Fine Woodworking* magazine (November 1985) 55:82-83

an advantage when subtle staining is desired. They are nonflammable and have no toxic vapors or bad odor.

Tinted penetrating oils are useful whenever an easy-to-apply, complete finishing system is needed. You apply the oil according to the package directions, then wipe off the excess. Additional coats can be applied before hand buffing the finish. Penetrating oils are not intended to be used with any other type of finish—some of these oils leave behind residues that may inhibit the drying time of varnish or lacquer. You can also make tinted oils by dissolving dye powders in tung or linseed oil, then thinning with 20% to 30% mineral spirits.

Varnish stains are synthetic or natural varnishes tinted with transparent dyes. This combination makes them highly transparent, and they intensify porous areas of the wood less than other stains. The first coat of varnish penetrates the porous area deeply, causing darker coloration, but then this coat blocks further absorbtion after it dries. Thus, subsequent coats will even out the color. Varnish stains have highly diluted tints, so you must apply several coats. The transparent color also makes it a good choice for softwoods such as pine and fir; inexpensive lumber can be livened up without ending up with the lurid colors and grain patterns that often result from oil stains.

Lacquer stain is similar to varnish stain but dries faster and has more toxic vapors. Ordinary clear lacquer can be colored by adding alcohol-soluble aniline dye, first dissolving the dye in a little methyl alcohol or lacquer thinner.

Chemical stains react directly with the wood and are somewhat unpredictable, so you must experiment with every species to see what color the chemicals will produce, especially if you want to reproduce the chemical stains on old pieces. Oak treated with ammonia turns a warm brown. Wood containing tannin becomes silvery gray when wiped with a solution of ferrous sulfate. Potassium dichromate, potassium permanganate and sodium carbonate (sal soda) will darken most hardwoods. The methods are simple: stir 1 to 2 tablespoons of chemical into a quart of lukewarm water in a glass jar (don't use metal, which may react). Except for ammonia, the chemicals are free of fumes, but they are poisonous if ingested. Wear rubber gloves and apply the solution with a rag or sponge. Let the stain dry overnight before sanding the raised grain.

Regardless of the product, staining can be a valuable technique in this age of high lumber prices and dwindling forest resources, when it's often necessary to salvage sap-streaked and bland boards. It's definitely not a sign of shoddy workmanship. □

George Mustoe is a geochemistry research technician at Western Washington University in Bellingham, Wash. Sources for stains include Sigma Chemical Co., P.O. Box 14508, St. Louis, Mo. 63178 (chemicals); Henningson & Associates, P.O. Box 6004, Rockford, Ill. 61125 (water-soluble dyes); Woodfinishing Enterprises, Box 10117, Milwaukee, Wisc. 53201 (stains and dyes), The Woodworkers Store, 21801 Industrial Boulevard, Rogers, Minn. 55374 (water- and oil-based stains, penetrating oils, NGR stains), H. Behlen and Bros. Inc., Route 30N, Amsterdam, N.Y. 12010.

Staining problems

Many staining problems are due to poor surface preparation, rather than a problem with the stain. No stain will work well unless it's evenly absorbed into the wood. Dull planer knives can glaze and compress the wood fibers enough to block stains. Thorough sanding parallel to the grain (to at least 120-grit) is essential. Even tiny swirl marks and scratches will absorb stain differently than smooth surfaces. Problems here can be cured only by sanding or hand-planing the wood to a fresh surface.

Dried glue won't absorb stain, so gluelines can show after staining, especially where the joint juxtaposes contrasting grain patterns. You can't fix these defects, so lay out stock so grain patterns match, and fit joints tightly so gluelines are thin.

The only way to remove ugly glue smears that appear after staining is to re-sand and restain the surface. If you suspect smears, you can make the glue temporarily visible before staining by dampening the wood with mineral spirits or lacquer thinner—use chalk or a pencil to mark areas that need more sanding.

End grain is highly absorbent and can sometimes turn almost black if you don't seal the open pores before staining. For oil stains, use linseed oil as a sealer. Shellac (3-lb. cut) diluted 1:1 with denatured alcohol makes a good blocking agent for most other stains. No matter how much sealer you use, large areas of end grain don't stain well unless you are trying to emphasize the contrasting textures.

Wood-patching compounds and fillers seldom absorb stain like the surrounding wood. Unless you have extraordinary luck, you must do a good deal of experimentation on scrap lumber to come up with a colored patching compound that dries to match the stained lumber. Some stainable compounds remain porous after drying, but if porosity of the patch differs greatly from that of the surrounding wood, these fillers may come out lighter or darker than you desire. Even if you get a good color match, the lack of grain patterns will reveal large patches. Instead of using synthetic patches, the best results often come from inserting a plug of matching wood. This means routing or chiseling out the defect to get smooth margins and thin gluelines. If synthetic patching compounds are used, hand-tint the repaired area with oil stains or artists' acrylic colors to match the adjacent stained wood. Apply the colors with a fine brush and streak them to follow the grain lines of the surrounding wood.

Wood fillers applied to smooth the surface of open grained woods usually work well with stains. The fillers come in many colors, so experiment to find one that matches the stain. Mineral-spirits based fillers can also be custom tinted with dry pigments or up to 30% oil stain. The paste-like filler is thinned to a creamy consistency with mineral spirits, then liberally brushed onto the stained wood, saturating the open pores. Wait a few minutes for the filler to dry to a dull luster, then rub with a coarse rag to wipe off the excess and smooth the surface. Let dry overnight, then sand lightly with 320-grit paper.

Once stain has been applied, don't let the colors bleed into later coats of finish. Your best precaution is to make sure the stain has a different solvent than the next coat of finish. For example, water-soluble dyes won't bleed into lacquer or varnish, but oil and spirit stains will. You could also let the stain dry thoroughly, then seal it with a thin washcoat of shellac.

Stained wood is vulnerable to surface damage because scratches and abrasions may penetrate the colored layer and expose lighter wood. You can't just restain a scratch—the microscopically rough walls pick up pigment and end up too dark. A better approach is to restore the color by applying a tiny brushful of diluted stain, tinted varnish or shellac colored with spirit stain. With extensively damaged pieces, it's better to strip off the finish and redo the whole piece.　　　　　　—*G.M.*

Aniline Dyes
Coloring wood with modern chemicals

by Michael Dresdner

Although natural dyes can be very appealing, the vast majority of contemporary finishers prefer to use modern dyes and stains. These materials are generally much more dependable than the natural dyes. In addition, the chemical mordants and organic materials needed to make natural dyes, which produce color by reacting with the wood itself, can be messy, unpredictable, dangerous and hard to obtain.

Aniline dyes, or dye stains, which are very similar to many modern fabric dyes, are usually sold in powdered form. Formulated for one of three common solvents, they will dissolve in either water, alcohol or oil. The dye works by saturating the wood with color as the solvent soaks in. Pigmented stains, which are basically pigments or tiny opaque particles of color that are suspended in a medium, color wood by depositing the particles in the pores and crannies of the wood's surface. Unlike the transparent dyes, which will remain in solution indefinitely, the pigment in stain will settle to the bottom of the container over time.

When any wood is stained or dyed, the resultant color is a combination of the original wood color plus the dye. Hence, if a blue stain is put on a yellowish wood, the end result is not the original blue color of the dye but rather a greenish hue. Most woods have some color to them, and most ebony dyes are actually dark blue or green, although better-quality black anilines have orange added to make the dye "blacker." As a result, simply staining a piece of maple with black dye will cause the wood to appear blue-gray under a finish; on oak it will come out greenish-gray. To get the true black referred to as ebonizing, it is easiest to use several layers of dye or stain, a process that also gives you more control of the color.

Because water penetrates wood so well, water-soluble anilines are the best choice for the first coloring operation. Sponge the wood with water to raise the grain; after it is dry, sand lightly with 220-grit paper to defur it. This will prevent the water in the dye from significantly raising the grain again when the color material is actually applied. Dissolve the aniline in moderately hot water and soak the wood with a rag or sponge. The amount of dye dissolved in the water and not the amount of solution applied will control the intensity of the color. Try to get the whole piece or section wet at one time, and then wipe off any excess liquid. If it is not dark enough, add more dye to the water and restain the piece after it dries, but remember, there is a limit to how much stain a piece of wood will take. After a certain point, excess stain will merely accumulate on the surface and form a layer of colored dust when it dries.

Nongrain-raising (NGR) stains (water-type anilines predissolved in an anhydrous solution) will also work, but because they are premixed, you have less control of the color intensity. Both alcohol- and oil-soluble anilines, which actually work with naptha and lacquer thinner as well as oil, are generally less lightfast, and depending on the solvent, may flash off faster than dyes mixed with water, making them harder to control. All types of dyes vary greatly in their lightfastness, but nonfading anilines are now available in a variety of colors and solvencies.

On very porous woods, such as oak and mahogany, the pores will not absorb water-soluble aniline very well, so the pores may remain lighter than the surrounding wood. If the pores are to be filled with semipaste filler before the final finish coats are applied, this will not be a problem: Simply use black filler; otherwise, you might want to color the pores by wiping on a black pigment stain that is compatible with whatever finish is to follow.

After the first coat of finish has been applied, if the surface is still not dark enough for your liking, you can shade it up by adding an aniline dye to the next coat of finish. There are transparent dyes available that can be added to virtually any finish—oil, lacquer, shellac, varnish, water-base lacquer and even catalyzed finishes. Proceed cautiously, though, as too much dye added at this stage will make the finish look painted.

Because ebony is rarely all black, you might want to ebonize to a different color by using a combination of stains. This layered method will allow you to achieve any look you desire. □

Michael Dresdner is an instrumentmaker and woodfinishing specialist in Zionhill, Penn., and a contributing editor at FWW.

Sources of Supply

Highland Hardware, 1045 N. Highland Ave., Dept. F, Atlanta, GA 30306; (800) 241-6748 or (404) 872-4466 in Georgia.

The Woodworkers' Store, 21801 Industrial Blvd., Dept. 1212, Rogers, MN 55374-9514; (612) 428-2199.

Woodcraft Supply Corp., 41 Atlantic Ave., Box 4000, Dept. FW39, Woburn, MA 01888; (800) 225-1153 or (617) 935-5860 in Massachusetts.

Wood Finishing Supply Co., 100 Throop St., Palmyra, N.Y. 14522; (315) 597-3743.

Black aniline dye is not actually black, but rather a mixture of oranges, blues and other colors, as shown below when dye powder is scattered on damp paper.

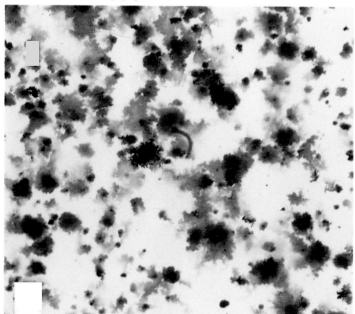

Raw wood | 1 tablespoon/qt. | 3 tablespoons/qt. | 6 tablespoons/qt.

Household lye penetrates into the surface of cherry, accelerating the natural aging of heartwood. The finish then intensifies the color.

Unlocking Cherry's Color

by Tom Dewey

Cherry heartwood darkens with age, eventually yielding a patina of rich, naturally varied color that no stain can duplicate. I have several antique cherry pieces that were restored by my father. Every time I made a new cherry piece "to match," regardless of whether I used oil stains or aniline dyes, the artificial and uniform tones of the new work made it look out of place among the clear, vibrant color of the old.

Five years ago, quite by accident, I discovered a chemical treatment that seems to duplicate natural aging. I had spilled a few drops of Easy-Off oven cleaner on the cherry countertop in my kitchen, and, although I quickly cleaned it off, there before my eyes was the 100-year-old look—several deep burgundy-brown stains. The treatment seems to color the wood according to the pigments and extractives that nature has deposited in it. Sapwood darkens only moderately, as it would over the years, but heartwood ages instantly. Boards from different trees color slightly differently, just as they do in old furniture.

I read the Easy-Off label: "Contains sodium hydroxide (lye)." Indeed, the label read like an OSHA alert: six "Do not's," four "Avoids." But, if you can use Easy-Off in the kitchen, why not in the workshop? Out I went to experiment.

Easy-Off proved troublesome because of its soapiness. Drano, another product containing lye, was out because it's mixed with aluminum chips, which react to produce intense heat and gas—fine for blowing out a drain, but rough on a candlestand. Straight household lye, however, worked fine.

The photo shows the results of various concentrations. The stronger the solution, the faster and deeper the color change. If the solution is weak, further coats don't darken the wood much more. You want a concentration that gives you the desired color in one application. It's a good idea to experiment, starting with one tablespoon to a quart of warm water; add more dry lye powder until the solution produces the desired color. Mix and keep the solution in a plastic bottle with a plastic lid, to avoid corrosion. I recommend plastic goggles and gloves, and protection for clothes and workshop surfaces.

Apply the solution with a nylon brush (natural bristles will be reduced to mush within minutes) or spray it on using a plastic spray-pump container, such as many household cleaners come in. Don't use conventional spray equipment for two reasons: first, the solution reacts with aluminum, and

even more important, overspray is very nasty stuff.

Try to cover a surface as quickly and evenly as possible. The process is moderately forgiving—apparent blotchiness during application tends to disappear when dry—but careful, overlapping, full-wet treatment is the key to success. In doing a small cherry pedestal table, for example, I begin with the work upside down. I spray all visible surfaces, then turn the work over and spray the pedestal and legs again. Drips and runs don't seem to matter; it's the full-wet initial contact that counts. For the top, I'll generally switch to a brush, mostly because by that time my finger is getting tired pumping.

Occasionally I've tried to neutralize any lye residue by treating the wood with vinegar, but I don't really believe that this is necessary. The active ingredient in the lye appears to use itself up working on the wood. I've never had trouble with final finishes either, whether oil or lacquer.

Clean your equipment with soap and water. Allow the work to dry, which may take overnight. Because the lye mixture is water based, it will raise the grain somewhat. I use 180-grit silicon-carbide paper to remove any fuzz. The color change penetrates the surface, but even so, be careful not to sand through at corners, etc., as touching up such areas is time-consuming and difficult. I usually work up to 400-grit paper before applying the finish.

Obviously, this method shouldn't be used on children's toys or items where there will be contact with foodstuffs. I'm not sure that even then there would be problems, but why take chances?

Try the treatment yourself on other woods. There are always offcuts to practice on. I've found it doesn't do much for maple, and for my money it darkens walnut too much. You may or may not like the brown color it gives to oak, or the intense red it produces on Honduras mahogany.

Colors can change with time, especially when exposed to bright sunlight, but in my house at least, the lye treatment has been the only way my projects could have blended in with my father's treasures. I'm reminded of my luck every time I pour a cup of coffee—those brown spots are still on the countertop. □

Tom Dewey has been designing and building furniture for ten years in Coudersport, Pa.

Old-Fashioned Wood-Coloring
Reviving the dyes of yore

by George Frank

There can't be much doubt about the advantages of using modern ready-mixed stains or dyes for coloring wood. They're readily available, easy to apply, reasonably fade-resistant and they yield consistent results. But if you're a one-piece-at-a-time wood artisan interested in obtaining a quality of color you can't get directly out of a can, there are great thrills and advantages to making your own homemade wood-coloring mixtures by following some of the old-fashioned, bygone ways of preparing natural and chemical dyes. I learned about various natural extractive dyes and chemical mordants in Paris in the days following World War I. Although the old woodworking section of Paris has undergone many changes since the unforgettably charming days of the 1920s, and while the old ways of dyeing wood are slowly disappearing, I haven't forgotten what I learned and still depend on many of these techniques today.

Why go to all the trouble of making your own coloring concoctions when you can get reliable, ready-made stains at the corner paint store? First of all, using a dye instead of a stain allows you to color the wood without adding a cloudy layer of pigment that can conceal the grain and cover up the wood's natural beauty. Unlike paint or stain, a dye consists of a liquid medium—usually water or alcohol—in which pigment particles are dissolved, not merely suspended. Thus, the pigment can't settle out. And since these dissolved pigments are less opaque than suspended particles, a dye solution is more transparent than a stain.

Furthermore, many of the techniques I'll describe produce their color by chemical reaction with the wood itself. The effect they achieve has a clarity and vibrant *quality* of color that, in my opinion, far exceeds that of their modern equivalents, such as aniline dyes. The old-fashioned dyes can also be the right way to get an authentic color when refinishing certain antiques.

The use of dyes to change the natural color of a material goes back to textile dyeing—a craft that evolved well before recorded history. Woodworkers undoubtedly gleaned the experience of these textile artisans in developing their own methods for dyeing wood, often to make light, inexpensive woods resemble the darker, more coveted varieties.

The palette of color-creating substances compatible with yarn and fabric is vast, yet relatively few of these materials have been adapted to the wood-dyeing craft. One of the most useful and well-known of these dyestuffs is brewed from the hulls of walnut shells by so simple a means as a pot simmered on the kitchen stove or by extracting the dyestuff with ammonia. This venerable *brou de noix* produces very handsome rich-brown colors when applied to wood.

But allow me to introduce you to the two most versatile stars for natural wood-dyeing, derived from various species of South American hardwoods: logwood (also known as "campeachy wood"), so called because it is imported from Central America in heavy, dense logs; and brazilwood, frequently referred to simply as "brazil." In the old days, these logs were reduced to chips or sawdust and marketed as dyestuffs. The product was boiled down, strained, bottled and stored for future use. Since these exotic chips are far from easy to come by these days, we must buy extracts of them (available as powders—see "Sources of supply," p. 27) ready to be dissolved in water. Yellowwood and cate-chu are also available as extracts, but they're far less versatile than logwood and brazilwood.

Applied by themselves, these extractive dyes will produce pleasant yellowish and reddish-brown tones. But combine them with chemical mordants and you open the door to a multitude of superb colors (see facing page). Mordants like sodium sulfate also help increase the fade resistance of brazilwood and logwood dyes. Before I provide a how-to on combining dyes and mordants, however, allow me to explain what a mordant is and how it works.

The word "mordant" comes from the French verb, *mordre*—"to bite." The mordant helps the dye penetrate into the fibers of the wood and bind there. Quite frequently, the chemical combination of dyes and mordants also gives birth to deep, rich, vibrant colors impossible to obtain in any other way. The reason is this: While a dye creates color with dissolved pigment, mordants create or change color by chemically reacting with dyes or other substances found in the wood itself.

Sometimes mordants are used without dyes to create color. For example, untreated oak becomes darker after being exposed to fumes from a heated ammonia solution. By "fuming" the oak in this manner (caution: the use of a vapor respirator with an ammonia cartridge is essential during this process), the natural tannin present in the wood reacts with the ammonia mordant to cause a color change. This effect can also be achieved on other woods lacking tannin by simply applying a tannic acid solution before fuming (see bottom right, facing page).

There are no hard-and-fast rules on how best to combine dyes and mordants. Typically, the dye is applied first, then the mordant when the dye is dry. Sometimes the mordant comes first and the dye follows, but rarely are the two mixed. In some instances, it's unknown which component—dye or mordant—actually creates the color change.

There are countless possible combinations of mordants and dyes, and the key to discovering the magic of brilliant color is experimentation. Experimenting is like creating a play on the stage: The actors are the ingredients; the plot is how you make

From *Fine Woodworking* magazine (September 1987) 66:52-55

Sample results using various dyes and mordants

This white ash sample shows some of the colors obtainable with logwood dye and various chemical mordants. All solutions were mixed in a 15% concentration.

An interesting range of colors can be created by using mordants in combination—with or without dyes. This entire white ash sample was first coated with tannic acid. Then, various second coats were applied, as indicated.

Ferrous sulfate
over logwood dye

Logwood dye alone

Ferrous sulfate
over tannic acid

Alum
over tannic acid

Alum
over logwood dye

Potassium dichromate
over logwood dye

Ferrous sulfate
over tannic acid with
logwood dye topcoat

Potassium dichromate
over tannic acid

After topcoating this white ash sample with brazilwood dye, different shades and tones were created by varying the concentration of potassium dichromate mordant used.

You can darken woods that have a natural tannin content (such as oak) by exposing them to ammonia fumes. Furthermore, non-tannin woods such as birch and ash can be fume-darkened by first topcoating the wood with a tannin solution.

Brazilwood dye only

5% solution

Oak

Birch

Ash

20% solution

10% solution

Your wood-dyeing experimentation kit needn't make your workbench look like Dr. Frankenstein's laboratory. The most important tools include: disposable mixing cups, mixing sticks and applicators; masks, goggles, gloves and other protective devices; and an accurate scale.

them perform. Here's the chance for you to do for wood-coloring what Shakespeare did for the stage.

The basic tools you need to begin are shown in the photo above. They include: a reliable scale to measure the weight of the powdered dyes and chemicals (mine was made by Kodak—I paid $15 for it in 1941); a graduated cylinder or beaker to measure the water; disposable plastic cups to mix small sample batches (I use small urine sample cups available from any hospital-supply store); a few dozen Popsicle sticks for stirring each mixture separately; cotton swabs or scraps of old foam rubber for use as disposable applicators; and a notebook for taking notes on the various combi-

nations of mixtures and the results they yield on different woods—so you can reproduce your best results in the future.

Before you do any mixing, however, a word of warning: Most of the chemicals described here are poisonous (see "Mordanting chemicals" below), so treat them with respect. Bottle the chemicals in safe containers, label them properly and store the containers in a locked cabinet or high out of reach. Keep kids and pets out of the shop while you're experimenting (mixed in solution, deadly potassium dichromate looks just like orange soft drink), and avoid all contact with these chemicals by wearing protective goggles, an organic-vapor/acid-gas particulate cartridge (available from MSA, P.O. Box 426, Pittsburgh, Pa. 15239), an apron and rubber gloves. And, most important, concentrate on what you're doing. Add the woodfinisher's most essential ingredient to every mixture: plain horse sense. In six decades of working with these chemicals, neither I nor any of my workers have had a serious mishap.

Start your experiments by cutting and smooth-sanding a number of thin sample boards or strips from whatever wood you plan to work with. Section off several separate areas on each one with masking tape. Now, fill the disposable cups with warm distilled water (or rainwater), and add small amounts of the various dyes and mordants. Use a separate Popsicle stick to stir each mixture (you can write the contents of each mixture on one end of the stick for quick identification). For most general experimenting, I mix dyes and mordants in about a 15% concentration. To speed the process of proportionally combining dry weight with liquid

Mordanting chemicals

The following is a list of common, readily obtainable chemicals that can serve as mordants in the wood-dyeing process. Please handle, store and use these substances with care.

Alum—Usually mined as a mixture of several metallic aluminum sulfates, alum is sold in drugstores as a white, astringent powder or crystal. Relatively non-toxic, it brings out purplish or dark-crimson tones when used over logwood and other dyes.

Potassium dichromate (potassium bichromate)—These orange crystals of chrome, available from darkroom-supply stores, are *extremely* poisonous (five grams can kill an adult) and are considered carcinogenic. Avoid all contact with the skin, and use them only in well-ventilated areas. Applied alone, they will darken the natural color of mahogany. When applied over logwood dye, they tend to create rich browns; applied over brazilwood dye, they produce deep reds and browns.

Copper sulfate—Also known as blue vitriol. Plumbers use large quantities of this turquoise crystal to kill the tree roots that clog sewer lines. Highly poisonous, copper sulfate can often be purchased at hardware or plumbing-supply stores. When used in conjunction with logwood, it produces dark gray and olive tones.

Ferrous sulfate—This toxic form of iron comes in tannish crystals that are poi-

sonous in the amounts used for mordanting, although minute quantities of the chemical are used in iron-supplementing vitamins. Ferrous sulfate will produce an ebony-like black when applied over logwood, or a deep gray over tannic acid.

Stannous chloride—A white crystalline form of tin, stannous chloride is moderately poisonous. Toxic fumes are generated when the chemical is mixed with water, so use maximum ventilation, or mix and apply it outdoors. Stannous chloride can be used in combination with alum, potassium dichromate or copper sulfate for color variations. It will produce a nice light red over brazilwood, and a deep yellow over yellowwood. When applied over madder dye (or alizarin, a synthetic replacement for madder), stannous chloride yields a pink color.

Potassium bitartrate—The most common form of this white powder can be purchased at the grocery store as cream of tartar. Since it's used in cooking and sauce-making, potassium bitartrate is obviously non-toxic. It will sometimes brighten red or yellow when applied over dyes of those colors. Over logwood dye, it creates a gray-brown; over brazilwood, a reddish-yellow.

Sodium sulfate—Also known as Glauber's salt, sodium sulfate is a white or colorless crystal that is thought to assist other mordants and dyes in molecularly bonding colors to the fibers of wood,

yielding better and brighter colors with improved light-fastness.

Ammonia—This is a clear liquid with powerful fumes. While the non-sudsing, household-grade ammonia sold in grocery stores will work, a 28% solution called aqueous ammonia (sold by industrial-supply companies) is most effective for darkening the color of oak with fuming. Ammonia will yield a dark violet-brown when applied over logwood dye, a light brown over brazilwood and a yellow-brown over yellowwood dye. It is hazardous to the eyes, skin and respiratory tract, so wear goggles, rubber gloves and an ammonia-cartridge-equipped vapor mask during use.

Tannic acid—This slightly toxic chemical can irritate sensitive skin. Tannic acid is naturally present in oak and is the "ingredient" that gives tea an astringent quality. It can be applied to the surface of non-tannic woods to make them susceptible to darkening by fuming, or it can be used in combination with other mordants to produce color—with potassium dichromate, for example, it produces a yellowish-brown.

Calcium oxide—Also called quicklime, calcium oxide can be employed by itself to enrich mahogany, walnut or cherry. Slake calcium oxide with warm water and coat the wood with the freshly made paste. Let it dry overnight. The next day, brush off the lime and wash off the residue with rainwater. Neutralize with vinegar. —*G.F.*

volume, nothing beats the metric system. Since 1 cubic centimeter (cc) of water weighs 1 gram, 15 grams of powder dissolved in 100cc of water automatically yields a 15% solution. Try calculating *that* with liquid and dry ounces!

With a foam applicator, brush on the first coat of dye or mordant. Once dry, remove the raised grain with 400-grit sandpaper, sanding on a slight diagonal to shear the fibers off rather than just pushing them down. Next, brush on an even coating of the mordant solution (or dye, if you used mordant on the first coat). With some applications, the color changes will be rapid; others—ferrous sulfate over logwood dye, for instance—will continue to darken for several hours. If you like the color attained but want to darken it, you can either mix a higher concentration solution of the dye and/or mordant, or you can try a second application of either mixture—or both mixtures.

Once you're satisfied with the hue and intensity of the color, sand the piece lightly and top coat it with the finish of your choice—acknowledging that most finishes will add a slight yellow cast to the color and that some may not adhere to the dyed wood. Although natural-dye colors are reasonably light-fast (particularly when fixed with a mordant), everything in life eventually fades—even the natural color of most woods themselves. These old-timers' dyes, however, will age with dignity.

If you don't get quite the color qualities you're after with the substances I've described, feel free to experiment with others. There are many possible substitutions for the mordanting chemicals discussed here. If you're familiar with safe procedures for using diluted forms of nitric, sulfuric or hydrochloric acid, for example, you might try them in lieu of other mordants. These acids yield a whole range of deep reds, purples or yellows, depending on the dye over which they're applied. Don't be timid in your experiments, but *do* be careful using these materials. And *never* attempt to dilute a concentrated acid by pouring water into it; instead, add the acid to the water gradually, stirring constantly.

There are many other possible sources for dyestuffs. Antique restorers, for instance, achieve a very subtle faded-gold hue in their refinishing by applying final coats of a dye brewed from Chinese black tea (available in brick form from Chinese food and gift shops). In the old days, some finishing masters knew how to use the stone and iron sediment from the bottom of the water trough under a sandstone grinding wheel to make three different color dyes: green, brown and red. They'd boil the mud in vinegar and, over a period of days, skim off liquid at different intervals to produce the three colors. Although I've never tried this formula, I've had success making a grayish-color dye from the aluminum oxide dust and steel particles gathered from below my bench grinder.

Although the old ways of wood-dyeing are usually slower, less predictable and sometimes more dangerous than the modern practice of "finishing by the numbers," they can add valuable tricks to the repertoire of the artistic woodfinisher. □

George Frank is a retired master woodfinisher living in South Venice, Fla., and is the author of Adventures in Wood Finishing *(The Taunton Press, 1981).*

Sources of supply

Dyeing materials and mordanting chemicals:
Olde Mill, R.D.#3, Box 547A, York, PA 17402 (also offers a kit of dyes and mordants).
Woodfinishing Enterprises, 1729 N. 68th St., Wauwatosa, WI 53213.

By letting a tree's natural circulation system absorb his pigmented solutions, LeRoy Frink is able to create a rainbow of unnaturally colored woods.

Dyed-in-the-wood pine

by Sandor Nagyszalanczy

The next time you have trouble getting the stain off your clothing or fingertips, think of LeRoy Frink. About 30 years ago, Frink got the idea that it would be neater and more economical to color wood while it's still in the living tree. It took him 10,000 experiments to perfect his unorthodox method of dyeing: Frink bands each tree near its base with a probe consisting of multiple hollow needles. Through these needles, he pipes a water-based pigment solution (the exact nature of which he's understandably secretive about) fed by a ⅛-in.-dia. hose connected to an oil drum reservoir. The tree's active transport system, which normally circulates water and nutrients through the living portion of the plant, pumps the dye solution into every inch of sapwood and right out into the leaves or needles. A 16-in.-dia. to 20-in.-dia. tree takes about a month to assimilate the color, sucking dry an entire 55-gal. barrel.

Although the process works on all types of trees (including hardwoods), Frink prefers Ponderosa pine since it's fast-growing and consists mostly of sapwood. He once dyed 2,000 aspen trees simultaneously for a production run of colorful paneling, but he rarely colors more than 500 trees "intravenously" at the same time.

Semi-retired at 68, Frink runs a thriving craft business and uses thousands of small pieces of the unnatural-colored woods for making earrings and pendants, which he sells in his shop in Loveland, Colo. In addition to dyeing wood, Frink has explored other applications for his process. With the help and advice of several chemical companies, for example, he has introduced fire retardants, insect repellents and fertilizers into trees. □

Sandor Nagyszalanczy is an assistant editor at FWW.

To emphasize the grain of this oak tabletop, Shaw works a mixture of plaster of paris, purple Japan color and water into the wood pores. After sanding off the excess, he finishes the wood with white shellac to seal in the color highlights.

Filling the Grain
Making wood as smooth as glass

by David E. Shaw

Filling the grain is one aspect of wood finishing that should be in the repertoire of every finisher and cabinetmaker. Even when contemporary styles lean more toward the natural look, a highly polished, smooth-as-glass finish, like the walnut shown in the photo at right, is frequently considered proof of elegance, especially with pianos, dining-room tables and other more formal furniture. But you can't simply sand and buff this glow onto the wood as you can on brass or silver. Compared to these fine-textured metals, wood is a pock-marked, torn-up country road, and all its grain irregularities and pores must be filled before you can get a breathtakingly flat, glowing finish.

Applying fillers can be tricky. If you're not careful you can ruin a few day's work and then have to strip the piece and start all over. A properly filled and finished surface, however, will look as if you could dive into it. You can run your fingernail

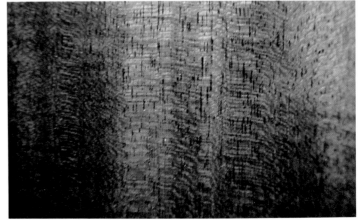

Filled and polished walnut is as smooth as glass.

From *Fine Woodworking* magazine (September 1986) 60:58-61

across the wood and never feel the grain telegraphing through, even with oak or walnut. Visually, the filler will be unobtrusive and subtle, and not affect the clarity or color of the finish.

The two most popular filling methods involve applying numerous thinned coats of the finishing material itself or rubbing in commercial paste fillers made from ground quartz. For special effects, the filler can also be colored to highlight the wood grain and create a decorative look, as shown in the photo on the facing page. As a professional finisher, clarity is one of the qualities I admire most in a finish, so I prefer using the finish itself as a filler. I dislike any finish that obscures the natural beauty of the wood, so I avoid paste fillers and other heavy, opaque fillers as much as possible. With tight, close-grained woods like cherry or maple, white shellac and high-solids-content, water-white lacquer sealer or lacquer work best for me. White shellac is sometimes hard to find, so you might be tempted to substitute orange shellac. That's fine, as long as you don't mind the way the finishing material will change the color of the wood. Experiment on scrap first. On oak, ash, walnut and other open-pored woods where heavier fillers are needed, I tint paste fillers to match the wood, vigorously work the material deep into the pores, then rub and sand off any excess before applying a final finish.

In contrast, when you use a finish for a filler, you apply a coat of finish and sand it down, then repeat the process until the surface is smooth. Both lacquer and shellac dry so quickly that you can apply several filler coats, as well as the top coats, in one day. Shellac can be a filler under almost any finish, except pure tung oil and penetrating oils such as Watco. It's okay under oil-based varnishes, but will make them less resistant to extreme heat, such as a hot pan being dropped on a table. Lacquer works well under lacquer, but not under much else. If you're building a pure polyurethane or varnish finish, use thinned coats of the finish itself as a filler. You still must sand with 400-grit paper between coats, and, since varnish and polyurethane dry so slowly, you can only sand down one coat per day. Any oil finish can be its own filler, but it's a time-consuming process because the oils dry so slowly.

When using a shellac sealer, it's best to mix your own solution with denatured alcohol and shellac flakes or buttons (available from the better finishing supply houses). This guarantees a fresh mixture, essential if the finish is to dry properly, and you can make a thicker "cut" than what's usually available at the hardware store. The "cut" of shellac describes the amount of raw shellac that's dissolved in a gallon of alcohol. A 6-lb.-cut—6 lb. of shellac in one gallon of alcohol—is best as a filler.

Sanding sealer is a good filler under lacquer, but you can use any heavy-bodied lacquer. Sanding sealer is just a type of heavy-bodied lacquer that has a higher percentage of solids and, therefore, fills the pores more rapidly than thinner lacquers. Make sure the lacquer or sealer is water-white clear; the natural amber tone of regular lacquers affects the color of the finish.

When using finish as a filler, remember that you want to level the thin coats of finish you have applied, but you don't want to sand into the wood itself. If you sand into the wood, you will remove some of its color and only the finest touch-up work will blend that spot in with the surrounding surface. This is a problem even when you haven't applied a stain or a dye to the wood. If you've left the wood its natural color, this heavy-handed sanding and filling eventually will lead to a finish that looks blotchy and uneven. If you've applied a stain or dye and sand into the wood, you can usually feather the colors well enough that few

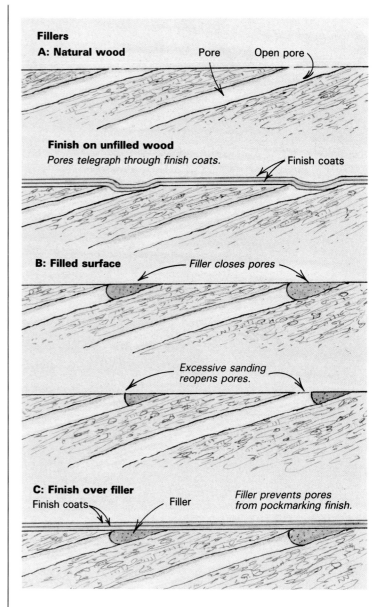

Fillers
A: Natural wood   Pore   Open pore

Finish on unfilled wood
Pores telegraph through finish coats.   Finish coats

B: Filled surface   *Filler closes pores*

Excessive sanding reopens pores.

C: Finish over filler
Finish coats   Filler   *Filler prevents pores from pockmarking finish.*

customers would notice it, but the odds are that you will always notice the repair. If you're aiming for perfection, however, you will have to strip off all the filler and color coats and start over. To minimize the risk of damaging the color coats, I rely on water-based aniline dyes when I want to change wood colors. These dyes penetrate more deeply than pigment stains and are available in a vast array of colors. But, even with aniline dyes, you'll get a color change if you sand through the surface of the wood. Don't make the mistake of assuming you can avoid the problem by staining after filling. Grain sealed with filler doesn't absorb stain well, so the finish will appear blotchy.

While great care is essential when sanding, you shouldn't be so timid about sanding through the finish that you end up laying five or six coats of material before you actually begin to level out the filler. This leads to a heavy look. If you want an unobtrusive filler, you should learn to fill grain with only a few coats. The key is to stay on top of the work at all times, checking your progress at least every minute or so. After a while you will get the feel of when the grain is full and the surface is ready for a coat of finish.

When your wood is sanded to at least 220 grit and ready for finish, brush or spray on a coat of shellac or sanding sealer. When this coat is dry, dry sand the surface carefully with 220-grit wet/dry sandpaper on a felt or rubber sanding block. The goal is to sand the material remaining on the surface of the wood while leaving the material that has settled into the pores and grain. Sand the entire surface evenly in the direction of the grain, being careful not to sand through the filler on the edges. Change the paper when it's clogged, and sand until you have smoothed out all the raised grain, dust and other impurities. Remove these impurities with a blast of compressed air or with a tack rag—excess dust on the surface will work into the pores, blocking the shellac and detracting from the clarity of finish. (I generally buy tack rags from the local paint store, but you can make them with rosin or colophony. Dissolve a teaspoon of the rosin powder in a pint of mineral spirits, add a few drops of linseed oil and soak clean rags in the mixture, then squeeze out as much liquid as possible.) After applying another filler coat and letting it dry, wet sand with water and 220-grit paper. Wipe the surface periodically to check your work (you can't accurately judge a wet surface).

Wet sanding is somewhat faster than dry sanding and the paper doesn't clog as fast. You don't have to wet sand with the grain as long as the paper is clean. I generally find it easier to wet sand with a circular or figure-eight motion. The important thing is to sand evenly. This sanding step will remove a large amount of material (more than the first step) and, with a close-grained wood like cherry, pine or birch, may be almost enough to fill the grain. If you're working with an open-grained species like walnut, oak, elm or mahogany, you probably have a way to go. To check if the grain is full, put a light directly over the furniture and look at the surface from about 2½ ft. in front of the piece and slightly above the level of the top. You shouldn't be able to see any shadows from the grain.

If you don't see any shadows, you can double check your work by looking for highlights in the material. If the surface isn't completely filled, you'll be sanding only the material on the surface, and the sandpaper won't touch the finish that has settled into the pores. These finish-filled pores will appear like shiny little dots. If the grain is full, the sandpaper will reach both the surface and the material in the pores and you won't see any shiny highlights. The entire surface will appear uniformly dull. If you run your fingertips over the surface, you won't feel any surface irregularities. When you think the grain is nearly filled, dry the surface, recoat and wet sand with 320- or 400-grit sandpaper.

With oak and other open-grained woods, it's faster to use a commercial paste filler. These fillers are mixtures of ground quartz (called silex), oil, thinners and other materials, and let you stain the wood at the same time you fill the grain. Check the label before you buy any filler. High-quality fillers are almost pure silex, but numerous low-cost brands are mainly starch or flour. These cheaper fillers are easy to work, but they're worthless because they shrink so much when they dry.

Have the paint store agitate the filler on a mixing machine to lift all the silex that will have settled to the bottom of the can, otherwise you'll spend an hour or so cursing and straining to mix the stuff by hand. You will also need a stiff, wide brush and some paint thinner (unless your brand calls for a specific thinning agent). If you can't buy the color you want, tint the natural filler with any oil-based stain, universal color or Japan color until it's just slightly darker than the desired color. It will lighten as it dries. Don't use any filler labeled "natural" without adding some color. I've always found "natural" fillers to be a bland tan, quite unlike any natural wood shade I've ever encountered. From the start, you should realize that some touchy finishes, such as catalyzed lacquers (see pp. 70-71) may not adhere to paste fillers. Most

finishes will adhere, but some may not be as strong as you expected. For example, polyurethane is very heat resistant, but, if applied over paste filler, will turn white or burn when exposed to extreme heat, just as lacquer or plain varnish would.

Thin the paste filler according to the type of wood being treated. Large, open pores, like oak and walnut, can absorb a lot of silex, so thin the filler just enough to make it brushable. Woods with small, tight pores, like cherry, maple and some exotic hardwoods, need a thinner filler about the consistency of a milk shake. After thinning and coloring the filler, brush it on heavily with a 3-in.-wide brush, as shown in the photo below. Brush against the grain, using the bristles to work the filler into the grain. Do small sections at a time, feathering each section into the next. The filler will have a slightly oily sheen at first

Brush thinned filler on heavily with a 3-in. wide brush.

and look terrible. As soon as the filler dries to a dull shine, rub off the excess with burlap or horsehair, as shown in the photo below. Don't let the filler dry so long that you can't rub it off. If you do, brace yourself for a miserable sanding job. Horsehair is the stuff found in the guts of many old, upholstered chairs, and the best material for rubbing off filler. If you use horsehair, roll it into a ball, dip the ball in some shellac and let it dry before

Vigorously rub off excess filler with a wad of burlap or horsehair.

using. The dried shellac will bind the horsehair together and keep tiny pieces from breaking off.

To remove the filler, grip your ball of burlap or horsehair tightly and firmly rub across the grain. As you're removing the excess filler, you'll be working more of the filler deep into the wood grain. As you remove the excess, gradually lighten your pressure and turn the direction of your rubbing until you are going very lightly with the grain. Next take a clean, soft rag and gently wipe the piece off, photo below, again starting across the direction of the grain and gradually falling into line with it. You should be able to rub the surface perfectly smooth just with the cloth and not have to sand the filler at all. Again, when the pores

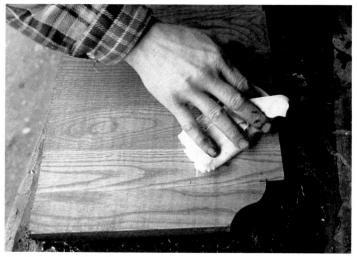

Gently wipe with clean, soft rag until surface is smooth.

are full, you won't see any shadows from the overhead light and the colored filler will be highlighting only the pores. Now leave it alone for a full 24 hours. The slightest handling can mess up the works. After the filler dries, I generally apply a coat of sanding sealer to lock it in, then sand the surface with 400-grit or 600-grit paper, as shown in the photo below, before applying the finish.

You can create some interesting effects by adding aniline

After filler dries, apply sanding sealer to lock it in, then sand.

dyes or other colors to plaster of paris for a filler that will accent the grain of the wood. It's a simple process, but the labor involved is endless. I generally do it only when it's necessary to accent wood grains with different colors. You can begin with a stained or natural board, depending on the effect you're after. Take a little bit of plaster of paris (available from most hardware stores) and mix it with water and a little lime powder to

inhibit the drying. Work the plaster of paris quickly into the grain with your fingertips, cover the whole piece and let it dry. To speed up drying, I sometimes uses an electric heat gun, as shown in the photo below.

The only colors that I find rich enough to use with plaster are aniline dyes. I add the aniline to the plaster while mixing it with water, and then work the plaster in with my fingertips. If you are squeamish about coming into direct contact with aniline, you can use watercolors or other water-based coloring

An electric heat gun speeds drying of plaster filler.

agents. If you simply don't want to have colored fingertips, you can seal the wood before applying the uncolored plaster. After the plaster dries you can brush on the stain. The dried plaster will be able to absorb the water stain, but the sealed wood will not. When the plaster is dry, gently sand the surface with 360-grit or finer paper until the plaster is level with the surface of the wood. This is a slow process. A small serving table can take as long as five hours.

My favorite formal finish is lacquer sprayed over a lacquer filler. If I don't have spraying facilities, I favor a shellac filler, a couple of coats of shellac, then two coats of varnish. You can also get a formal look with just tung oil, but it takes time. You can increase the oil penetration and make it a better filler by heating the oil before you apply it. Boil a pan of water, remove the pan from the stove, then put a coffee can of oil into the water until the oil warms up. I use shellac and varnish over paste fillers, but these fillers are seldom my first choice. Putting colored solids into the wood pores detracts from the appearance and clarity of the finish, which I think is the hallmark of a really fine job. ☐

David Shaw is a writer and finisher in Kelly Corners, N.Y.

Sources of supply

Among the finishing products used by Shaw are:

Natural paste filler No. 101, colored fillers, Japan colors by Ronan and Universal colors, available from Industrial Finishing Products, 2624 Pitkin Ave., Brooklyn, NY 11208.

Behlens Pore-O-Pack paste filler, natural No. 99-P-03.01, colored fillers, shellac and aniline dyes, available from Mohawk Finishing Prod., Rt. 30 North, Amsterdam, NY 12010.

Behlens Pore-O-Pack paste wood filler, shellac and dyes, available from Garrett-Wade Co., 161 Ave. of the Americas, N.Y., NY 10013.

Dri semi-paste filler natural No. D70T1, available from Sherman Williams Co., 101 Prospect Ave., Cleveland, OH 44115.

Polyurethane Finishes
Price tells as much as the label on the can

by Otto Heuer

Companies manufacturing polyurethane describe it as a stunning finish that is unbelievably tough. Even though some craftsmen complain that the glossy finish has an artificial, plastic look, it does wear well, resists scratches and other abrasions, and is virtually impervious to household chemicals and detergents, alcohol, even boiling water.

Picking the right polyurethane for your job can be a bewildering journey through a maze of cans: Urethane Finish; Polyurethane Varnish; Clear Gloss Urethane; Spar Urethane; Polyurethane Liquid Plastic; Polyurethane Reinforced Varnish; Spar Urethane Varnish. The composition labels on the cans are difficult to understand, and at times, remind me of the old saying about well-organized confusion. I know one man who was so confused he wasn't sure if he bought polyurethane or something being compared to polyurethane (he bought oil-based varnish).

Part of the confusion comes from the chemical complexity of polyurethanes. They are not merely blends of solvents and resins, but highly reacted chemical compounds. In contrast, lacquers are relatively simple mixtures of nitrocellulose (as a film-former), hard resins (to increase gloss), and plasticizers (to make the film more flexible). Traditional varnishes, mixtures of vegetable oils and natural or synthetic resins, are slightly more complex than lacquers. The varnish is heated during the manufacturing process, promoting chemical reactions among the components.

Because of the elaborate equipment needed to produce the complex polyurethane, many small- to medium-size finishing companies don't even manufacture it. They buy "concentrated" resins from some of the country's major chemical companies, blend it with their own ingredients, and market it under their own names. This may explain why I found so many similarities among various brands. I tested 15 clear gloss and 12 satin luster polyurethanes on wood and glass panels as I researched this article. The finishes were so consistently clear and strong I concluded that most of the differences in quality of finish had to do with application methods. Price is also an important factor. If you buy a brand-name product, you improve your chances of getting a good finish. If you buy a bargain-basement brand that's considerably cheaper than the brand-name ones, you're tilting the odds in favor of an inferior result.

The terms polyurethane and urethane have nothing to do with quality—both terms, along with names like urethane polymer and isocyanate polymer, refer to the same type of finish. The name game seems to be mostly a sales gimmick—a label advertising isocyanate polymer might scare people away. "Plastic" is another sales pitch. Although polyurethanes are chemically similar to plastics, the term "synthetic" would be more correct in describing polyurethane, epoxy, and other modern finishes.

Oil-modified polyurethanes are based on vegetable oils (linseed, soya, safflower and others) that have been reacted with polyhydric alcohol (glycerine or pentaerythritol) and diisocyanate. An alkyd-modified polyurethane is composed of the same oils and polyhydric alcohols, but the phthalic anhydride, which is the usual acidic ingredient reacted with the oils and alcohols, is partly replaced by a portion of diisocyanate. In both oil-modified and alkyd-modified mixtures the amount of diisocyanate, the most expensive ingredient in the mixtures, affects the hardness, chemical and abrasion resistance, and drying speed of the film.

The chemical reaction that produces polyurethane must take place in a large (1,000 gallons or larger), closed, stainless steel reactor. The air in the vessel usually is replaced with carbon dioxide before the tank is heated, to prevent discoloration of the raw materials during the reaction. After the reaction is completed, the resinous mixture is cooled, then pumped from the reactor vessel into a thinning tank, where it is reduced with mineral spirits (or other petroleum distillates) until it is about 60% to 70% non-volatile solids by weight.

I have formulated oil-modified polyurethanes for several small companies by blending these "concentrated" polyurethane resins with alkyds to improve adhesion and reduce cost, and for semi-gloss and satin mixtures, silicates as flatting agents to reduce gloss, and anti-settling agents to keep the silicates and the solvents from separating. At this point, small amounts of metallic dryers (cobalt, calcium and zirconium) are added. To prevent the polyurethane from skinning over in the can, anti-oxidant agents are also added. Then the mixture is thinned with mineral spirits until it is 45% to 50% solids by weight.

The type of oil used in the manufacturing process is a good guide to several aspects of finish quality. Polyurethanes are never water-white clear, but they have a tendency to darken to an amber color as they age. This is especially true if linseed oil is the base. With soybean oil mixtures, the dried film will be slightly lighter and have less tendency to darken with age. Polyurethanes based on safflower oil darken the least, and, therefore, are most suitable for finishing furniture and interior woodwork made of light-colored (not stained) woods like white pine, birch and maple.

Gloss polyurethanes tend to be tougher than the satin finishes, which contain transparent, inert silica powder that serves as a flatting agent. The light, fluffy silica has a tendency to float to the surface while the polyurethane is drying. Light rays striking these transparent particles tend to scatter, thus reducing the gloss. This loss of strength is insignificant on interior finishes, and you may decide you prefer the satin look because scratches and defects in the finish are less noticeable. Gloss finishes tend to magnify any

From *Fine Woodworking* magazine (July 1986) 59:70-73

imperfections; satin finishes are more forgiving.

Manufacturers rate the durability of polyurethanes as an exterior finish at fair to good, depending on the climate. Linseed-based polyurethanes are slightly better than the other types and I'd recommend you use only these as an exterior finish. Patio furniture left outdoors during the spring and summer, but stored inside for the winter, should look good for several seasons with this finish. This toughness also makes the linseed-based formulas better for floors and other heavy-wear areas.

Other types of polyurethanes are available, but are not recommended for small production and home shop use. These two-component industrial coatings are used on laboratory equipment, skis and tennis rackets, and as anti-graffiti shields in schools and on subways. Some stores specializing in automotive refinishing paints and enamels handle these finishes, but they're expensive, tricky to mix and apply, and usually available only in large quantities. Once the clear resin and catalyst are mixed, the finish thickens within 2 to 8 hours and even the strongest solvents can't stop it.

You might also find moisture-cured polyurethanes at your local hardware store, but avoid them unless you plan to work fast and use the whole can in one application. These polyurethanes harden quickly after being exposed to the air, and will continue to harden after the can is resealed. They're also very sensitive to impurities and tend to flake off if contaminated during application.

In trying to gauge the strength and quality of various polyurethanes, I applied the finishes to small panes of glass and a series of 6-in. by 12-in. panels of mahogany, walnut, cherry, and other woods. Since the glass won't absorb finish the way wood does, it is a good surface for checking the drying time of the film and determining if it is seedy (contains impurities), cloudy, or too viscous to flow out evenly. To check flow out, I poured a little bit of each sample on clean pieces of 6-in. by 10-in. window glass held in an upright position so the excess would flow off. Flow out can be a problem with polyurethanes. Their fast drying time prevents the film from flowing out and "bridging over" very small pores in the wood. If you hold the panels on an angle, you can sometimes see little pockmarks beneath the surface. I found these imperfec-

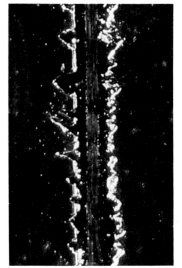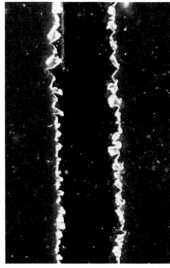

To compare flexibility and chip-resistance, scratch the dried finish off a pane of glass with a coin. A brittle finish fragments (left). A more flexible one (right) peels off as a smoother strip.

tions occurred when the finish was too thick—either it wasn't thinned properly or was applied in a too-cold room. For best results, the finishing area should be from 70°F to 80°F. If you find your finish hasn't flowed properly, you may be able to wash off the partially dry film with mineral spirits. Otherwise, let it harden, then sand it with 600-grit wet/dry paper before applying another, thinner coat.

A good way to gauge the hardness or adhesion of a sample is to hold a nickel on end between your thumb and index finger and scratch the finish. It may take two or three passes to scratch through a very hard finish. If the dried finish scratches into little flakes or fragments, I'd call the film brittle. If the edge of the coin cuts through the film and takes off a soap-like cheesy strip, I'd call the film flexible. A flexible film will most likely be a better finish on wood, since it will not chip easily. All of the brands I tested produced a film that was strong and flexible enough to be re-

Reading the label

Confirms product is a urethane. Another commonly found term is isocyanate polymer.

Linseed-based polyurethanes make the most durable finish, but tend to darken more than other types. Soybean oil mixtures slightly lighter and darken less. Safflower mixtures darken the least.

Metallic solutions (cobalt, calcium and zirconium) to speed drying.

Flatting agents (silicates) to reduce gloss. Found in satin-type finishes. The silica decreases film strength, but the effect is insignificant for most interior applications.

Composition by Weight
Non-Volatile 46%
Polyurethane fortified Linseed Oil Alkyd Resin 41.0%
Driers 0.3%
Silicates 2.5%
Ultra Violet Light Absorbers & Additives 2.2%
Volatile 54%
Non-Photochemically Reactive Petroleum Thinners ... 54.0%
MO–159   100.0%

Percentage of solids, the finish material left on the surface when the solvent dissipates, indicates thickness of film.

Additives include anti-settling agents in satin finishes (to prevent silicates from separating out of solvent) and anti-oxidants (to prevent finish from skinning over in can).

Added to exterior finishes to increase resistance to sunlight.

Solvents complying with state and federal air pollution regulations. Thin with mineral spirits for maximum cutting power, use regular spirits, not odorless kind.

Spraying polyurethanes and other varnishes

by Nancy Lindquist

In our furniture shop people ask for "that plastic finish" on their fine furniture, so they can enjoy the beauty of the wood without "doing anything" to take care of it. "Miracle" finishes don't exist, but apparently miracles happen everyday in the marketing of furniture finishes. Urethanes are known for their toughness, but like any other finish, they're only as tough as the wood they protect and I don't think they are the best choice for every piece of furniture. I choose polyurethane for interior floors, trim work, bar tops and table surfaces subjected to heavy wear, marring, heat and water exposure. The best way I've found to apply polyurethanes and varnishes is spraying, which eliminates brush marks and many of the contamination problems that can mess up a finish.

Because of their high solids content, polyurethanes and varnishes have tremendous "build." Unlike lacquers, in which each coat dissolves the previous coat to form a single or monolithic film, varnishes and polyurethanes form distinct layers that are stacked on top of each other. This makes adhesion to the wood and between coats a primary concern.

For good adhesion, use the same polyurethane or varnish finish for the entire job, from the first sealer coat to the final top coat. Commercial sanding sealers are less expensive, faster drying, and easier to sand, but they may reduce the bond between the wood and the top coats. In contrast, a thinned coat of polyurethane will penetrate deeply into the pores of the wood to provide a better grip for subsequent layers. A heavy coat of the finish, however, may bridge the wood pores and reduce adhesion. The wood should be clean and free of wax, grease or oil. I wash the raw wood with naptha and clean rags before I begin. Scuff-sanding between coats gives the polyurethane layers a mechanical bond that helps adhesion. Heavy oil glazes floated between the finish coats, thick staining, or fillers will cause adhesion problems.

I spray polyurethane and other varnishes with a conventional cup gun with a general purpose or standard lacquer fluid nozzle and either a standard lacquer air cap or a lacquer primer air cap, if the finish is a little cool to spray. The gun must be clean. Before using it, I clean the gun by spraying and backflushing with lacquer thinner, and then blow air through the gun until the solvent has evaporated. After spraying, I clean the gun with mineral spirits first, then lacquer thinner.

Not all brands of finish spray easily. I've had good results with Pratt & Lambert products. I thin the material as little as possible and deliver it at the lowest air pressure that will make it flow without obvious spray texture. (For technical fanatics this is a viscoscity of between 14 to 16 seconds at room temperature with a #2 Zahn cup. My air pressure at the regulator is between 30 and 35 PSI with a 25-ft. hose.) It's no problem on tabletops to adjust the flow by trial and error—thinning the finish to reduce viscosity and manipulating the fluid valve to change the spray pattern. On vertical surfaces, though, you risk applying finish that's too thin and runs, or of spraying such a heavy coat that it sags. If you're accustomed to spraying lacquers, polyurethane will feel heavy and clumsy because of its higher solid content and lower viscosity. I always test the finish first on a vertical sample board so I can adjust my spray pattern and see how much I can apply before it sags. If you run out of patience before you get

moved from the glass after 24-hours drying time by lifting one edge of the film with a razor blade. After 72-hours drying time, none of the films could be easily peeled off the glass.

In applying the finish on wood, I followed the instructions on the labels, let each coat dry as directed, then sanded lightly between coats with 600-grit paper. Make sure you follow the manufacturer's instructions on recoating times. If you let polyurethane cure more than about four hours, the film becomes so hard and inert that the solvents in the following coats won't soften the previous coats enough to allow the new material to adhere. If you wait too long between coats and have to scuff-sand before applying another coat, do so carefully—you don't want any scratches in the film. Avoid using steel wool for the scuff-sanding—the fuzzy fibers will stick in the finish. In most cases, the best looking and most durable finish comes from three to four thin coats rather than two heavy ones.

Most of the manufacturers recommend that polyurethanes be reduced 10% to 20% by volume with mineral spirits for a first coat on unfinished wood. This thinned mixture penetrates the wood much more effectively than unreduced polyurethane, which is viscous enough to stay on the surface. Subsequent coats may be applied without thinning, but I recommend you thin the top coat about 5% if the label states that the finish is 45% to 50% non-volatile solids. Always use regular mineral spirits, which has more cutting power than the odorless kind. This will enable you to thin the polyurethane without drastically altering the percentage of film-forming solids, thereby interfering with proper drying.

For applying the top coats, I used a foam-type applicator instead of a bristle brush. Even the best brushes leave some marks on the surface, whereas the foam brush (urethane foam) produces a very smooth film. For best results, dip the applicator in the finish, just as you would a brush, and apply it cross-grain, feathering out the strokes in opposite directions. The finish should flow together smoothly. If you soak the foam applicators in mineral spirits you might be able to clean and reuse them, but they're so inexpensive I just discard them.

Labels on many brands warn the user: "Do not shake the can, but stir the contents of the can before using." Shaking may prothe gun adjusted, you can always brush the verticals and try a different brand next time.

Apply the finish in a clean, controlled environment and keep the area dust-free while the finish is drying. Before spraying, I sweep sanding dust and overspray in my spray booth, then sprinkle water on the floor around the project to reduce static that might attract dust. A plastic drop cloth suspended over my drying area prevents direct fallout from my tar roof. I also like to change into clean clothes and wear a cap to keep personal touches out of the finish. Eliminate traffic in the area until the surface is "tack free." Your nose is a good guide on when the finish is dry. If you can't smell solvent, it's safe to touch the surface. (The rest of the time I wear an organic solvent respirator.)

Besides the bugs and junk in the air, watch for contaminants in the can. You may have problems if you leave the lid off while you're sweeping up, or if you use an improperly cleaned brush containing traces of old stain or dried varnish. Varnish won't redissolve after it dries. You must strain out the dried specks of cured varnish, called seeds, by filtering the finish through a paper-cone strainer. Some finishes just come seedy; it's a measure of quality for the finish to be clear in the can. If the finish looks cloudy or foamy, something is probably wrong. When you thin the finish, always use the solvent recommended by the manufacturer, who's the only one that really knows what's in that can.

One brand's "satin" sheen looks like what another brand calls "semi-gloss," so you may have to experiment to find the look you want. The manufacturer's idea of what's "satin" may not match yours. Mix the finish just enough to lift any flatting agents that have settled to the bottom of the can and blend them evenly with the solvents. Overmixing may create bubbles that will pop and make craters in the finish film. Undermixing may produce an uneven sheen. Make a sample chip for each product you use to serve as a reference for future jobs.

When you apply the finish, it helps to use the automotive technique of first spraying a light "tacky" coat with very little overlapping on verticals. When you come over this with a wet coat, it will hold easier without sagging. On tops I want an even film thickness and texture, not only for a smooth finish but for an even sheen. I'll first spray across the grain and then, with a second pass, go with the grain for an even, full wet coat. It is very tempting to put on more in one coat because it looks so great when you spray the tops, but thin coats dry most evenly.

Temperature and humidity also affect finish quality. With polyurethanes and other varnishes, temperatures below 65°F and high humidity slow drying time and invite runs and sags. I think the labels should read, "dries in four hours unless you live in Missouri where it may take three days!" Temperatures above 85°F may cause the finish to dry too quickly, leaving a skin over the surface that

traps solvents and uncured finish underneath. Direct sunlight or strong drafts on the wet finish also trap solvents and prevent even drying. The older the finish, the longer it takes to dry. If the finish is too thick and cold to apply, warm it by placing the can in a sink full of warm water.

Polyurethanes also differ from varnishes in that they don't rub out or flow under friction. A gloss finish will polish well if you apply liquid polishes and buff. For lesser sheens, practice until you can spray cleanly enough to avoid rubbing the surface. If you do try to rub the surface, you risk uneven glossy or hazy patches and scratches. If you want a rubbed finish, apply varnish.

It's ironic that one disadvantage of varnishes and polyurethanes is that they do build so fast. The biggest complaints about polyurethane involve putting too much on. If you spray the surface, you'll be using thinner coats and be able to control the thickness of the film more easily than if you were brushing it on. If you spray or wipe a couple of really thin coats of urethane on a nice piece of wood, most people would never question your saying it was an "oiled" finish. This is something most purists would hate to admit, but others know it's true and use this fact to their advantage. □

Nancy Lindquist operates Kansas City Woodworking with her husband, John, and Integrated Finish Systems, an architectural millwork finishing shop in Kansas City, Mo.

duce air bubbles in the applied films. When these air bubbles burst, they create small pinholes, or, if the finish dries before the bubbles break, you're left with air pockets in the film. The labels also warn against applying polyurethane over lacquer sealer, shellac, traces of varnish removers containing paraffin, wood fillers or pigmented wiping stains containing stearates or other waxy substances that will prevent the polyurethane from adhering.

Adhesion problems arise whenever polyurethane is applied over another finish. For the polyurethane to adhere, you must scuff the old finish enough to provide a mechanical bond between the roughened surface of the old finish and the fresh coat of polyurethane. Sand the old finish carefully, using 400-grit paper for gloss and 320- or 280-grit for satin. Follow the direction of the grain, but don't go down to the bare wood. Remove dust and debris with mineral spirits on a clean, lint-free rag. This will clean the surface as well as a tack rag, and you don't risk leaving any oily residue to contaminate the surface. Touch up any surface defects, such as scratches and bare spots. Apply a thin coat of polyurethane, and let it dry several hours before

sanding with 600-grit paper and applying another coat.

Proper ventilation is needed whenever you apply polyurethane. Dry, cured polyurethane films are non-toxic, according to federal guidelines, but be careful with the liquid. With spray applications, use a respirator—every label I saw indicated that breathing the spray was harmful and dangerous. Don't get any in your eyes and avoid prolonged skin contact. If the label states flammable, do not use the material near open flames, pilot lights electric sparks or similar hazards. Throw used rags into a pail of water to prevent possible spontaneous combustion.

Polyurethane can look as good as most varnishes, and offers a number of advantages over varnish. It dries faster, thereby reducing the chance of dust contamination, cures at a lower temperature, has a higher gloss, and has better wear and water resistance. Polyurethane is also easy to maintain. You don't even have to worry about waxing the finish—just buff it with a soft cloth periodically. □

Otto Heuer is a finishes consultant in Waukegan, Ill.

Versatile Varnish

A *reliable finish* for a small shop

by Craig Deller

Brushing varnish can yield good results. To avoid air bubbles in the finish, don't scrape the brush on the side of the can, but allow excess to run off, as shown by the author.

One difficulty of running a small shop, either as a hobby or a business, is producing a flawless finish without a huge investment of time or money. Lacquer is first choice in many operations, but the potential health and fire hazards of lacquer mist require special booths, exhaust fans and spark-proof electrical components for spraying this highly volatile material. Varnish is not as explosive, although it doesn't set or cure as quickly as lacquer. Also, varnish can be applied easily with a pad, brush or by spraying, making it an excellent, reliable finish well suited for use in the small shop. You can also mix varnishes of various sheens to create the exact gloss and toughness needed for a particular job. Even though it's less explosive than lacquer, varnish should be sprayed only with adequate ventilation, and users should always be aware of any local fire codes.

Modern varnishes offer advantages over other traditional finishes as well. I prefer it over shellac and lacquer because it's more durable and more resistant to heat and alcohol damage. A kitchen table in a house full of "wee ones" demands the tough, elastic finish of varnish that shellac cannot achieve. Oil finishes, due to their deep penetration, are irreversible and therefore unsuitable for restoration work I do on historic objects. Linseed oil is the worst because it darkens the wood initially and continually darkens it until the piece is almost black. My ethics will not allow me to use a urethane–no plastics in this shop–so a high-quality varnish fits the bill perfectly. A purist may argue that synthetic resins are, in fact, ingredients of plastic, but I don't consider them in the same category of liquid plastics as urethane.

The long and short of varnishes–Although varnishes have been used for more than 2,000 years, early varnishes were mainly spirit varnishes, such as shellac, dammar or mastic dissolved in alcohol. These spirit varnishes were brittle, susceptible to alcohol and water damage, and difficult to polish to a high gloss. It wasn't until the middle ages that a German monk, Theophilus Presbyter, developed a way to heat and mix amber, a fossil resin, and linseed oil to create what I refer to as drying-oil varnishes. Based on oils such as linseed, safflower or other vegetable-based oils, these varnishes dry by chemical change through oxidation, polymerization and evaporation. The fossil-resin varnishes have two major disadvantages: the resins are rare and expensive, and the linseed oil yellows and darkens the wood. Fortunately, the mid-20th-century development of much cheaper and cleaner syn-

From *Fine Woodworking* magazine (July 1989) 77:64-67

thetic alkyd resins in a soya oil, safflower oil, other vegetable oil or china-wood oil vehicle has given the use of drying-oil varnishes a new lease on life.

All modern drying-oil varnishes can be divided into two groups: long oil and short oil. Long-oil varnishes, commonly known as spar varnishes, have a high proportion of drying oil in relation to resin. High oil content retards the curing of the varnish, but makes the cured film tougher and more elastic, rendering spar varnishes ideal for exterior work and boats. Short-oil varnishes, with lower proportions of oil to resin, are more appropriate for furniture. They are the only type I use because they produce harder, faster and more completely cured finishes and thus polish better. Cured varnishes are impervious to their original solvent and removable only with methylene chloride or a similar solution. Such a harsh removal procedure would be unacceptable for an object of historical value, making varnish an inappropriate finish for these pieces. The insolubility of varnish, however, offers some distinct benefits, especially when spraying.

I have been spraying a variety of off-the-shelf and commercial varnishes in my restoration work for years. I've found that Pratt & Lambert's #38 Clear Finish works best. It can produce nearly any effect from a subtle, waxed glow to a hard, mirror-like shine by mixing various sheens. All varnishes come in a naturally glossy state. Manufacturers make varnishes satin or dull by adding flatting agents, such as aluminum stearate and silica, to break up the light reflection and produce the softer look. Even though all commercial varnishes are prepackaged as gloss, satin or dull, the amounts of the flatting agents can be adjusted simply by mixing gloss with satin or satin with dull in various combinations. I buy varnish in gallon cans, but break it down into quart containers because they are easier to work with and increase the varnish's shelf life by decreasing its exposure to air. I also mix various sheens to achieve the desired degree of gloss. I have found a 50:50 mix of gloss and satin is best for most situations. A straight satin is good for projects with lots of turnings and carvings. You can steel wool and wax the finish to produce a good luster without beating your brains out trying to tone down the shine from the gloss or even the 50:50 mix. If you are looking for the simple elegance of a soft, waxed glow, apply a thin coat of dull varnish to seal the wood before waxing. By using the same mixture of varnishes for each coat of a project, you can eliminate variations in sheen and the possibility of rubbing through one layer to a different sheen.

Ease of application—Varnish is a good brush-on finish because its 15-minute working time is sufficient to do a fairly large table top. Although I prefer spraying whenever possible, brushing is the only choice for some jobs, such as on-site finishing of cabinets or paneling. The first consideration here is the brush. I prefer a well-broken-in china-bristle brush; I've been using one for years and I'm comfortable with it. You might prefer a foam brush because it doesn't generate as many air bubbles and it eliminates problems with brush marks and loose bristles. Although I use the varnish straight from the can, thinning with a good-quality turpentine will slightly retard setting time.

Air bubbles are a major concern when brushing varnish because they leave little pockets in the finish. Bubbles can be introduced when mixing sheens, stirring the varnish or loading your brush. While the big bubbles go away fairly quickly, it may take the little ones overnight. I stir the varnish gently with a regular paint stick. Proper loading of the brush, as shown in the photo on the facing page, however, is dependent upon the quality of the brush you are using. Better brushes will hold more varnish without dripping, allowing you to apply a more even, consistent coat with fewer trips to the varnish can. Start off by dipping your brush into the varnish about 1 to 1½ in. If the varnish runs from your brush, you have too much and will end up with runs and sags. Don't put so much on that you must scrape the brush along the edge of the can as this will fill the brush with air bubbles. Too little varnish will result in more frequent trips to the varnish can. I've always found it best to brush against the grain, then lightly "tip-off" with the grain using long, light, even strokes. This helps to work the varnish into the open grain, provides a more even distribution and avoids trapping any air bubbles. Remember, applying a number of thin coats, rather than a couple of thick ones, avoids the sags, runs and wrinkles that are sure signs of an amateur.

Since drying-oil varnishes polymerize, the subsequent coats do not "melt" the previous layers as the spirit varnishes do. I hand sand between coats, starting with 220-grit silicon carbide paper for the first coat and then use 320-grit and 400-grit for subsequent coats, which levels the finish and provides a physical "key" for the next coat. An electric palm sander works well if you stay with light grits to avoid orbital marks. I wipe off the sanding dust between coats with a homemade tack cloth, which is made by spraying a small amount of varnish on a lint-free cloth, and lightly dust the piece. Don't blow the sanding dust off because it will just land on something else. Avoid commercially prepared tack cloths as some contain non-drying oils, like mineral or raw linseed oil, and any residue may impede the drying of the next coat. I generally allow 16 hours to 48 hours between coats depending on drying conditions. If the surface is still a bit soft (the sandpaper clogs), I lightly sand the surface using the current grit paper to break open the skin and allow further solvent evaporation and oxidation before proceeding with the next coat. You will find curing from the outside in, known as "skinning over," to be a problem if you try to speed up drying with a fan. Without driers, standard short-oil varnishes require about 30 days for a full cure.

Spraying varnish is faster, speeds up drying time and eliminates brush marks, air bubbles and foreign matter that comes off a brush. And no, it does not destroy the spray gun. Basic equipment is all that's required (see photo at left). The air compressor doesn't have to be big and expensive, but should be rated at about 100 psi and have an in-line filter to prevent water and oil from mixing with the varnish. My compressor is about 30 years old and the

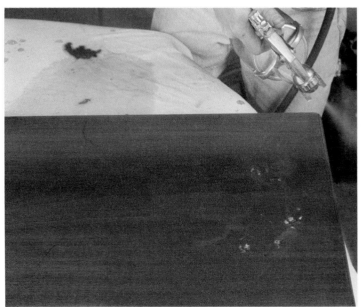

Spraying varnish requires a minimum investment in equipment, is easy to do and yields extremely good results.

motor needs an occasional smack with a hammer, but it works just fine. The spray gun is important enough to warrant a good one, so stay away from the toys. I have a stainless-steel, siphon-feed type gun available from any of a number of manufacturers such as Binks, DeVilbiss or Grainger (see sources of supply box on p. 39). In addition to the spraying equipment, I have constructed a room with an old furnace blower inside a sealed box to pull the air through a series of filters to trap the solids and prevent the overspray from settling on other projects. Again, you should check to be sure you are in compliance with any local fire codes. And even though the vapors aren't anywhere near as obnoxious as lacquer, you should have a high-quality face mask to protect yourself. I use a Pulmosan #10768 with a 17160 CAM charcoal cartridge, available from Reliable Finishing Products Inc.

Before pouring the varnish into the gun cup, it should always be strained, for even the smallest particles will cause the gun to clog and spit. The simplest strainer is made from panty hose. I use a relatively low spraying pressure (40 psi), which minimizes overspray, reduces the amount of material wasted and eliminates "pooling," which is caused by excessive air pressure pushing the varnish around. I spray in a normal crisscross pattern, about 12 in. from the piece, keeping the pattern tight to ensure even coverage. Although varnish, unlike lacquer, will build easily, it is still best to spray more light coats than few heavy ones. I find commercial varnishes spray quite easily without thinning even at 40 psi. If you prefer a thinner mix, I recommend adding a high-quality naptha until the varnish is thinned to the consistency of loose honey. It will take very little naptha, perhaps ½ oz. per quart, to achieve this consistency. The naptha will also speed up the drying process slightly. Because turpentine extends the drying time, it would be a mistake to use it as a thinner when spraying.

To further enhance drying, one of varnish's touted "problems," I add a metallic drier; I prefer Grumbacher's Artist's Oil Medium Cobalt Drier over the more common and inferior japan driers because it doesn't crack, crawl, alligator or darken. I add the drier to each quart container of varnish; one drop, maybe two, per quart is

Varnish finishes can also be colored to match old work or to achieve an antiqued appearance by adding oil-based stains before spraying.

plenty, as too much drier can actually retard the drying process. Then I mix thoroughly with an ordinary kitchen blender on low. Don't worry about the air bubbles because they'll be eliminated when sprayed. By shortening set-up time, the driers help eliminate sags and dust collection. Even with the drier I still allow 16 hours to 48 hours between coats, sanding as previously specified. I allow about a week before doing the final rub out.

The fact that varnish does not melt the previous coats allows greater freedom during spraying. By inspecting a piece after spraying, I can catch those drips, sags and fly tracks that may appear, level them with my finger without removing previous coats and lightly touch up with additional sprayed varnish. Although working time to catch these drips will vary depending upon the amount of driers or thinners used, I find about 10 minutes to be optimal. This allows time for the sags and runs to develop, but allows you to catch them before they start to set.

The non-melting advantage can also help in the constant battle against silicone contamination, the most common source being spray-on waxes like Pledge. Cleaning the piece with TSP (trisodi-

Silicone damage, shown at right, can be covered by "dusting," spraying several light coats, and allowing five minutes drying time between coats until the silicone is sealed in, as shown on the left. Additional coats can then be sprayed on without fear of fisheye and other defects.

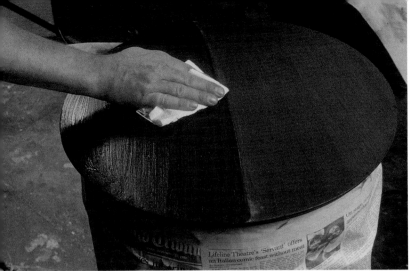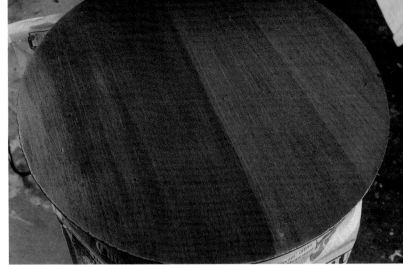

Glazing is done by thoroughly sanding the first coat of varnish and then wiping with an oil-based stain (above, left). Remove any heavy build-up before spraying additional coats of varnish. The subtle tone change obtainable is evident in the photo above, right.

um phosphate), available from most hardware stores, will not solve the problem, but will lessen the severity of the reaction between the new finish and silicone. I never use commercial silicone eliminators, such as fish-eye eliminators, because these products are pure silicone themselves, merely making the finish compatible with silicone and contaminating your equipment. If silicone damage does show up, wipe off the offending coat and begin "dusting." Spraying very light coats from 18 in. to 24 in. will merely dust the surface, not allowing the varnish to flow and separate. After five minutes, dust again, then repeat until you have an adequate coat to seal the surface and any residual silicone. Once thoroughly dry, the dusting coats are sanded and leveled for the next coat. Since the fresh coat of varnish will not melt the previous one, the first coat will not flow and separate. But should the second coat still show some reaction to the silicone damage, simply wipe it off and dust again. Although the stability of any finish over silicone is unknown, I've never had any trouble with a finish I've dusted. The bottom photo on the facing page demonstrates the results obtainable by the dusting technique.

After each spraying session, your spray gun should be cleaned thoroughly no matter what you are shooting. For cleanup after varnishing, I use the highest-grade gum-spirit turpentine because it effectively dissolves varnish in ways mineral spirits, or even naptha, cannot. Occasionally it will be necessary to thoroughly clean the gun with a mild, liquid, non-flammable methylene-chloride mixture by soaking, not spraying, then rinsing with lacquer thinner to remove all the dissolved residue. Don't allow the gun to sit too long in the methylene chloride as it may damage the seals.

Additional techniques—Varnish can also be colored with a certain degree of success by using chemically compatible oil-based stains, such as Fuller O'Brien's. Adding a small amount of additional oil to the varnish mixture may prolong the drying slightly. Dry pigments work well also, but require more mixing to achieve natural tones. Because it can be difficult to achieve the proper mix, I use dry pigments only when trying to match a finish or for custom work. Although not recommended for heavy coloring, this technique is helpful for subtle tone changes, as shown in the top photo on the facing page. If you do not wish to color the varnish directly, you can do a simple glazing. After a thorough sanding of the first coat of varnish, dip a paper towel into the desired color of oil-based stain and wipe down the piece; don't allow any heavy buildup to remain. Allow the piece to dry and proceed with the next coat of varnish. (See the two photos above.)

Another good feature is that varnish can be used as a light filler

on open grain wood. I spray on a fairly heavy coat of varnish, allow it to set slightly, then, using a lint-free rag, work the varnish into the grain and wipe off any heavy excess. While this does not fill the grain completely, it doesn't change the color tone as most fillers do. Also, varnish can be used as a sanding sealer by thinning slightly before spraying. While some people will use alcohol-based shellac for this purpose, I feel it is chemically prudent to stick with a single class of finishing products throughout the project, such as the oil-based varnish for filler and/or sealer and the top coats.

I always rub out the finishes starting with fine-grit sandpaper, 320 for brushed finishes and 600 to 1200 for sprayed surfaces, using paraffin oil as a lubricant. This is followed by buffing with any one of a variety of rubbing compounds, from pumice and rottenstone to automotive compounds. See Michael Dresdner's article "Rubbing out a Finish" on pp. 50-52 for appropriate techniques in applying these compounds. Even though varnish tends to be much tougher than shellac or even nitro-cellulose lacquer, it still needs proper care after rubbing out. The best protection for any finish is a superior-quality paste wax. After much experimentation in my shop I have settled on "Beauté Satin Creme Wax," available from Roger A. Reed Inc. It can be very easily colored by mixing in a bit of artist's oil colors, a particularly helpful trick for coloring marks and sealing leather. The wax can even be made into a rubbing compound by mixing in pumice or rottenstone for that final, satin-smooth shine. □

Craig Deller owns and operates Deller Restorations Ltd. Inc. in Geneva, Ill. He specializes in fine antique furniture restorations.

Sources of supply

Fuller O'Brien and P&L products are available from most hardware stores or write for the location of the nearest distributor:
Fuller-O'Brien, 450 E. Grand Ave. S., San Francisco, CA 94087.
Pratt & Lambert Inc., Box 22, Buffalo, NY 14240.

For spray guns and pneumatic equipment, write to the following suppliers for the location of the nearest distributor:
Binks Manufacturing Co., 9201 W. Belmont Ave., Franklin Park, IL 60131.
The DeVilbiss Co., Box 913, Toledo, OH 43692.
W.W. Grainger Inc., 5959 W. Howard St., Chicago, IL 60648.

Cobalt driers are available from most artist supply houses or from the following supplier:
Grumbacher, M. Inc., 30 Engelhard Drive, Cranbury, NJ 08512.

Face masks and filters are available from:
Reliable Finishing Products Inc., 2625 Greenleaf Ave., Elk Grove, IL 60007.

Beauté Satin Cream Wax is available from:
Roger A. Reed Inc., Box 508, Reading, MA 01867.

Water-Based Varnishes
How they compare to the old favorites

by Don Newell

Though you might not have heard of water-based "latex" varnishes, they've been around for about ten years. But they've been easy to overlook because they haven't been advertised very much. I decided to find out if these finishes are good enough to use on a valuable piece of furniture, and, if so, why I should choose one instead of a tried and true conventional varnish. I did some experimenting with different brands to see how well they performed.

Why make a water-based varnish? Two reasons: Brushes clean up in soap and water, as long as the varnish hasn't hardened; and, unlike conventional solvent-based varnishes, water-based materials don't pollute the air with hydrocarbons as they dry. Because these water-based formulas contain negligible amounts of organic solvents, they provide an alternative for woodworkers concerned about exposure to toxic conventional finishes.

The water-based clan are not varnishes in the traditional sense. With conventional varnishes, after most of the solvent has evaporated, the film begins to harden by first absorbing oxygen (a process called oxidation), then polymerizing: the molecules cross-link to form a hard film that, once dry, is no longer soluble in the original solvent. In contrast, water-based varnishes consist of a solution of film-forming polymers (usually acrylic resins) dispersed in a carrying medium of water. When the water evaporates, the dispersed polymer particles coalesce to form a coherent, protective acrylic film—much the same way that PVA glues cure.

Water-based latex varnishes, as a group, are still evolving. Some have come and gone, while others are still available. Both Valspar and PPG Industries, for example, marketed water-based products in the mid 1970s, but eventually withdrew them because they didn't perform well.

I bought a can of every brand of clear water-based varnish I could lay my hands on, which amounted to five: Sears Interior Latex Varnish, Deft Interior Acrylic Wood Armor, Flecto Varathane Ultra Plastic Finish, Fuller O'Brien Pen-Chrome Super-V Varnish, and Benjamin Moore VaquaKleer. As a benchmark for comparison, I used ZAR Antique Polyurethane Varnish, which is a conventional polyurethane. In general, the price of water-based varnishes is somewhat higher than that of regular varnishes.

All the water-based clears I tested contained about the same percentage of solids, a level considerably below that of their conventional counterparts. And all carried virtually the same directions on the can labels, such as the need to use nylon-bristle brushes or short-hair rollers to apply the material. Although the labels don't mention it, some manufacturers recommend spraying as an alternative to brushing.

I applied two coats of each brand on pine, walnut and mahogany boards, allowing the first coat to dry overnight before laying on the second. I tried to duplicate the brushing of an actual piece of cabinetry by applying the varnishes to both

Each brand of water-based varnish tested had its own brushing characteristics. Some were watery, others were much like regular varnish. Brushing all five brands on the same board allowed Newell to compare the quality of the films side-by-side.

horizontal and vertical surfaces. It was under these real working conditions that I discovered the vast difference in workability between the brands. The Sears Latex and Deft Wood Armor were so thin-bodied that they brushed on like water, though they stayed on the surface with little apparent absorption into the wood. The Flecto Varathane, Pen-Chrome Super-V and VaquaKleer were thicker in consistency, and could be applied in much heavier brush coats, more like regular solvent-based varnish. Before attempting to do serious work with either of the runny varnishes (Sears Latex and Deft Wood Armor), it's a good idea to get the feel of them first. Initially, I found myself trying to load on too much varnish in an attempt to produce a decent film thickness. This was a mistake: heavily applied, the thin varnishes ran and sagged on vertical surfaces. When brushing these thin-bodied latexes, it's best to err on the skimpy side, applying several thin coats (allowing drying time in between) instead of one heavy coat.

Because of the lower solids content, you'll need about two coats of any of the clear latexes to equal the dry-film thickness of a single coat of regular varnish. Since water evaporates more slowly than volatile lacquer thinners, water-based mate-

From *Fine Woodworking* magazine (July 1984) 47:65-66

rials don't quickly "flash" as lacquers do. But compared to regular varnishes, the clear latexes do dry quickly. The brands I tested dried to the touch in about one hour. With most, a second coat can be applied after two to three hours, though the first coat will still be somewhat soft. Thus, you can apply two coats in the time that it takes to apply and let harden one coat of solvent-based varnish.

These latex finishes contain about 70% water, and I discovered that every brand raised the grain severely when the first coat was applied. After this coat had hardened, I scuff-sanded the raised grain with 400-grit. No further grain-raising occurred with subsequent coats. Since wood finishers often deliberately raise the grain and sand off any whiskers before applying the finish material, I don't consider this to be a negative factor.

According to the manufacturers of some of the varnishes, a water-based acrylic clear will not completely cure in less than two weeks. For the finisher's purposes, however, overnight is dry enough for doing about anything you want with the finish. After eight hours, I could wet-sand most of the films with 400-grit paper in the same manner as I would with a conventional varnish after it had dried overnight. I tried both water and mineral spirits as a sanding lubricant, with equal results. After wiping off the sanding slurry, I polished with a fine, white automotive polishing compound, and most of the finishes polished out well. None of the labels mentioned this technique, but I recommend at least wet-sanding to remove brush marks and dust specks.

Though all the varnishes except the Flecto Varathane contain acrylic-resin polymers—the Varathane is an oil-modified, water-soluble polyurethane—I found that each brand has its own characteristics.

Sears Interior Latex Varnish: Thin and watery when applied, this product dried to a hard, even film with few brush marks. The dry film, however, was dead flat in appearance and hid much of the wood's figure. Polishing removed the brush marks, but didn't do anything to help the lackluster surface tone. I wouldn't recommend this one.

Deft Interior Acrylic Wood Armor: Another extremely thin, runny material, this finish produced a film that showed brush marks, and that was uneven and wrinkled where heavily applied. These surface flaws were too deep to sand out. Thus, I found Wood Armor's performance unsatisfactory.

After I reported the test results on off-the-shelf Wood Armor to Deft, they sent samples of a new, experimental Wood Armor, in both glossy and satin finishes. The experimental Wood Armor brushed well (though Deft recommends the use of a foam-brush applicator, which I didn't try) and built an excellent film. It dried without wrinkling, and the finish had a first-rate appearance. Sanding and polishing removed tiny imperfections, but dulled the gloss. (Editor's note: This new finish is now available from Deft. See the article "Painting Furniture" on pp. 120-122 for more information on Wood Armor.)

Flecto Varathane Ultra Plastic Finish: This product is a water-soluble form of polyurethane which brushed and handled much like a conventional varnish. Flow was good, with almost no brush strokes in the dry film. While this varnish eventually dried to a very hard film, complete curing required several days instead of the average overnight drying time. When I checked with Flecto, they told me that the particular lot I had purchased was quite moisture-sensitive, resulting in a prolonged drying time. A newer lot presently on the market apparently doesn't have this problem.

Fuller O'Brien Pen-Chrome Super-V Varnish: This finish, which contains some polyurethane in addition to acrylic resin, appears to have everything going for it. It brushed like a conventional varnish, leaving only a few brush marks, and had a good film build. It wet-sanded and polished as well as the ZAR polyurethane varnish I used as a standard. Of the varnishes tested, this was my favorite.

Benjamin Moore VaquaKleer: This material brushed very easily, appeared to produce excellent film build, and gave good flow with few apparent brush marks. Drying time seemed a bit longer than that needed for the other acrylic materials, especially the Pen-Chrome Super-V and the experimental Wood Armor.

•   •   •

In general, except for the flat-drying Sears Latex and the wrinkle-prone Wood Armor, the water-based varnishes I tested performed satisfactorily. After final-polishing, it was impossible to distinguish the better ones from a conventional varnish finish. They also seem about as tough as ordinary varnish, and I believe they'll hold up as well. I found that scratches could be easily touched up.

To test durability, I applied a drop of ethyl alcohol to the hardened film, to simulate a spilled alcoholic drink. A distinctive ring remained on every one of the water-based finishes after the alcohol had evaporated, though the Flecto Varathane was less severely marked than the others. I also tested all the finishes by leaving a wet glass full of water on the surface for five hours. Each finish exhibited some whitening and dulling, especially under the outer rim of the glass. After the glass was removed and the film allowed to dry overnight, however, all the finishes returned to a nearly normal appearance, but the ring mark was still clearly visible.

I didn't conduct any heat-resistance tests, but acrylic resin is thermoplastic, and these finishes probably won't resist marking from a hot pan or cup as well as a conventional varnish will.

Because these products contain such a high percentage of water, I ran a separate set of tests to measure how much water actually remained in the wood after the finish had dried. The results showed that the application of a water-based varnish increased the wood's moisture content less than 1%. As these finishes introduce a lot of water into the wood surface when first applied, however, I don't recommend that you use them on veneer or on very wide, thin boards—the wood is liable to warp.

Despite the excellent results I got with the Fuller O'Brien Pen-Chrome Super-V, for serious finishing work I still prefer conventional lacquer or varnish. As a group, the old standards offer a wider choice of properties (e.g., the chemical resistance of polyurethane). From a performance standpoint, there isn't anything that the water-based varnishes can do better, except keep hydrocarbons out of the air. □

Don Newell is a finishes chemist and consultant who lives in Farmington, Mich. Photo by the author.

As a furniture conservator, the author keeps many grades of shellac on hand for matching finishes. In the foreground is a dish of sticklac, short sections of twigs encrusted with the secretion of the lac bug. To the left of that is some wool yarn and the lac dye, once commercially important, used to color it. The round disc in the center, partially obscured, is a piece of buttonlac.

Shellac Finishing
A traditional finish still yields outstanding results

by Donald C. Williams

Almost everybody has heard the old wives' tales about shellac: It's not easy to use, it doesn't look good, it isn't durable, and so on. These notions are easy to refute. Shellac, for starters, is the main ingredient in most contemporary French polishes, arguably the most beautiful finish known. In addition, shellac resists ultraviolet-light degradation better than most unpigmented finishes, and it is tough enough for floors and bowling alleys, two traditional uses. It is more resistant to water-vapor transmission than polishes, oils and many lacquers and oil varnishes, making it a good choice where humidity levels swing widely (see the article on pp. 17-19). Moreover, shellac is an excellent sealer, able to cover waxes, knots and many existing finishes. Shellac dries quickly by evaporation and doesn't need the curing time required by oils and oil-base varnishes. Also, and it's no minor point, damaged shellac finishes are easy to repair because hardened shellac can be redissolved in alcohol.

Shellac is the most widely used finish in the conservation of historic furniture and is also a good choice for finishing contemporary woodwork. It can be used as a finish without needing any other sealers or topcoats. If applied as a sealer only, most other finishes will adhere to the shellac either with a chemical or a mechanical bond, provided the sealer coat is applied thinly

enough that it dries matte rather than glossy. Shellac can also be padded over many finishes for spot repairs. A heavy shellac coat over an existing oil-base floor finish, however, would very likely crack because the materials "move" differently. Combining layers of finish that have different solvents and resins is risky, unless common sense, experience and testing tell you otherwise.

The only "secrets" to successful shellac finishing are to mix your own solution using quality shellac flakes, which ensures that the shellac is fresh and will dry properly, and to use an alcohol solvent of sufficient purity. Application methods don't require sophisticated equipment. Any careful beginner can produce a surface of remarkable clarity, depth and luster. In fact, in my opinion, shellac is the most attractive finishing material around.

Before discussing some techniques of shellac finishing, I would like to talk briefly about the history and properties of shellac and the methods of its preparation. This overall picture will go a long way toward explaining the varieties of shellac—both ancient and modern—that you may encounter in the marketplace today.

The shellac trade between the Orient and Europe began in the early 17th century with lac dye—a scarlet by-product of shellac (see photo above)—as an inexpensive substitute for costly cochineal dye. The resin itself did not achieve widespread use in the

From *Fine Woodworking* magazine (July 1988) 71:56-59

West for nearly two centuries. Shellac finishes on furniture became fashionable at the beginning of the 1800s, and their popularity continued unabated until the development of synthetic resins, particularly nitrocellulose lacquers, in the 1920s and 1930s.

Late in the 19th century, aniline dyes replaced lac dye, thus eliminating a large part of lac commerce. Coincidently, new production methods made shellac resin available in great quantity. This led to its increased use in a number of applications, including electrical insulators and gramophone records (most old 78s are solid shellac). Following the discovery of the first synthetic resin, Bakelite, the importance of shellac as an industrial resin diminished. Nevertheless, it's important today as a coating for such diverse things as electric-motor windings, fruit (shellac wax is what makes supermarket apples shine), candy (M&Ms, for one), pharmaceuticals (time-dissolving capsules), leather and wood.

Shellac processing and properties—Lac, the raw material from which shellac is made, is refined from the secretions of the tiny insect *Laccifer lacca,* which is indigenous to Indochina and India. Lac bugs live on trees, sucking out nutrients from the sap and secreting a protective shell that eventually covers the twigs and branches. When these deposits are abundant, the branches are cut off and the resin is prepared for processing. This raw material, "stick-lac," is crushed and washed in water to remove twigs, dirt and the lac dye in the insect carcasses.

Sticklac is a complex mixture of several resinous components that fall into two major groups: one soft and the other very hard. The soft resins (along with another natural component, shellac wax) act as a natural plasticizer, giving shellac a great deal of flexibility; the hard resins give shellac its toughness and durability. Shellac can be bought as either a solid or a liquid, which is simply solid shellac dissolved in alcohol by the manufacturer. Solid shellac is available in various grades in three forms: flake shellac, which looks like amber or orange cornflakes; buttonlac, which comes in a variety of diameters and thicknesses; and crushed or ground shellac, which is a coarse powder. None of these forms is appreciably different from the others when used in finishes. What is important is not the form of the shellac, but how it has been processed.

After the initial processing and cleaning of sticklac to remove the lac dye, it is called "seed-lac." Seedlac looks like dirty maroon beads and can be used in the same manner as refined shellac in finishes, although it should be filtered to remove dirt particles. Seedlac is further refined to become shellac through two main processes: heat refining and solvent extraction.

In heat refining, seedlac can be refined through hand processing or industrial processing. In hand processing, seedlac is placed in cloth filtering tubes near a fire hot enough to slowly melt the resin. As the resin softens and begins to liquify, the cloth tubes are twisted and the molten resin, now called "shell-lac," is wrung out. (Processing by this method limits the purification to the porosity of the cloth used in the filter tubes.) If the desired end product is flake shellac, the semi-molten material is stretched by hand into large sheets and crushed into flakes when cooled. To make buttonlac, the material is pressed into molds and allowed to cool.

Varnish made from hand-refined shellac will appear cloudy because of the presence of shellac wax, which cannot be removed by this method. Hand-refined shellac is still a cottage industry in India, although it has been superceded almost completely by two industrial refining processes. One of these, industrial heat refining, is essentially the same as hand processing, with the exception that the seedlac is melted with steam.

The other industrial method, solvent extraction, is the primary refining process today, and it provides an end product that can be fundamentally different. Seedlac is dissolved in methanol and then filtered. The solution is then heated to remove the alcohol, and the remaining shellac is stretched and pressed in rollers. All or part of the natural lac wax can be removed, yielding dewaxed shellac with greater clarity and moisture resistance.

The final refining step is the assignment of grade, or quality, which is based on host tree, time of year the sticklac is harvested, wax content, color, clarity and hardness. Grading is usually done by eye, and there may be minor differences between shellacs of the same grade. There appears to be general agreement that the most prized resins from India are the Kusmi Aghani, coming from the kusum tree during the month of Aghan (late November to early December). The grades of hand-processed shellac range from TN, which is the lowest grade, to Kusmi Superior, which is the highest. TN resin is reddish-brown, tough, with moderate hardness. Kusmi Superior is amber in color, with excellent clarity. Intermediate grades are known as Lemon #1 and Lemon #2. These are available from WoodFinishing Enterprises, 1729 N. 68th St., Wauwatosa, Wis. 53213; (414) 774-1724.

The shellacs found in most woodworking catalogs are supplied by Behlen and rated by color and wax content. The higher the color number, the darker; the higher the wax number, the more wax. The following are the four available Behlen grades: ButtonLac, which varies because it is essentially unrefined; GarnetLac (roughly equivalent to TN), with a color of 30 and a wax content of about 3%; Orange (equivalent to Lemon #1), with a color of 13 and a wax content of 4.5%; Super Blonde (derived from grades such as Kusmi Superior), with a color of 0.8 and virtually no wax. One source for Behlen products is Wood Finishing Supply Co., 1267 Mary Drive, Macedon, N.Y. 14502; (315) 986-4517.

Natural wax particles present in the dried shellac film make it less resistant to water, and they slightly dull the gloss. Super Blonde would be a good choice when gloss and the clarity of the wood surface matters. Orange would be a good choice when power-sanding the surface is anticipated, because waxes act in a manner similar to stearates (dry lubricants added to lacquer sanding sealers), preventing the film from overheating and becoming gummy when sanded. The darker colors of GarnetLac and ButtonLac can be blended with the other shellacs to match old finishes, although I use alcohol-soluble dyes for this purpose so as not to change the properties of the shellac I'm using.

Super Blonde is clarified by filtering it through active carbon; shellacs known as "bleached" have been treated in an alkali bath with chlorine. Such bleaching makes the dry resin unstable and drastically shortens its shelf life—both dry and in solution—and accelerates the degradation of the finish. Despite these shortcomings, bleached shellac made from high-grade resins remains a favorite among French polishers because of its clarity, although its inherent instability makes it unsuitable for any of my needs.

Drawbacks—Shellac resists water-vapor penetration very well, but water in liquid form presents problems. The most frequently expressed complaint about shellac is the formation of white rings from water condensed on drinking glasses. The severity of the damage is frequently dependent on the amount of wax in the shellac, just as water spots in other finishes are sometimes in the wax polish rather than in the finish itself. Repairing water damage can be easy, particularly with newer finishes (less than 20 years old) that are in good overall condition. Apply alcohol to dissolve the surface, as shown in the photo on the next page, and the water will evaporate as the surface dries. However, it is critical to note that the application of solvent may change the texture and

Although shellac may turn white from water or heat, in many cases the damage is easily repaired by redissolving the surface with alcohol. In cases of severe damage, a subsequent coat or two of shellac may be needed to restore the surface.

appearance of the finish, which may need further attention. The success of this technique declines if the film is degraded. In addition, indiscriminate intervention with historically important surfaces is to be discouraged as unethical.

Another drawback is that shellac begins to plasticize, or become malleable, at about 150°F. Imagine the damage caused by a steaming tureen of stew carelessly placed directly on a beautifully French-polished surface. Yet even this damage can be speedily repaired with alcohol and perhaps a subsequent padding of more finish.

Perhaps the worst complaint against shellac is that it sometimes fails to dry hard. Anyone who has had experience with shellac that would not dry is unlikely to recommend it or use it again. The cause of this problem is age: Shellac is acidic, and if left too long in alcohol, it produces esters, which are chemical compounds that leave the shellac gummy. This problem can be entirely avoided by mixing your own shellac and using it within a reasonable period of time, as will be discussed shortly.

Shellac's final characteristic is that it remains soluble in alcohol, which is both an excellent feature (allowing future removal, repairs and color blending) and a drawback (liquor acts as paint remover). Shellac can be made more alcohol resistant with the addition of nitrocellulose, and most commercial French-polishing varnishes (padding lacquers) contain lacquer, but even these are not impervious to alcohol damage.

Preparing and using shellac—Solid shellac can be purchased in all grades and as waxed or dewaxed, bleached or unbleached. Liquid shellac is generally available only as white (bleached) or orange (unbleached). Liquid shellac comes in solutions with designations such as "4-lb.-cut shellac" or the like. This indicates a solution of four pounds of resin per gallon of solvent, but is no clue to the grade of the resin. The primary problem with purchasing liquid shellac is that the consumer usually has no idea when the liquid was formulated. Some manufacturers date the containers, but this does not guarantee the environment in which the container has been stored. If the temperatures are too high, even shellac that's just a few months old can degrade to the point where it will not harden. This is particularly true of bleached shellac. In moments of desperation while working away from home, I have purchased liquid orange shellac, but I wouldn't buy premixed bleached shellac under any conditions.

Dry shellac has an indefinite shelf life if kept cool and dry. If exposed to moisture, the resin may solidify into a block, but this can be broken up and used. If dry shellac has chemically degraded because of improper storage, it will not dissolve in alcohol.

The extreme toxicity of shellac's best solvent, methanol (wood alcohol), prompts me to use ethanol (grain alcohol), the alcohol in liquor, instead. I find that the alcohol generally sold as "shellac thinner" in hardware and paint stores contains contaminants and is useful only as a cleaner for my brushes and the surfaces of objects on which I am working. I don't recommend alcohol sold by finishing supply companies, because I have had more than one bad experience with contamination, which ruins the varnish (one exception to this is Behkol, a Behlen product).

The best bet for making good spirit varnish is to use either reagent alcohol or pure grain alcohol. Reagent-grade alcohol is denatured alcohol sold by chemical companies and is pure enough to be used in laboratories. "Denaturing" of alcohol means contaminating the alcohol so it becomes non-drinkable and therefore exempt from liquor taxes. Generally, reagent alcohol is 95% ethanol and 5% methanol or other toxic additives.

You can buy reagent alcohol if you choose, but grain alcohol is never farther away than the closest liquor store. Just ask for 190-proof grain alcohol, pay the man, go home and mix up some shellac varnish. Be prepared for alcohol in this form to be more expensive, because you are paying liquor taxes. Keep in mind that an open container of any alcohol rapidly absorbs moisture from the air, regardless of how pure it may have been when first bought.

As mentioned earlier, shellac varnish is rated in pound cut. You can mix precise proportions by volume and weight, but I seldom bother. As a furniture conservator, I like to keep a number of grades on hand in concentrated solution. This allows me to blend colors as needed and then immediately dilute the mixture to proper viscosity for the job. To make the concentrated solution, roughly equivalent to a 6-lb. cut, I fill a small glass container with shellac flakes. Then, I fill the container with alcohol and allow it to stand in a cool, dark place for a couple of days. I may speed up the process by occasionally shaking the container vigorously. I increase the alcohol content by one half for powdered shellac and double for buttonlac, because they are both denser than flake.

I keep only a couple of months supply of orange shellacs on hand. While I never use bleached shellac, if you need to use it, mix only what you need for the next couple of weeks, after which, discard it. The minor inconvenience of preparing new solution pales in comparison to the aggravation of using old shellac that won't dry properly.

There are three main techniques of applying shellac finishes: spraying, padding and brushing. I'll discuss the particulars of each in a moment. Regardless of the application method, there are some characteristics of liquid shellac that are beneficial. Alcohol-soluble dyes can be added to shellac, allowing very careful manipulation of the finish color for touching up, shading or controlling overall tone. Because shellac remains soluble in alcohol, mistakes in the application procedure can be corrected easily.

Spraying—I spray shellac when I am using it as a sealer or when I want a surface that can be finished off simply by rubbing with 0000 steel wool. Spraying shellac is much like spraying nitrocellulose lacquer (see pp. 89-95), so if you spray lacquer, you can spray shellac. I spray a 1½-lb. to 2-lb. cut, which means I dilute one part of my stock solution with three or four parts alcohol. I set the pressure to about 30 lbs., use a moderately wide fan pattern and keep the gun moving constantly.

There are a couple of problems in spraying shellac that can be avoided easily. First, don't apply shellac heavily, or you will get drips and runs. Shellac doesn't always set as fast as lacquer, so don't always assume that similar applications will dry the same as lacquer. If the gun is too far away from the surface, the pressure too low or the material flow inadequate, the result will be an uneven surface called "orange peeling." If the gun is too close to the surface or the pressure too high, you can get runs and possibly pinholing, which is the result of the sprayed shellac being agitated so much that it froths and air bubbles get trapped in the film as it dries. Shellac, like any other solvent-release finish, can blush if the finish is applied when the humidity is too high or when there is too much moisture in the solution or on the surface. Finally, take special care to clean out the gun frequently. Shellac reacts with metal, a reaction that makes the shellac turn dark and interferes with its drying. My gun is aluminum, which is less reactive than steel. If I'm spraying shellac on a daily basis, I disassemble and soak the gun in alcohol every couple of days. I'd clean a steel gun every day. If you spray infrequently, the gun should be cleaned thoroughly after each use.

I smooth the surface as necessary between coats with sandpaper, pumice or 0000 steel wool. If the shellac is dewaxed, use steel wool; sandpaper may overheat the surface, although this is not likely if you are sanding by hand. Steel wool is not a bad idea on waxed shellac either, as the wax may clog very fine paper. The shellac dust from smoothing can be left in the pores of the wood as a filler. The introduction of alcohol with new coats will dissolve the dust and lead to a smoother surface.

Padding—Applying shellac with a cloth is known as padding, or more popularly as French polishing. This process, the application of a great many very thin coats, is covered on pp. 56-59, so I won't give a long exposition on my technique, but instead I'll give you a quick review of the build-up process.

French polishing is possible because shellac is a solvent-release finish with excellent adhesion qualities. As the polishing rubber is moving over the surface, several things are happening simultaneously. First, shellac is being deposited on the surface. Second, the solvent in the shellac is softening the layers below, allowing some of the shellac already down to be pushed around from high areas to low areas, filling the grain. Starting with a 1½-lb. cut, the amount of resin in the varnish is decreased by adding alcohol—not shellac—as the varnish is consumed. Eventually, the surface coating is simply being moved around by the solvent and the abrasion of the fabric (or pumice), resulting in the familiar mirror-like smoothness.

Parts of a piece that cannot be easily padded, such as intricate carving, certain table pedestals, etc., may be sprayed or brushed thinly as described below. A final treatment using steel wool and wax, buffing hard enough to produce heat, will get the finish close to the high gloss of the French-polished areas. If carved areas are adjacent to padded areas, do all brushing first, then pad, overlapping onto the brushed parts to blend the two.

Brushing—The best brush for shellac is a very fine artists' brush, the kind usually employed in watercolor painting. The bristles should be flat and moderately soft: golden nylon, badger or red sable. Artists' brushes come in a variety of sizes up to 2 in., which is as big as you'll ever need. New brushes should be thoroughly washed in mild soap and water to get out any dirt, oil or loose bristles. Brushes should be cleaned with solvent after use.

The importance of the shellac cut cannot be overstated. Many people make the mistake of applying a couple of heavy coats of shellac followed by laborious rubbing out after drying. Although I

Shellac can be refined to various grades. From the left: bleached, dewaxed; dewaxed blonde; Kusmi Superior; Siam seedlac. Note that shellacs containing wax will appear cloudy and may settle into strata with hard resin on top.

have seen finishers use up to a 5-lb. cut with success, my own experience suggests that anything heavier than a 2-lb. cut can lead to an uneven, streaky finish. I use a 1-lb. cut for most brushing, so my stock solution is cut 5:1 with alcohol. The light cut allows for excellent flow-out of the shellac, providing a smooth, glossy finish. Admittedly, the buildup of finish can seem slow, but the coats can be applied in rapid sequence. Besides, the objective is to produce a beautiful finish, not a thick one.

Have enough shellac in the brush so it'll flow well, but not so much that it drips. Determine an application pattern and stick to it. Aim to cover all the surface evenly without having to go back over areas where shellac has already been applied. Unlike oil varnishes, where you can rebrush the wet surface to even it out, all this will accomplish with shellac is the pulling back up of the semi-wet finish. This produces a lumpy, ribbed surface. If the brush is worked too vigorously and froth builds up, pinholing may result.

When you've come to the end of the application pattern, test the beginning point with your fingertip (first clean any tacky shellac off your finger). If the shellac at the beginning point is stiff (slightly tacky) or dry to the touch, begin again and apply a complete new coat. Repeat this process until the starting point is too tacky to apply more finish. I can generally apply six or eight successive coats on large objects. Allow the final application to dry overnight, then rub the surface down. You may choose to leave this as a final rubbed finish, or you may apply another coat or two of shellac without rubbing to achieve a finish of high gloss. Two coats of paste wax completes the job. □

Donald C. Williams is a conservator at the Conservation Analytical Laboratory of the Smithsonian Institution in Washington D.C. and is a contributing editor for The Wood Finisher, *P.O. Box 64, Rosemount, Minn. 55068. Photos by the author.*

Further reading

Try large libraries for these out-of-print books:

Shellac and Other Lacs by William Howlett Gardner. Chapter in *Protective and Decorative Coatings Vol. I.* John Wiley & Sons, Inc., New York, NY 10158; 1943.

Shellac: Its Origin and Applications by Edward Hicks. Chemical Publishing Co., New York, NY 10011; 1961.

Shellac by James Martin. Chapter in *Treatise on Coatings Vol. I, Part 2.* Marcel Dekker Inc., New York, NY 10016; 1968.

Shellac: Its Production, Manufacture, Chemistry, Analysis, Commerce and Uses by Ernest Parry. Sir Isaac Pitman & Sons, London, England; 1935.

Shellac (referred to as the "Blue Book") by M. Russell. Angelo Brothers, Calcutta, India; 1965.

An Oil and Varnish Finish

by Lothar Baumann

I mill a lot of my lumber from walnut logs and crotches, and can control the figure in the wood according to how I cut it. When I've uncovered a really fine feather figure, I go to the trouble of stretching it; I resaw the block several times, bookmatch the grain, and veneer the best looking wood over solid walnut for wall-cabinet doors and other furniture. When I've finally gotten a piece made, I aim for a finish that brings out the hard-won feather to best advantage.

Oil is my favorite. It penetrates the wood and makes the most of the wood's ability to reflect and bend light, creating depth and allowing the figure to shimmer. But a lot of my customers don't want pure oil—they grew up with durable polyurethane, and won't settle for anything else. Combining oil with polyurethane gives some of the benefits of both. The idea isn't new, and lots of people have different ways of mixing and applying the blend. I've settled on a system that takes more work than a lot of people seem willing to go to, but the results are worth it.

First, I sand the raw wood smooth, working up through progressively finer grits until I reach 220- or 240-grit garnet paper. In theory, each grit scratches the surface efficiently and uniformly, and the next grit size removes the first set of scratches, replacing them with slightly finer ones. You use one grit, say 100- or 120-grit, to remove major machine marks, fuzzy grain and other irregularities. (I use a 4-in. by 24-in. Makita belt sander, but occasionally turn to a hand plane or scraper.) You sand until the wood is completely even, then move up to the next finer paper, 150-grit, and sand until the first set of scratches is gone and the surface looks even. Work through the remaining grits in the same manner. If you skip grit sizes or start with too fine a paper, you'll waste a lot of time. Even worse, flaws you thought you'd sanded away will reappear in the finish. This whole initial-preparation process shouldn't take more than half an hour for a pair of cabinet doors.

Sandpaper is a precision tool and deserves to be taken seriously. Each piece of grit is bedded in a layer of adhesive that holds it to the paper backing and exposes just so much cutting edge. If you tear or fold the paper, you'll break into the layer of adhesive and expose more cutting surface than was intended on the grit particles along the edges, putting yourself back a grade or two if the edges hit the work. Grit can also become dislodged from the paper, and if you don't dust the wood between grits you can end up with wrong-size scratches that will mar the pattern. If this happens, it's best to resand with the previous grit. People who use power sanders often complain about swirl marks on the wood. These may not be the machine's fault, but the result of loose grit left on the work.

Beware of buying cheap stuff. I got a bargain on some paper not too long ago and bought hundreds of sheets, but I discovered that the 220-grit is full of larger particles that make the paper useless; it's too fine for coarse work, and too scratchy for finish-sanding.

I don't usually stain the wood because it already looks the way I want it to, nor do I apply fillers—the finishing process fills the pores as much as necessary. When the surface has been taken to 220-grit dry, I apply clear Watco oil as a primer coat, rubbing it in with 220- or 280-grit wet/dry paper wrapped over a block of Celotex. The Celotex distributes the pressure just as a cork block would, but it's cheaper. When saturated with the oil mixture, Celotex becomes spongy and may disintegrate. If you set aside damp blocks and allow them to dry, they will become harder and more durable. When I feel the sandpaper begin to slip on the wood instead of biting, I know that it's almost finished its job and that most of the 280-grit scratches are gone. I switch up to 320-grit and sand again, then repeat the process with 400-grit and 600-grit.

The wet-sanding produces a slurry of wood dust and oil, which is forced down into the pores. I wipe the slurry off the surface before beginning each new grit, but leave the 600-grit slurry on the surface until it begins to thicken. Then I wipe the wood across the grain until it's almost dry and set it aside for the oil in the remaining slurry to dry completely. This takes about three days in hot weather and up to a week and a half in the winter, when it's cool and damp. One test for dryness is to put the work briefly in the sun or near a heat source; if it bleeds oil, it's not ready yet.

When the oil is dry, remove the slurry film with steel wool, working in the direction of the grain. Polish the wood to remove any oil residue from the surface. If the surface quality is uneven, with dull spots where the oil has been absorbed, apply another coat. Work it in with 600-grit paper, sanding with the grain. Wipe off the excess with paper towels and let this coat dry. If you are determined to completely fill the pores, you can sand again to build up a slurry and let it dry again on the wood, repeating until the surface is flawless. I don't mind a few open pores because they keep the wood looking like wood.

I complete the process by applying an oil-and-varnish mix. The mix is 3 parts polyurethane, 2 parts boiled linseed oil and 2 parts mineral spirits, applied with a rag. I usually sand-in the first coat with 600-grit paper, just a little—too much sanding at this stage will only open up new pores. I apply two or three coats, although I have used up to eight, wiping each coat clean and almost dry, and allowing drying time between coats. I don't sand after the first coat unless there's an imperfection that I overlooked earlier. I have used several commercially prepared tung-oil mixtures, such as Hope's, Gillespie's and Formby's, instead of my oil-varnish mix, and they work equally well. The sanding of the finish into the wood seems to be the critical factor to obtain the results I want. Applying the top coats of finish takes time, but you can't call it much work. It's more like a reward for all the preparation that went into getting the wood ready for it. □

Lothar Baumann is a woodworker in Berea, Ky. He uses the same finish when he works on the lathe.

From *Fine Woodworking* magazine (May 1985) 52:53

Finishing with Oil
Modern products for an age-old process

by Michael Dresdner

An oil finish's beauty, as well as its easy and forgiving application qualities, make it an ideal finish for woodworkers who have little finishing experience or who don't want to invest in spray systems or other specialized equipment.

The expression "hand-rubbed oil finish" conjures an image of the venerable craftsman practicing an ancient craft to bring beauty to a fine piece of woodworking. Oil finishes trace their lineage to "China wood oil," an Oriental tung-oil mixture reputed to go back 800 years. Although they are still widely used today, oil finishes must compete for space on the paint-store shelves with the most advanced chemical soups and coatings that the wizards of technology dish up.

Without question, oil's long suit is its simplicity, both in terms of its subtle appearance and its ease of application. Oil is generally the first finish a fledgling woodworker will attempt, because it requires virtually no equipment and will yield excellent results to the most inexperienced hand. Many consider a basic oil finish to be the only finish that allows wood to look "natural," imparting the rich color characteristic of freshly surfaced wood, while leaving the pores open and the surface feeling uncoated. And for those who view finishing as a necessary evil, the wipe-on, wipe-off modern oil finish is perhaps as close as you can get to not finishing at all.

Oil finishes have come a long way since the old days, when applying an oil finish was an involved process, requiring hours of arduous labor. The old-timers who taught me about woodfinishing had been trained to rub boiled linseed oil into the wood with their bare hands, following the "rule of two:" twice a day for a week, twice a week for a month, twice a month for a year, and twice a year for life. Unquestionably, this process still will produce an excellent finish, but few woodworkers, and fewer customers, are willing to agree to the sustained effort needed. As a result, the "modern" oil finish, one buffered with resins and prepolymerized oils, has taken its place. But just as few old-timers understood what boiling had to do with linseed oil, most craftsmen today have a dim understanding of what modern oil finishes are all about. I recently investigated about a dozen oil products and talked to several

manufacturers, and I'd like to share what I learned about oil finishes: what they're made of, how they cure, how to go about applying them and how to use them when repairing and refinishing.

Oil mixtures – In spite of what manufacturers claim in their advertising and literature, various brands of oil finishes are more alike than they are different. Most commercial products, including "Danish-oil" finishes by Minwax, Watco, Waterlox and Deft, are mixtures of oil, resin, driers and a solvent. The natural oils most commonly used are linseed oil, pressed from flaxseed, or tung oil, from the nut of the tung (Montana) tree. The oil finishes made by Minwax and Watco, two of the best-known brands in the field, are of a linseed-oil base, while Deft Danish oil and Waterlox's "Transparent" are based on tung oil. Although there are many other natural oils, linseed and tung are inexpensive and readily available.

Resins added to oil mixtures may be natural or synthetic. The most common are modified alkyds, which are often added to linseed oil, and phenolic resin, which is used with tung oil. These resins are solids—in many cases the same solids used in varnishes and lacquers—and add bulk to the oil mixture. They result in a harder finish, one that builds film thickness quickly, because the solids fill the pores of the wood more readily than oils alone. The solvent dissolves all the components of the mixture and reduces its viscosity, which makes the finish easier to apply and increases its ability to penetrate the wood. The most common solvent used in commercial products is mineral spirits, though some products use turpentine.

Curing—Most oil mixtures include driers, heavy-metal salts that speed up the drying process. Although both natural linseed and tung oil will dry by themselves when exposed to air—a reminder to keep oils in closed containers with little airspace—raw oils may take weeks or even months to dry. By adding driers, this time is reduced to a matter of hours. The driers, sometimes referred to as "Japan driers," include zinc, cobalt, magnesium, manganese and lead. Some of these work as "top driers," causing the oil to form a "skin;" others act as "through driers," causing the oil to dry evenly throughout.

Linseed oil, as well as tung oil, can be purchased as raw oil, without driers in it. Linseed oil also comes boiled, with driers added. In spite of its name, boiled linseed oil is not actually boiled: The metal salts are added with the help of a chemical catalyst. The reference to boiled is probably a throwback to an early process in which oils were heated to help dissolve the metal salts. Used alone, boiled linseed oil makes a credible finish, and there are some purists who will use nothing else to finish their woodwork (see the sidebar on the facing page). Another method manufacturers use to shorten oil's drying time is polymerization. In fact, most commercial tung-oil products are partially polymerized. The process involves heating the oil, causing a percentage of its molecules to bond, which increases the oil's viscosity and shortens its drying time.

Application—The first thing most proponents of oil finishes rave about is oil's most alluring feature: It is easy to apply. You simply wipe it on, and after a short time to allow for penetration and solvent evaporation, you wipe off the excess. The time this takes may vary, so it's best to go by the manufacturer's recommendations on the label. It is almost impossible to get bad results; the amount of oil applied and the speed, pattern and method of application have virtually no effect on the result. You don't even need special equipment or a dust-free room to get excellent results.

However, because oil finishes don't hide surface imperfections very well, you must sand to a finer grit than necessary for surface-coating finishes, such as lacquer or varnish. Final sanding should be to at least 220 grit, but it may need to be 400 grit or 600 grit with fine-grain woods, such as rosewood or ebony.

The first and second coats of oil tend to be completely absorbed into the wood's surface and act as a sealer. Once the wood is saturated with cured oil, successive coats will start to form a film on the surface. You can get an effect that ranges from a barely perceptible finish in a single sealer coat to a glossy film, which can take from two to five coats. Because oil is a reactive finish (once it dries, subsequent coats will not redissolve it), a dried oiled surface can be recoated by wiping, brushing or even dipping, without fear of disturbing the dried layer. Some woodworkers prefer to do fine sanding while the surface is drenched with oil, which helps to build the finish quicker, because the wood's pores get filled with a slurry of wood dust and oil. I don't care for this approach though, because it puts sanding dust and grit into the pores and spoils the clean look I like my oil finishes to have.

About the only major mistake you can make with oils is neglecting to wipe off the excess before the oil dries. This will result in a sticky mess, which must be scrubbed off with steel wool. Although acetone or lacquer thinner might help lubricate this abrading process, neither is a true solvent for cured oil. If you need to remove an oil finish by redissolving the film, about the only thing that will work is methylene chloride, the active ingredient commonly found in paint and varnish removers.

The one common glitch that users of oil finishes often run into is "bleeding." On large-pore woods, such as oak, there is a tendency for the extra oil trapped in the pores to leach out and form shiny spots on the wood's surface. This generally occurs only on the first coat or two, until the cured oil seals the pores. Bleeding can often be avoided by applying the oil early in the day and rewiping the surface every hour or so until the leaching stops. Once the spots are left to harden, there is no way to remove them except by sanding the surface with fine paper (400 grit) or by stripping the finish entirely.

While oil's simple nature is its advantage, it also contributes to its downside. An oil finish is an inherently weak finish, which wears off easily and has a very low moisture-vapor resistance. Because oil is largely absorbed into the wood rather than becoming a film over it, the wood surface is given little protection from abrasion or staining. Although some people contend that an oil finish can case-harden the wood surface, evidence suggests that the effect is due to resins added to the mixture and not the oil itself. Because of its low moisture-vapor resistance, water molecules can penetrate easily, and oil also offers little protection against alcohol and other liquids. This makes oil a poor choice for furniture, cabinets, tabletops, counters or other wooden objects used in wet or humid conditions. Due to oil's poor performance as a vapor barrier, it also offers little protection from changes in humidity—one of the most important functions of any wood finish. Therefore, designing with regard to expansion and contraction is essential for work that's to be oil-finished.

Despite the easygoing attitude finishers have toward oil finishes, there is one very serious warning: *Oil-soaked rags or paper towels are ready prey to spontaneous combustion; if left in a pile, they can heat up and burst into flames on their own accord.* Therefore, any oily rags or paper should be disposed of quickly and carefully by incineration or by being completely immersed in water. If you can't do this immediately after oiling, hang the single-thickness rag up to dry until it can be disposed of properly. Although oil fumes are not as hazardous or offensive as those produced by most lacquers, you should work in a well-ventilated area, wear a vapor respirator and rubber or neoprene gloves when handling or applying oil mixtures. Also, many commercial oils are toxic, and unless otherwise indicated on the label, they shouldn't be used for wooden eating utensils or children's toys that are likely to be chewed, such as baby blocks or rattles.

Repairing and refinishing—Oil's reactive drying properties and forgiving application qualities make it a finish that's extremely repairable. A white water ring or a damaged spot can be lightly sanded or steel wooled, and new oil can be applied. Due to its inability to redissolve itself, the newly applied oil will not affect the undamaged finish in the surrounding area and will blend the spot almost invisibly, even if the finish is many years old. With oil's repairability comes a responsibility for maintenance. Ideally, an oil finish should be rejuvenated with a new coat every year or so, depending on the amount of wear it's subjected to.

While oil may be the ideal solution for a new project, it is often a poor choice when refinishing. Bob Flexner of Norman, Okla., an expert in antique conservation and repair, points out that the original finish on most old pieces was seldom oil. He considers oil an inappropriate replacement finish for most commercial and even pre-industrial revolution handmade furniture. Few commercial furniture producers today use oil finishes on their furniture (see the sidebar at right for some exceptions). Even woodwork that is commonly believed to be finished in oil, like Swedish and Danish-Modern furnishings, is more often than not finished with a thin film of catalyzed lacquer. In spite of oil's low cost, ease of application and moderately innocuous fumes, it remains the province of the individual craftsman. There, an oil finish's subtle good looks continue to be the earmark of handmade furniture. □

Michael Dresdner is an instrumentmaker and woodfinishing specialist in Zionhill, Penn., and a contributing editor at Fine Woodworking. *A number of other articles by Dresdner are included in this book, including "Rubbing Out a Finish" on pp. 50-52.*

Using oil finishes: two approaches

While oils are often the finish of choice for beginning woodworkers, there are many professionals who prefer to use them as well. I recently discussed oil-finishing methods with two woodworkers who represent completely different-size shops: woodturner David Ellsworth, who works alone, and Tom Moser, founder of Thos. Moser Inc., a 90-person furniture- and cabinet-building company.

Ellsworth, one of the most prominent turners in the world, produces a variety of work, including the hollow forms that are his hallmark. Woodturners are a strong bastion of allegiance to oil finishes, and like many of his peers, Ellsworth finishes his pieces with a tung-oil product, specifically Waterlox Transparent.

After power-sanding with 320-grit paper on a foam-back disc, a process Ellsworth claims is equivalent to hand-sanding with 600 grit, he soaks the outside of the piece with Waterlox, spreading it on evenly but not wiping it off. Because he generally turns wood while it is still green, the oil is being applied to the outside of a relatively wet turning even before the inside has been turned. Ellsworth leaves the inside of his pieces unfinished.

As the turning dries, more coats of oil are added, the exact number depending on the wood's porosity. When both the oil and wood are thoroughly dry, he buffs off the oil residue using tripoli or white-diamond compound applied to a 6-in. stitched-cotton buffing wheel spinning at 3,500 RPM. This is followed by further polishing with a clean buff. The process removes all of the surface oil, leaving only finish that has been absorbed by the wood. The turning's exterior looks as if the wood has no finish on it at all. The ability to get what Ellsworth calls a "natural" appearance is what led him to choose oils over other finishes he had tried. While his application methods may be unorthodox, the results are excellent, as witnessed by this oil-finished vessel at right (above).

A notable exception to the fact that most commercial furniture companies don't use oil finishes is Moser. His company grosses millions of dollars yearly building Windsor and Shaker-style chairs, such as the one pictured at right (below), tables and case goods that are finished in linseed oil.

Flying in the face of the furniture industry's conventional wisdom, Moser proudly points to the beauty and durability of the boiled linseed-oil finishes on thousands of his tables and chairs. The soft, natural appearance gives each brand-new piece the feel of a vintage classic; in fact, Moser says that chairs that are 10 or 15 years old look

After turning this 24-in.-tall, 13-in.-dia. vessel from redwood-pitch burl, Ellsworth applied tung oil to give it a soft, rich finish. The inside is left unfinished.

A simple finish of boiled linseed oil on top of a polished surface of cherry wood sanded to 400 grit gives Moser's 'reader's side chair' a soft appearance that ages gracefully.

better than the new ones. This is especially true on the arms and back, which are enhanced by repeated contact with human skin and the sebaceous oil it secretes.

Moser admits that offering only oil-finished furniture was a sales obstacle at first, because potential customers were used to seeing lacquer and varnish finishes in the furniture stores. With time, however, his buying public came to associate his style of furniture with what he calls "an extremely low-tech finish." But after trying dozens of finishes, including lacquers, polyurethanes and oils other than linseed, Moser settled on the finishing procedure he still uses today.

Preparing a wood surface for an oil finish is considerably more time-consuming than for any other kind of finish. A full one-third of his shop's production hours are spent sanding the pieces up to 3M's 40-micron Imperial Microfinishing Film paper, a polyester film-backed sanding material that 3M says is equivalent to 300-grit paper. (The product comes in sheets and self-stick 5-in. and 6-in. discs, ranging in grits from 9 microns [1,200 grit] to 100 microns [150 grit]. It is available from 3M, Box 33053, St. Paul, Minn. 55133-3053.) Moser's wood surfaces are indeed smooth and feel finished even before the oil is applied.

To increase penetration, Moser's finishers heat the boiled linseed oil to 120°F before applying it to wood. The oil is applied with fine Scotch-Brite pads and allowed to dry for about four hours before it is wiped off with special industrial-quality paper towels. To avoid the danger of spontaneous combustion, the oil-impregnated towels are burned after use. After the first coat, the wood is resanded with 400-grit paper, then a second coat is applied, and if needed, a third coat. When the oil is dry, two coats of Butcher's Wax are applied and rubbed down with 0000 steel wool. The wax gives the surface its characteristic sheen, and incidentally, helps repel water slightly. Moser's customers receive a furniture-care kit consisting of sandpaper, steel wool and a small jar of wax.

How does Moser deal with oil's poor moisture-vapor protection and low abrasion resistance? Wood movement is accommodated for in case goods by making a different fit for drawers and doors in winter than in summer—"a nickel fit versus a dime fit," as Moser puts it. As for abrasion resistance, Moser sees the marks of wear that furniture accumulates as part of its overall charm. He tells of a table in his house that bears the imprint of a Spirograph drawing his son did as a 6-year-old child. "It is a beautiful signature on that table," Moser remarks, "and that's priceless." —M.D.

Rubbing Out a Finish

Fine abrasives, soap and elbow grease

by Michael Dresdner

Many finishers opt to save time by not rubbing out the final finish coat of a completed piece. As a consequence, running your hand over an otherwise flawless tabletop reveals the existence of tiny specs of dust and other particles cropping up defiantly but invisibly from the plane of the finish. High-quality furniture deserves better than this. A creamy-looking satin finish, for example, should have a sensual smoothness that conveys to the fingers the very image it presents to the eye.

I don't think you can achieve this special visual and tactile quality without rubbing out. I'll get to the specifics shortly, but as a quick overview, rubbing a finish is the process of abrading away any small imperfections in the surface so it is completely smooth and level, with uniform sheen. The surface is sanded with fine paper and then rubbed with a lubricant and a fine abrasive to produce a subtle but even pattern of minute scratches. The difference between gloss and satin rubbing is one of degree: The coarser the rubbing material, the deeper the scratch pattern it creates.

The glossiness of a finish is a function of the amount of light that is reflected and the direction in which it is reflected. Think for a moment of a bright new aluminum pot: You can see your face in it almost as well as in a mirror, because the light hitting its polished surface is reflected straight back to your eyes. The same pot, as scouring pads and oxidation begin to etch its surface, becomes gradually less reflective, because light hitting the surface bounces off randomly. Finally, after a few years, the minute scratch pattern covers the surface completely, and the pot is not reflective at all. In a satin finish, the scratch pattern is quite obvious, looking somewhat like the pattern in so-called brushed brass and other metals. In fact, a top rubbed to a satin sheen will look different depending on whether it is viewed head on, with the scratches going toward and away from your line of sight, or from the side, with the scratches crossing horizontally.

While one *can* change the sheen of a finish by rubbing (such as when removing the plastic-like glare from some polyurethanes), it is a good idea to begin with a finish that's already at the intended level of gloss or flatness. Some shops finish tabletops in gloss and then rub them down to satin in the conviction that gloss lacquer or varnish is harder, and therefore more durable, than satin. While this may be partially true, the difference is not significant to justify the added work. Gloss lacquer is clearer than satin, however, so rather than building up the entire finish with satin lacquer, just spray a healthy margin of satin topcoats over a gloss base. Rub carefully to avoid cutting through.

Keep in mind that there is no sense in trying to save any improperly applied finish by rubbing. If the final coat is not smooth and level, scrape or sand it flat and recoat.

Hard cures – Virtually any finish can be rubbed, provided it is thick enough (rubbing does remove some finish) and it is cured. Air-drying finishes, both evaporative ones like lacquer or shellac, and polymerizing ones like oil or polyester, generally dry from the outside in; they may still be soft underneath even though they have formed a dry skin. The curing time will depend on the material as well as on how thick the finish is and how quickly it was applied. For example, a six-mil-thick (0.006 in.) lacquer finish that was applied in six thin coats over a six-day period (one coat per day) will cure considerably faster than the same six-mil coating applied in three sprayings within one day, primarily because there is less solvent entrapment. If your thumbnail can leave an impression in the film, it is not yet ready for rubbing.

Non-air-drying finishes, such as catalyzed lacquer or conversion varnish, usually cure much more quickly, often overnight, and the cure time is not affected by the film thickness. Because they cure through a chemical reaction, they harden uniformly rather than from the outside inward. The quick-and-easy test to figure out whether or not a catalyzed finish has set up enough to rub is to scuff a sample area with 320-grit sandpaper. If the sandpaper clogs up with gummy clots, it is not ready to rub. Manufacturer's directions provide important clues. For example, we use one type of catalyzed lacquer in our shop that dries as fast as regular, but it takes seven days to cure. While it will pass the sandpaper test in a day or two and can be rubbed then, much better results are obtained by waiting past the seventh day.

Certain oil varnishes, and shellacs used for violin finishes, contain chemicals that keep the finish flexible even after it has dried. These finishes can be difficult or impossible to rub out, but it's sometimes possible to do it after they've been topcoated with a thin layer of shellac applied by French polishing (see pp. 56-59).

Abrasives and lubricants – Before rubbing, the finish should be cured and level without a lot of brush marks or orange peel, but it probably will have some tiny dust pimples. Remove these by lightly sanding with the grain; for a low-luster, open-pore finish, 320-grit self-lubricating paper is adequate (such as 3M's Tri-M-ite Fre-Cut). For filled-pore or medium- to high-gloss finishes, however, it's best to work up to 600-grit wet-or-dry sandpaper with a lubricant (we use naptha or mineral spirits). Most any lubricant can be used with the sandpaper provided it does not harm or redissolve the particular finish.

As long as the scratch pattern goes in one direction (with the grain), it will diffract light evenly and give a smooth satiny appearance. The scratching is done either with 0000 steel wool or 3M's grey ScotchBrite (3M, 3M Center, Contractor Products, Bldg. 223-4N-06, St. Paul, Minn. 55144-1000; 612-733-1140), the

From *Fine Woodworking* magazine (September 1988) 72:62-64

Rubbed satin finish | **Rubbed gloss finish**

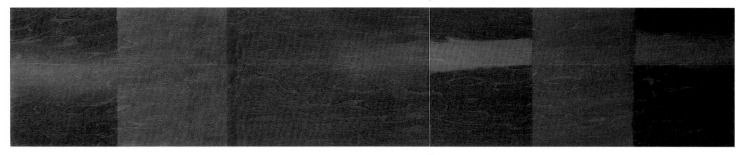

This sample board shows, from left to right, satin lacquer as sprayed; next has been sanded with 320-grit paper followed by dry steel wool; third has been rubbed with steel wool and a lubricant; fourth has been rubbed with steel wool using polishing compound.

Far right shows moderate orange peel in gloss lacquer. Sanding with 600-grit paper produces a flat surface (center), which can be polished with automotive rubbing and polishing compounds (left).

finest grade. Avoid using steel wool with visibly uneven fibers; it will cause deep scratches.

As with sandpaper, the abrasive pad is kept from clogging by a lubricant. There are many possibilities here, but I'll just offer four. Probably the most common is Wol-Wax (pronounced wool-wax), available from Star Chemical Company, 360 Shore Drive, Hinsdale, Ill., 60521; (312) 654-8650. It is a translucent gelatinous paste that turns into soapy suds when mixed with water. Contrary to its name, it is not a wax, but just furniture soap, and as such, offers the bonus of cleaning your hands while you work. My favorite is No. 61 Dull Wax Polish (available in gallons only, from Industrial Finishing Products, 465 Logan St., Brooklyn, N.Y. 11208; 718-277-3333). Unlike the water-base Wol-Wax, it is a dark-brown wax-base liquid that can be used right from the can or diluted with naptha. Referred to as "black wax" in the industry, its dark color makes it ideal for rubbing open-pore finishes on dark woods such as walnut or mahogany, where a light-color lubricant might leave an obvious white residue in the pores. A similar but more commonly available alternative to black wax is Butcher's Wax thinned with naptha. Finally, there is automotive rubbing or polishing compound, which when used with 0000 steel wool, leaves a slightly more polished surface—sort of a semi-gloss rub—after its residue has been buffed off. This is due to the fine abrasive in the compound. Of the four, the automotive compound leaves the most obvious residue and should therefore not be used with open-pore finishes. I'll talk more about compounds in the section on rubbing to a gloss finish.

In my shop, these new materials have almost displaced the old method of mixing dry, powdered abrasives such as pumice (for satin) or rottenstone (for gloss) with light oil or water on a felt pad. These are messier, and the pumice can clump up. Nevertheless, I often use pumice for spot rubbing, using my bare fingers and palm (for maximum control) with water or oil to feather out a problem area.

Rubbing a satin finish—Top surfaces, being the most obvious, require the greatest care. The edges of the piece present a problem: Because of surface tension, a wet finish tends to pull away from a sharp edge, leaving the finish thinner there. Normal rubbing strokes, if allowed to roll over the edge at the end of the stroke, will cut through. If this happens, there is no quick fix; the only proper solution is to clean off the piece and recoat the area. Out of a natural caution to avoid rubbing through, it is easy to shortchange areas such as the short edges of a tabletop. For this reason, I start by dipping the abrasive pad into the lubricant and carefully rubbing 8 in. to 10 in. of the ends of a tabletop with short strokes, working with the grain and keeping the pad flat to avoid breaking through the film on the corner.

Now, with edges done, you can rub out the top. With both hands stacked above the pad and pressing flat, rub with long, straight strokes with the grain, starting at one edge and overlapping strokes in much the same pattern you would use when spraying, but with more (90%) overlap per pass. Avoid making arcs with the pad, and try to go all the way to the ends without touching the sharp corners. On a top, I like to repeat this process, going side to side from bottom to top and back again at least six times to ensure ample overlap and uniformity. Be liberal with the lubricant, rewetting frequently, and don't be shy about applying the pressure; rubbing a top is a respectable aerobic workout.

Where two pieces of wood join with grain going in different directions, such as a miter joint or a butt joint, it is best to protect one of the members with masking tape while you rub the other. Similarly, a bullnose on a tabletop should follow the grain; roll over the edge at the ends of the boards, and go along the sides. On smooth turned legs, it is easiest to wrap your hand and abrasive pad around the leg and go up and down with the grain. On an intricately turned spindle, it is better to rub around the circumference, as you would if you were sanding the piece on the lathe. Endgrain can go whatever way looks best.

After rubbing, wipe off the excess lubricant while it's still wet (to avoid leaving a film) using a clean, soft, dry cloth. I prefer washed, bleached cheesecloth, because it doesn't scratch, is lint-free and absorbs moisture well. If you've used a wax-base lubricant and not removed it adequately, the surface will look smeary and take fingerprints easily. Sprinkle the surface with water (it will bead up like rain on a newly waxed car), take a fresh pad and *lightly* make one more even pass. You'll notice the wax accumulation on the pad, and the water beads will break up and not regroup. Dry it as above.

Now take a step back and admire your work. Depending on which way the light hits the top, it should look like the even graininess of brushed metal with no excessively shiny or dull spots. Now for the best part. Run your hands over the surface. Nice, huh? Your hands should skate across the surface smoothly, with little friction or resistance, and it should feel smooth and "soft" to your touch. That feeling is the lure of a well-rubbed satin finish.

Rubbing a gloss finish—Rubbing a finish to gloss is a lot like rubbing to satin, only more so. It takes more time, more work, requires more finish thickness, and more things can go wrong. A gloss finish is like a mirror; it shows every imperfection, adds depth and reflects a great deal of light, so it must be clear, hard, dry and—because gloss rubbing tends to remove more material—comparatively thick. As a general rule, the more brittle a film is, and the drier, the higher the gloss to which it can be rubbed.

Because most gloss lacquers do not do a very good job of sealing the wood, the first few coats will necessarily be some sort of sealer, but the bulk of the film should be gloss so you don't risk rubbing through the topcoat into the duller film beneath.

Because gloss illuminates irregularities, such finishes are usually restricted to filled- or closed-pore woods. On porous woods, such as walnut and mahogany, the grain should be filled with a nonshrinking material that does not redissolve with the application of the finish coat. It is always wise to use a nonreactive material, such as a filler containing silex, rather than attempt to fill the pores by sanding back successive coats of lacquer, a method that will significantly extend the film's curing time and cause the pores to sink when the finish is buffed.

High-gloss rubbing, or buffing, generates a good bit of friction, and thus heat, so it is especially important that the finish be completely cured. An uncured finish scratches easily and seems to resist getting really shiny. The thumbnail test is a good guideline here, and it is always better to err on the side of safety. On a gloss nitrocellulose or butyrate finish, I generally like to wait about six weeks after the last sprayed coat. Again, different finishes require different cure times. At the opposite end of the spectrum, there are many gloss polyesters that are ready to buff in 48 hours or less. Of course, you can convince yourself that a finish is ready to buff when it should by rights sit longer, and the finish will be, strictly speaking, gloss. But, you will notice that the longer a film is left to cure, the easier the work and the brighter the gloss. On large-pore woods, this extra waiting time also allows the lacquer in the pores to settle before they are sanded smooth, so there will be less pore shrinkage after the final buff.

As with satin finishes, there are many variables. The type of resin, the amount of plasticizer and several other factors will affect not only how soon a finish can be buffed, but also the level of gloss you can achieve. Waiting time is also affected by the thickness of the finish and the way it was applied, as mentioned above. One of the more insidious factors—controlled as much or more by the finisher than by the finish manufacturer—is the use of a so-called retarder or blush chaser. Retarder (usually amyl, ethyl or butyl acetate; sometimes called banana oil because of its smell) is frequently added to lacquer in damp weather to prevent blushing, that annoying whitish haze resulting from moisture trapped in the film. By retarding the drying time of the lacquer (hence its name), it appears to allow the moisture to escape. This also allows the lacquer more time to flow out, resulting in less overspray—the roughness caused by partially dried lacquer droplets settling on already sprayed sections—as well as less orange peel, and results in a generally smoother and glossier sprayed film. Brushing lacquer is often heavily laced with retarder, allowing it to be handled more easily and limiting brush marks. However, increased drying time also means increased curing time, and a finish pumped up with retarder may look glossier off the gun but will require more waiting time and be more difficult to buff. If you are building a gloss finish and are using retarder for its blush-chasing properties, you might be wiser to substitute one of the solvents that tend to eliminate blushing without causing so much softening or extending of the cure time, such as MAK (methyl amyl ketone), IBIB (isobutyl isobutyrate) or "No Blush" solvent, which is available from Hood Products, Box 163, Freehold, N.J. 07728; (201) 247-2177.

Because gloss sheens are so unforgiving, the surface must be virtually perfect before the rubbing starts. Sand the finish with fine-grit wet-or-dry paper (at least 600 grit, or finer if it is available) and a lubricant that will not redissolve the finish. Water, either plain or slightly soapy, works well for most finishes; for lacquers, I prefer naptha or mineral spirits.

It may seem a backward step to dull a gloss finish before polishing it, but this is absolutely necessary to show imperfections. As soon as you start sanding, all of the low spots, pits and other defects, will stand out as bright areas. These must be sanded down level, or the final finish will have the appearance of a funhouse mirror. Squeegee the area that you are sanding frequently with your thumb or a bit of rubber to remove the film so you can check your progress; you are removing finish, so you don't want to go any further than necessary, but you do want to remove all of the flaws. When the dullness of the surface is perfectly flat and even, it is time to graduate to rubbing compound.

In contrast to finishing materials, where industrial suppliers often provide materials that are better and fresher than those found in hardware stores, the rubbing compounds available off the shelf in automotive stores appear to be identical to those available in bulk from finishing-supply houses. Two grades are commonly available. The coarser-grit paste, usually orange in color, is called rubbing compound, while the finer white paste is generally referred to as polishing compound. The color is not necessarily indicative of grit, though; I used to buy a black polishing compound for use on ebony and dark finishes. The coarser-grit paste will remove material faster, hence defects and scratches as well, but must be followed by the finer polishing paste to bring the surface up to the higher-shine and to remove the minute scratches left by the coarser grit. Depending on how finely the surface was sanded (or in those rare cases when you can buff right off the spray gun), you might be able to save some time and effort by going directly to the polishing compound. You can always go back to the heavier grit if the buffing is going too slowly. As with sandpaper, this material is an abrasive and it *is* removing finish, albeit slowly, so it stands to reason that the less you remove, the better.

Surprisingly, the instructions on the rubbing-compound can are quite adequate. Using a pad of soft, dampened cloth, apply some of the compound and rub it in a circular or back-and-forth motion. You will notice that as long as the mixture remains a slurry, it tends to abrade away finish, but that the actual shining up occurs just at that point when the slurry dries and turns chalky. Although you don't have to rub very hard, it is important to continue buffing briskly. As the shine comes up, switch to a clean, dry, soft pad to remove the last vestiges of chalky residue and to bring up the final shine. This is the type of work where extra elbow grease pays off in better results—buffing a gloss finish is a lot of work.

Because you are trying to eliminate all visible scratches when polishing to a high gloss, the direction you rub is inconsequential, so rubbing rounded or coved sections can simply be done whichever way is most convenient. I like to use my bare hands dipped into a bit of compound to get into hard-to-reach areas. It is easier to feel what you are doing so as to avoid rubbing through sharp edges, easier to control than a pad in tight spots, and I find that for small areas, the finish actually comes up faster.

For that little something extra, many people like to add a final polishing step with wax or an automotive commercial glazing liquid. The glazing liquids, many of which contain silicones, claim to fill minute scratches to give the appearance of an even higher shine. They do impart a shiny glare to the surface, at least temporarily, but for good looks and endurance, you probably won't do much better than a well-applied coat of paste wax rubbed out to a shine.

Now, turn on a bright light, step up and look deep into your work. If the rub was right, you'll see your tired but smiling face staring right back at you. *That's* what it's all about. □

Michael Dresdner is a contributing editor at FWW. *His guitar-making shop is in Perkasie, Pa.*

Demystifying Wax
Clearing up some cloudy questions about an ancient finish

by Bob Flexner

I've used wax for years to restore the luster of the finish on the furniture I repair. But it wasn't until I started testing some of the popular brands that I realized what a thoroughly misunderstood material wax is. Consider, for example, the following statements made by well-known polish manufacturers and authors of books on finishing: "A finish must breathe, and wax prevents this." "You should remove wax twice a year because it builds up and softens the film with age." "This traditional polishing wax ...feeds the wood." "Wax tends to get gradually darker over the years." Despite the authority of the sources, I've found all these claims to be utter nonsense.

The ad hype concerning wax products is so prevalent that I think many people are confused about using wax to polish, protect and care for wooden furnishings. In my quest to clear up confusion about waxes, I interviewed a dozen finish chemists and professional wood finishers. I hope the following explanations will clear the air about what wax does (or does not do), how it works and how to use it.

First, a quick introduction to the waxes. Manufacturers today can choose from many natural and synthetic waxes to obtain a good wax product—one that protects well and is easy to apply. Among the most popular waxes: Beeswax is a soft wax secreted by bees for comb building and was historically the primary wax for woodwork; carnauba wax comes from palm leaves and is the hardest of the natural waxes; candelilla, from a desert plant found in northern Mexico and southern Texas, is often used in blends because of its low cost and compatibility in mixing with other waxes; and paraffin refined from petroleum is a very soft wax that's often blended with harder waxes to make them easier to apply.

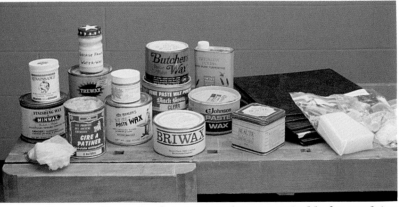

Dozens of brands of commercial waxes suitable for applying over furniture finishes are available. Among the most common raw ingredients are the ones shown in the plastic bags at the right. From left to right: beeswax, candelilla and carnauba.

The key to understanding wax lies in knowing its natural properties: It's a substance that's insoluble in water; a thin film of wax is capable of withstanding wear because it creates a low-friction surface things slide off of; wax bonds with tenacity to almost any solid material, but not to itself; and wax can be easily dissolved in a solvent, such as mineral spirits. The first two characteristics are important for understanding how wax protects, the third and fourth for understanding how to apply and remove it.

Wax protection—The primary finish on a piece of furniture, whether it be oil, lacquer or varnish, protects the wood from liquids or abrasion and reduces the exchange of moisture vapor between the wood and the atmosphere. Contrary to the all-too-commonly held belief, wood does not need to breathe, nor does it need to be fed. In fact, ideally, we would want to seal it off entirely from the atmosphere if we could. This moisture exchange, which will occur no matter what type of finish is applied, may cause the wood to warp, veneer to come loose, joints to come apart, and if the moisture is severe enough, wood to rot. Keeping the finish in good shape will postpone these problems, and wax is the best material I know of to accomplish this. It will repel liquids and deflect blows that might otherwise destroy the finish. Most waxes are inexpensive and easy to apply, and a wax finish is simple to keep in good repair. Further, a well-buffed wax coating imparts a soft, pleasing luster to a finish that can accentuate both the wood's color and grain.

Most woodworking finishes bond well to themselves and offer more protection if a thicker layer is built up with several coats. On the other hand, wax used as a polish is a material where less is better. To understand this, take a colored wax crayon and rub it on a piece of glass. If you keep rubbing long enough, all the wax ends up on the glass. But if you try to remove the wax from the glass with a cloth, you'll find that all of it wipes off except for a film so thin you can't see it. No amount of rubbing will remove this. Though wax crayons are softer than most waxes, the analogy still holds. Wax adheres with great strength to almost any solid surface, but it doesn't bond well to itself.

When the excess wax isn't properly buffed off, the effect is somewhat like the crayon on glass. As more coats are added, the wax layer becomes thicker and, like the crayon, will smear and mar easily. Further, this gummy layer collects dust and darkens over the years due to the dirt that becomes embedded in it. This has led many to believe that it's the wax itself that darkens with age. But if only one or two coats of wax are applied and rubbed down to the thinnest possible layer, a water-repellent and mar-resistant surface that will not smear or collect dust is produced. There's no reason to apply more coats of wax, since additional coats won't necessarily add protection and they will probably rub off when you buff it out. So despite the claims of polish manufacturers, a well-buffed wax finish will never develop wax buildup.

Applying wax—You can apply wax with steel wool, a dry or dampened cloth, or with a lump of wax inside a cloth. They all work decently, but there are some distinctions worth noting. Steel wool guarantees a duller sheen when waxing over a glossy finish. It's good if you want to dull a too-shiny surface and apply wax at the same time. But a steel-wool applicator shouldn't be used if you want the final finish to have a maximum gloss. Using a dry cloth works fine, but a dampened cloth makes application smoother. My favorite way of applying wax, however, is to put a chunk of it inside a cotton cloth. I hold it in my hand for a minute or two, warming and kneading the wax so it will spread evenly through the cloth. I can wax a fairly large surface quickly, without having to constantly reach back in the can to pick up more wax.

Obtaining an optimally thin coat of wax on a surface isn't difficult when you understand how solvents are used to make wax work. Solvents such as turpentine, mineral spirits and naptha are added to wax blends to create workable pastes and liquids. (CAUTION: Because these solvents are flammable, never heat commercial or homemade waxes over an open flame.) After the softened wax is applied and the solvents evaporate, the wax resolidifies. If you allow this thicker-than-desired wax layer to dry completely, it will take a lot of rubbing to get the excess off. If, however, you catch the wax at the point where it's bonded to the surface but the excess is still soft, then it wipes off easily—even if you've applied a very thick coat. You can't predict how long this drying process will take, as instructions on most wax products would lead you to believe. The appropriate moment to buff out the wax occurs relatively soon after application, but varies with the temperature and evaporation rate of the solvents. Visually, you can see it happening when the wax loses its wet shine and hazes over. If you wipe the wax before it dries, you'll remove too much. If you wait too long, you'll get streaks that will be difficult to remove, save with an electric buffer or polisher. You can also remove streaks by applying a new layer of wax to redissolve the hardened one, allowing it to be buffed out evenly. If you can smear the surface with your finger, then you have not removed all the excess wax.

In the same way that fresh wax can redissolve dried wax, the solvents used to make wax can also be used to remove it. A rag moistened with naptha or mineral spirits will quickly remove all the wax on a surface. Naptha leaves little residue and evaporates quickly, so it's my favorite solvent. Neither naptha, mineral spirits or any other commercial wax I know of will damage any primary finish, as long as the finish is more than two or three days old.

Solvents—not waxes—are the main ingredients in most liquid-spray and wipe-on polishes sold in supermarkets and department stores. Therefore, never apply one of these polishes to a waxed surface, because the polish might cause the wax to streak or remove it altogether. Waxed woodwork should be dusted with a dry cloth or feather duster and cleaned, if necessary, with a damp cloth. If a waxed surface becomes dull or marred, try rubbing out the marks and buffing up the luster with a soft cloth. If this fails, try another application of wax. This might be needed once every three months to a year on a tabletop that gets constant use and much less often on surfaces that see less use. If marks don't come out with re-waxing, the damage is likely in the primary finish.

Reviving a finish—Wax also can be effective for reviving the appearance of an old, worn finish. You can apply the new wax right over the old, because the solvents will redissolve any remaining old wax. It may be advisable to clean the piece first with mild soap and water to remove any dirt that has accumulated on the surface. It may even be necessary to rub out the piece with steel wool or sand lightly if the primary finish is lightly scratched or crazed. But this should never be done to a very old finish that has historic value. To hide scratches and recolor worn or damaged areas, you can apply pigmented waxes that come in wood tones. Most clear waxes can be colored with regular oil-based pigments. Experiment on a small inconspicuous section of a finished piece to determine the procedure that will get the best results. Remember though, a wax coating is very thin and won't hide imperfections on a badly cracked or worn finish. It should seldom, if ever, be necessary to remove the wax completely from an older piece, and could be ruinous on an antique: It might destroy some of the patina and reduce the value of the piece.

In addition to its use as a polish on an existing finish, wax can be used as a primary finish, as it was in the 16th to 18th centuries. But unfinished woods can absorb a great deal of wax, so it will be necessary to apply many coats. Just as with the wax crayon analogy, wax that builds several layers thick in the wood's pores and crevices does not bond well to itself. But these areas are so small that they have little effect on the overall wax surface. To reduce the number of wax coats needed to finish a piece of woodwork completely, it's best to seal the wood first with a coat of thinned shellac or oil. No more than one coat of wax should ever be needed on a sealed surface, but there are almost always small areas that don't get waxed the first time. A second coat ensures complete coverage and an even luster. □

Bob Flexner repairs and refinishes furniture in Norman, Okla. His videotape, Repairing Furniture, *is available from The Taunton Press, Box 5506, Newtown, Conn. 06470-5506.*

Putting wax to the test

I've used many commercially made waxes during my 15-year career as a furniture restorer and also made up my own concoctions from old formulas. I never noticed any substantial differences between waxes, but I always assumed I would find them if I looked closely enough. So, when I tested 13 waxes for this article, I was a little surprised at how close the overall results were, despite the differences in the waxes' cost and composition.

The waxes I tested (shown in the photo at the bottom of p. 53) included floor waxes, general-purpose paste waxes, waxes designed to clean and polish fine furniture and liquid wax polishes. Behlen's Blue Label, Minwax, Trewax, Butcher's Wax, Johnson's Paste Wax, Liberon Black Bison, Briwax and Livos Bekos waxes are paste waxes with a stiff consistency out of the can. Renaissance,

Beaute and French Buffing Wax are cream waxes, with a consistency between a paste and a liquid—like cold cream. The Liberon Beeswax Polish and George Frank's Water-Wax are both liquid waxes. The Water-Wax is a homemade mixture of carnauba and candelilla waxes emulsified in hot water by a formula given in Frank's book *Adventures in Woodfinishing* (Taunton Press, 1981). The majority of commercial wax prod-

From *Fine Woodworking* magazine (May 1988) 70:66-68

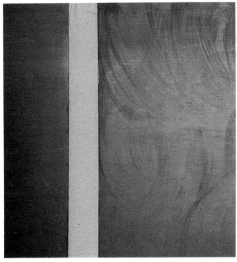 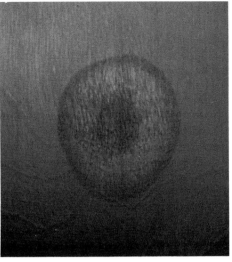

Above, left: If a wax is left on too long before the excess is buffed away, streaks will result, as seen on the right side of this test piece. Reapplying wax will soften the swirled coat so it can be buffed out evenly. Above, right: Wax will cause water to bead up and flow off, but it cannot protect against hot water after a spill. Despite the two coats of wax applied to this test sample, the grain of the maple plywood was raised and the wax dissolved after less than a minute of contact with hot water.

ucts are a mixture of waxes, including paraffin, beeswax, carnauba and candelilla dissolved in solvents. Renaissance wax is a petroleum derivative, like paraffin. The manufacturer says its refining process creates a "microcrystalline" or more compact crystal structure, making the wax tougher and with a higher melting point than paraffin.

I prepared wooden test pieces by staining 1-ft. squares of maple plywood a dark walnut color, then applying a number of coats of shellac. I used shellac because it would quickly show signs of water damage, and I stained the samples dark to show up wax streaking and unevenness in luster. The first test I performed was for sheen, and I compared the 13 waxes by putting two wax coats on each test piece. I was expecting waxes containing mostly soft beeswax, like Livos Bekos, to produce a duller finish than waxes made with a high percentage of harder waxes. But I couldn't see any difference in sheen at all between the samples. I tried the experiment again, but this time on a cherry hutch I had in my shop for repair. I put a different wax on each of the six drawers, two raised-panel doors, two sides and top and still couldn't see any difference in surface luster. However, the cherry hutch had a slightly higher gloss than the newly shellacked and rubbed-out plywood test pieces. Therefore, I decided that the final sheen depended more on the luster of the primary finish than on the type of wax I applied over it.

I performed a scuff test by subjecting each of the samples to repeated glancing blows from the corner of a book. The scuff marks buffed out easily, unless the wood was hit hard enough to damage the finish underneath the wax. There was no noticeable difference in

how the 13 waxes resisted scuffing. There also wasn't any difference in the way the waxes repelled water. The waxes offered very little protection when I allowed small puddles of water to stand on the sample piece, and none prevented the penetration of water for more than a minute or so. After one or two minutes, the maple plywood's grain would start to rise. After each sample was dried, the wax finishes always remained intact—with no blushing or change in color or luster—despite the damage to the plywood. For comparison, I tested Pledge, a spray polish containing silicone; Oz, an emulsified cream polish; and Simoniz II, an automobile wax. All of them yielded the same results as the 13 sample waxes.

Although none of the waxes are impervious to moisture, they do bead up liquids and make them run off easier, reducing the contact of the liquid with the surface. Ultimately, however, water-resistance depends on the kind of underlying finish and its condition. Older varnished and lacquered surfaces with deteriorated finishes may watermark, because the surface film has begun to fail. But on newly-lacquered surfaces, cold water stayed beaded up on the wax for hours with no apparent damage to either the finish or the wax.

Applying hot water to the waxed samples produced more dramatic results. The heated water started to melt the wax at about 140°, and all the samples showed a dull luster where the water had made contact. The dull spot could be eliminated, though, by applying a new coat of wax over it and buffing it up. Water above 150° damaged the shellac and dulled the wax film.

I tried several different methods of wax application during the testing to see if the liquid polishes were more

prone to streaking or leaving an uneven sheen than the harder, paste-wax types that have less solvent in them. Once again, all the waxes performed the same and predictably left streaks if left on too long before buffing. I tried using steel wool to remove the excess wax, as advocated by some wax makers. I found it almost impossible to keep the steel wool from removing all the wax, as well as a bit of the primary finish. I also tried following the directions on some wax-container labels, which recommended waiting from 5 minutes to 20 minutes and up to 24 hours before buffing off the excess. In all cases, hand buffing was very hard work, and I often resorted to my electric polisher. In contrast, it was easier to buff the excess immediately after the wax formed a haze, and I couldn't see any difference in the final results.

When evaluating my results, you should remember the tests I performed were under workshop conditions, not laboratory conditions. Even though there are scientifically measurable differences between the hardness and melting points of the components in each mixture, I couldn't detect significant differences in appearance or protection. Further, the tests convinced me that the differences between wax brands are not great enough to have any practical value for the woodworker and surely don't justify buying some of the more expensive brands. Nor do they justify the trouble and danger of making your own wax mixtures. —B.F.

Sources of supply

Beaute: Roger A. Reed Inc., P.O. Box 508, Reading, MA 01867.

Behlen's Blue Label and French Buffing Wax: Garrett Wade Co., 161 Ave. of the Americas, New York, NY 10013.

Black Bison and Beeswax Polish: Liberon Supplies, P.O. Box 1750, Mendocino, CA 95460.

Briwax: Briwax Int., P.O. Box 3327, Redwood City, CA 94064.

Butcher's Wax: The Butcher Polishing Co., 120 Bartlett St., Marlborough, MA 01752-3013.

Johnson Paste Wax: S.C. Johnson & Son, Inc., 1525 Howe St., Racine, WI 53403-5011.

Livos Bekos: Livos PlantChemistry, 614 Agua Fria St., Santa Fe, NM 87501.

Minwax: Minwax Co. Inc., 102 Chestnut Ridge Plaza, Montvale, NJ 07649.

Renaissance: Cereus Inc., 184 Warburton Ave., Hastings-on-Hudson, NY 10706.

Trewax: Trewax Co., 11641 Pike St., Santa Fe Springs, CA 90670.

Water-Wax: Ingredients for George Frank's Water-Wax are available from the Olde Mill Cabinet Shoppe, RD#3, P.O. Box 547A, Camp Betty Washington Rd., York, PA 17402.

French polishing, the venerable technique for applying a shellac finish, produces a high-gloss sheen as yet unmatched by any modern finishing technique. Here, George Frank checks for flaws in the finished surface.

French Polishing
Applying the ultimate finish

by George Frank

It was 1922, over 60 years ago, when I was first introduced to French polishing. My teacher couldn't hear or speak, but she was expert in the arts of French polishing and communicating through sign language. When she twirled both ends of her imaginary moustache she was talking about the boss, twirling just one end meant the foreman. She had unprintable words to chastize me for my errors; hugs and kisses were my reward when I was doing well. Two months later, French polishing had no secrets for me. If I could join the areas I've French polished since, I could easily cover three football fields.

In the olden days, before modern lacquers and varnishes, French polishing was the ultimate finish, reserved for fine luxury furniture. Even today, the beauty of this glossy shellac finish is unparalleled, but the skill is not an easy one to acquire. Here, I will convey to you the true French way of French polishing.

Materials—Shellac is the main ingredient in French polishing. Shellac's solvent is denatured alcohol. A French-polished finish is extremely durable, but because alcohol is the solvent, a spilled drink can damage it.

Hardware stores sell pre-mixed shellac in cans, but I mix my own so I have complete control over the quality of the ingredients. Dry shellac comes in many grades. I use a grade called superfine orange flakes. These flakes have an unlimited shelf life while dry, and almost as long a shelf life when they are dissolved in alcohol (don't store it in metal containers). On light colored woods, where I want a water-clear finish, I use bleached, or white shellac instead. Dry bleached shellac must be kept very cold and even so, it won't keep long. For this reason, I buy white shellac already mixed, and not more than I can promptly use up. Super blonde flakes, which have an unlimited shelf life, can be substituted for the perishable white shellac.

Shellac's "cut" refers to the ratio of shellac to alcohol. Three pounds of shellac flakes dissolved in a gallon of alcohol is called 3-lb.-cut, 5 lb. in a gallon is 5-lb.-cut, etc. For French polishing, I make 2½-lb.-cut shellac. For moldings, carvings and turnings I make a heavier, 3½-lb.-cut solution. After mixing, I filter the 3½-lb. cut solution through a clean cloth.

Mineral oil, a petroleum by-product, is used in French polishing as a lubricant. Light-density oil is the best for French polishing—baby oil and lemon oil are also acceptable.

Pumice stone is pulverized vulcanic stone used as an abrasive in French polishing. I buy the finest, the FFFF grade.

The French name of French polishing is *vernissage au tampon* (varnishing with a tampon). The tampon, in English, is called a pad, rubber or fad, but none of these are used exactly the same way a tampon is, so allow me to use the French word. The tampon is the French polisher's main tool. It holds the liquid shellac and alcohol and releases them as you squeeze it, or press it against the object to be polished. The inside of the tampon is wool, preferably some old, often-washed knit wool, such as part of a sweater or some white woolen socks. (According to my old notes the best tampons are made of virgin lamb's wool). Before making a new tampon, the wool has to be soaked with the 2½-lb.-cut shellac and hung up for about two hours. Before it dries completely, it must be stored in a tampon can (a tin can with a tightly fitting lid) or in a screw-top jar. A tampon must never dry out completely or it will be ruined.

The tampon is not complete without its outer wrap, which I will call by its old name "linen." Nowadays, our linen is mostly cotton and/or some untraceable man-made cloth. The linen, as we will soon see, plays a crucial part in French polishing.

An array of small secondary items makes the polisher's task easier. On my workbench, I have within easy reach two bottles (about a pint) and a third smaller one. All three have cork stoppers with a thin V-cut in the cork to slowly dispense the contents. I fill one pint bottle with denatured alcohol, and the other with the 2½-lb.-cut shellac. The smaller bottle contains the filtered 3½-lb.-cut shellac. On the workbench are two small tins, one containing 4F pumice stone, the second mineral oil. For dark or red woods (like mahogany) I fill a third tin with mineral oil tinted red or reddish brown with an oil-soluble aniline dye (in the old days, we colored the oil red with alkanet root). First, I dissolve the dye in a small amount of lacquer thinner, then filter out the sediment before adding the dye to the oil.

Under the bench I keep a toolbox containing three or four natural-bristle shellac brushes, a duster-brush, sandpaper (220 grit through 600 grit) and some cheesecloth.

The most important step in mastering the art of French polishing is to understand the theory. A single flake of shellac, when dissolved in alcohol, can be spread over an unbelievably large area. When the alcohol evaporates, the film of shellac remaining on the surface is incredibly thin, dry within seconds, and you can spread a second layer on top of it, a third, fourth or hundredth, and all these layers will melt into one almost immeasurably thin layer. In French polishing, the tampon holds and dispenses the dissolved shellac as it rubs over and over the surface. Meanwhile, the linen retains a bit of pumice and transforms itself into a fine sanding cloth, smoothing the surface simultaneously as it lays down countless layers of shellac.

French polishing a flat surface—French polishing could be compared to playing a musical instrument, and no music teacher

would start a beginner with an elaborate tune. Likewise, I strongly suggest that you practice on large, flat boards before you attempt to finish a piece of furniture. The technique is the same for a practice board or the little tabletop in the photos. The legs of the table require a different technique, as I'll explain later.

After sanding thoroughly with 120-grit paper, I sponge the surface sparingly with water to raise the grain. When it's dry, with one-quarter sheet of fresh 150-grit aluminum oxide sandpaper wrapped around my hard rubber sanding block (carpet layers use such rubber blocks to kneel on), I sand at a slight angle to the grain, so as not to push the raised grain back down, but rather to shave off the whiskers. I sandpaper the edges carefully, and break all the sharp corners. Then I sweep away the dust with my dust brush, and check my sanding. Not with my finger tips, but by laying my open palm on the board and moving it around. This way I can detect imperfections not otherwise perceptible.

At this stage, the wood may be dyed, and that's what I did to my little mahogany table. I mixed a water-soluble red/brown aniline dye in water and applied it generously with a piece of soft rubber sponge.

When dry, I sand again with 220- or 280-grit paper. I dust it off once more (not too carefully, since dust does not interfere with French polishing, especially not at the beginning) and I am ready to apply mineral oil.

At this point, I would like to explain that there is a marked difference between the Italian, English and American schools of French polishing and the true French way. These methods coat the raw wood with a heavy layer of shellac and don't use oil at the beginning. The French way always starts by oiling the surface. Using some cheesecloth, I spread on a coat of mineral oil and immediately wipe off the excess.

A finisher always expends his best effort on the surface that will show. Since no one will closely examine the underside of a tabletop, I don't lavish the same attention there as I do on the top. After oiling, I brush the underside with the filtered 3½-lb.-cut shellac. When dry, I build up a film of 2½-lb.-cut shellac with a piece of cheesecloth. It takes about five minutes to build a nice film on the underside. I'm ready to start polishing the top.

French polishing is usually done in three phases. The first phase is the filling of the pores. From my shellac-soaked wool I cut off enough to make a tampon about the size of an egg (larger for a big surface). Then, digging in my box of rags I pull out a piece of linen the size of a small handkerchief. I shape the wool

to fit my hand, cover it with the linen and twist the linen tightly around it. From the alcohol bottle, I dribble alcohol onto the bottom of the tampon, and squeeze it into the tampon. The rule of thumb for applying alcohol—the tampon should be moist, but you should not be able to squeeze drops out of it. The downward pressure applied to the tampon shall always be the opposite of the tampon's load. A just fed tampon—very light pressure, a nearly dry tampon...let me quote Olga, my teacher: "When your workbench sinks a half inch into the floor, the pressure is almost enough." I hold the tampon firmly so the thumb, index and middle finger can squeeze it to force out the moisture.

To begin, I fasten the board securely to the workbench, raised

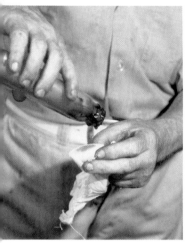

After dusting a pinch of pumice stone across the surface, the tampon is wet with alcohol and rubbed over and over the surface, filling the pores with pumice and wood dust. When the pores are filled, shellac is introduced to the inside of the tampon, and the rubbing continues, eventually building up a film of shellac.

on cleats so I can have easy access to the edges. Now, before my tampon contacts the wood, I pick up a pinch of pumice and sprinkle it across the surface. I glide the tampon onto the wood, like a plane coming in for a landing, and keep it moving once it has hit the surface. When I want to stop, I glide the tampon off the surface like a plane taking off. Just putting down and picking up the tampon will leave a mark. Gliding the tampon on, I start pressing the pumice into the pores of the wood, moving the tampon around the board in swirls, endlessly writing WOW, WOW, across the surface, with a few figure 8s thrown in. The tampon must never stop on the surface. This writing isn't limited to the board, in fact, half of the tampon is almost always off the edge of the board. Olga taught me, "Don't worry about the center of the board, it will be done by itself, worry about the edges and the corners."

As I rub, some of the pumice powder enters the microscopic pores of the very smooth wood, but a fair amount sticks to the bottom of the tampon and goes into the openings of the linen. This abrasive linen cuts off the protruding microscopic fibers of the wood, and mixes them into a paste, combining shellac (from the pre-soaked wool inside the tampon), pumice and wood-dust. This compound fills the pores of the wood, blending into it, matching its color and texture to perfection.

After 10 to 15 minutes of rubbing, filling and refilling my tampon with alcohol alone (no shellac) and sparingly salting the board with pumice (very little amounts, but frequently), the surface begins to change. It becomes like frosted glass, smooth and dull. At this point, I have to explain about the light. Imagine the surface as a mirror. I place it so as to see in it some source of light that will allow me to see all details of my progress. Are all the

pores properly filled? Am I leaving heaps of pumice? Did I wash off one coat with the next one? Without proper light, successful French polishing is impossible.

What happens if you put pebbles into a glass of water? Simple, the more pebbles you put in, the more water you force out. At the beginning, the pores of the wood were filled with oil, and now I am refilling them with pumice, shellac and wood dust. The oil spills out and reappears now on the surface, causing it to look like frosted glass, and helping my tampon to glide easier.

When the pores are filled, I begin adding shellac to the wool inside the tampon. I peel off the linen, feed the alcohol first, shellac next (always more alcohol than shellac), then re-cover my tampon, giving the linen a tight twist. I tap the tampon against the back of my hand a few times to even out the moisture. Now I work the shellac and alcohol into the wood. (I never apply shellac to the outside of the tampon, although I will sometimes add alcohol to the outside.)

Whenever the tampon is very dry, I feed it with alcohol and a few drops of shellac and dust a trace of pumice across the board's surface. I am achieving a beautifully smooth surface on which I can easily trace every move of my tampon, since its moves are as readable as the moves of your pen on paper. The oil being forced out of the pores forms faint clouds on the surface that tell me "everything is going well." The finish should always feel dry to the touch.

After I've refilled my tampon three or four times, the shellac buildup is already perceptible and quite shiny. When it is, I touch a drop of oil on the outside of the tampon and continue rubbing. Things begin to happen. Until now, faint clouds marked the passage of my tampon. The droplet of oil that I put on the bottom of my tampon transforms these clouds into easily visible ones. By now the first phase, the filling of the pores, is almost finished, and I've already started the second phase, the bodying. (I timed myself on the tabletop. The filling stage took me approximately 25 minutes, the bodying stage about 15 more.) Now I begin to increase the amount of shellac I add to the inside of my tampon, but never more shellac than alcohol. I also reduce the amount of pumice and, every so often, touch a single drop of oil to the bottom of my tampon. I concentrate on the clouds, which *must* be present on the surface at all times. French polishing has a wonderful rule: Whatever goes wrong, the remedy is alcohol. Remember this well, and practice it. I hardly put any pressure on my freshly filled tampon, but I increase the pressure as the tampon dries. Underneath the clouds, the wood becomes alive and beautiful, it pays me back every bit of effort I put in so far, and with interest.

The edges get a different treatment. In my tampon can, I keep a piece of cheesecloth about 1 ft. square. I wet this generously with 3½-lb.-cut filtered shellac and wipe it over the edges. Repeating this about every five minutes builds up a fair coating on the edges. With my tampon, I skim over the edges time and again. I don't use pumice on the edges, and a bit more oil than on the flat surface. By the time the surface is well bodied up, the edges are in good shape also.

I end up my bodying by filling my tampon once more with alcohol alone and rub until it is quite dry. The alcohol improves the shine and thins the clouds. Incidentally, by this time, the bottom of my tampon is always clean. (If not, the remedy is alcohol). The board is now ready for an overnight rest, and the tampon goes in the tampon can.

The next day I scrutinize my work for poorly filled areas. Beginners frequently have pumice heaps within the finish. These must be sanded off lightly with 600-grit wet or dry paper wet sparingly with soapy water then dried off well. It is a good idea to go over any and all problem areas with this sandpaper.

The second day operation takes about 20 minutes. The purpose is to correct the shortcomings of the first application and then complete the bodying by adding shellac. I start by feeding the tampon with alcohol only and dusting the board with pumice. The only difference is the quantity. Both alcohol and pumice have to be used much more sparingly than at the beginning. On the other hand, even more care is needed than the first day because the film of finish can be easily ruined. I apply hard pressure and space the "O"'s and "W"'s so that no spot will be hit again before it has time to dry.

Alcohol, little pumice, great care and the problem areas are fading away. The clouds are appearing again, meaning that once more I am on the right road and that I can resume the bodying. I slowly increase the shellac content of my tampon and add a dab of oil to its bottom.

After about 15 minutes, I replace my linen with a clean, softer "linen" (soft cotton). I stop using oil. This forces me to use extreme care as I land my tampon on the board. I use as little pressure on the tampon as possible. Now, as my tampon dries out, the clouds are thin and they become iridescent. The last two feedings of my tampon are with alcohol alone. I use up every drop of it and the surface smiles at me.

At the start of the third day, the beautiful gloss is somewhat veiled by the clouds of oil. If I am satisfied with the body of my polish, I can proceed with the final clearing. If I feel that additional bodying up would improve the job, I wet my tampon with shellac and alcohol (and maybe a tiny drop of oil, too) and keep up the bodying. When I'm satisfied, I will ease up the shellac feeding and once more, using alcohol alone, I thin-up the clouds to bring up the shine.

My goal now is to eliminate all traces of these clouds and to clear the glossy surface perfectly. For the final clearing, I park my tampon in the tampon can and reach for my special finishing tampon, which I keep in a special tampon can. This special tampon looks just like my regular tampon, except that it is new, and contains no shellac and no oil. The heart of this tampon could be made of a clean, white cotton undershirt or a piece of cheesecloth instead of wool.

First, I sprinkle a light pinch of tripoli earth (a very fine abrasive) on the surface. Wetting the tampon with alcohol, I land it on the board so gently that the board doesn't notice what I did, and wipe off, with imperceptibly increasing pressure, all remainders of the clouds. The job is finished.

French polishing the pedestal—Moldings and carved surfaces get a different finish, one more like the English style of French polishing, and I used this technique on the legs and column of my little mahogany table. Had I turned the table column myself, I would have sanded and finished it on the lathe.

After dyeing the pedestal, I sand with 220-grit paper. After applying mineral oil, I brush on a coat of the filtered 3½-lb.-cut shellac. When that is dry I wipe on 2½-lb.-cut shellac with a piece of cheesecloth. Here, I'm trying to fill the pores of the wood with shellac instead of pumice and wood dust. Where I applied only drops to the tampon when I polished the top, here I am liberal with the shellac. After a few minutes, I add mineral oil to the cheesecloth—much more than I used on the top, and a drop of alcohol. The shellac builds quickly and I have a nice shine in a few minutes.

On the second day, I sand the legs and column with 400-grit

A thicker coat of shellac is built up on the table legs and column using a piece of cheesecloth as an applicator. Then, after sanding with 600-grit paper, a final coat of shellac is applied with a piece of soft foam rubber.

paper. After brushing off the dust, I rub the legs with cheesecloth using more shellac and more oil. On the third day, I gently sand over the rough spots with 600-grit paper. Using the tampon this time, instead of the cheesecloth, I wet the inside liberally with shellac, apply some alcohol to the outside of the linen and smooth up the legs and column. When that coat is dry, I'm ready for the last step. I add the final gloss by dipping a piece of soft foam-rubber sponge in the filtered 3½-lb.-cut shellac and gently stroking on one smooth, heavy coat of shellac.

For the first 50 years, dusting is the only care that a French polished surface requires. After that, an occasional light wipe with lemon oil or lemon oil cut with turpentine will do fine. □

George Frank, of South Venice, Fla., is a retired master woodfinisher and author of Adventures in Wood Finishing *(1981, Taunton Press).*

Sources of supply

French-polishing materials are available by mail from Lee Valley Tools, Garrett Wade, Constantines, Highland Hardware, The Woodworkers' Store and the following companies:

Wood Finishing Supply Co., 1267 Mary Drive, Macedon, N.Y. 14502

Olde Mill Cabinet Shoppe, RD 3, Box 547A, York, Pa. 17402

Mohawk Finishing Products, Inc., Route 30 North, Amsterdam, N.Y. 12010

The Finish Crack'd
Conservator's fix for a fractured film

by Gregory J. Landrey

The restored dressing table.

What a face lift does for an aging movie star, finish restoration can do for a piece of furniture. In my work as a conservator at the Winterthur Museum, I use a variety of restoration methods on many period pieces. But the technique I'll describe here will work just as well on grandma's favorite dresser as on a collector's treasure.

When the 200-year-old mahogany dressing table shown above arrived in my shop this past summer, it had an extremely degraded varnish finish, exhibiting the yellowing, crazing and film shrinkage that can occur with time. Since the crackle pattern (a result of oxidation and subsequent contraction of the finish layer) extended through only the top part of the film, we decided that the finish was restorable. Crazing generally doesn't develop with thin-film finishes, such as French-polished or contemporary oil finishes, but it's fairly common with the thick, hard, resinous films characteristic of period varnishes and modern shellacs, lacquers and polyurethanes. The method I used to restore the table's finish—cleaning the film, abrading off the degraded portion, and polishing the remaining finish—is an acceptable conservation procedure because it preserves the original finish, leaving the patina of the wood undisturbed. The same process can be used on any reasonably thick finish in need of cosmetic repair.

Several factors contribute to finish deterioration: chemical instability, solvent loss, humidity, temperature, wear and tear, poor care, and, perhaps most damaging, exposure to light. Both natural and artificial light accelerate finish breakdown, which is why valuable furniture should be displayed in areas with moderate light levels, out of direct sunlight.

In dealing with an eroded finish, you have two choices: strip off the old finish and apply a new one, or repair the existing film. If a significant amount of the finish is gone, extremely discolored or seriously water-damaged, refinishing is probably called for. But, when possible, conservators prefer to save the old finish, doing only what is necessary to repair any damage and to retard further deterioration. The objective is not to make the piece look brand-new, but to let it age comfortably, preserving the whispered history of days gone by. This requires a fair amount of patience and even more finesse, but in most cases it takes less time, space and money than complete refinishing would.

Types of finishes—To determine the best way to repair a damaged finish, be it period or modern, you must first consider the original finishing materials and the finisher's intent. Through the centuries, a great many finishes have been concocted to enhance the beauty of wood, and to protect it from the ravages of moisture, sunlight, insects, and everyday wear. The earliest finishes in America were oils such as linseed, poppyseed and walnut, and waxes such as beeswax. These did little to protect the furniture, however, and often dulled its appearance. On period furniture—furniture built prior to 1830 and the advent of commercially available finishing products—three major types of finishes were commonly used: fixed-oil varnishes, spirit varnishes and essential-oil varnishes. Eighteenth-century cabinetmakers most often applied some type of fixed-oil varnish, consisting of a drying oil, usually boiled linseed, and a resin, such as copal, sandarac or amber. In the 19th century, spirit varnishes were more widely used, with alcohol as the common vehicle, and sandarac, copal, mastic or shellac the usual resin. An inexpensive essential-oil varnish, actually a type of spirit varnish, consisted of turpentine and rosin, a pine resin also known as colophony. Applying a spirit varnish over a previous, sometimes incom-

patible, finish was also common practice.

What effect were these early finish chemists after? According to Isaac Byington, a late-18th-century carpenter/cabinetmaker from Bristol, Connecticut, the ideal was "a varnish which stands water and shines like glass." In stylish homes, illuminated only by candlelight and subjected to constant fireplace soot, a high-gloss furniture finish was highly desirable.

Most of today's finishes can be divided into two types: solvent-release and reactive. Shellac, nitrocellulose lacquer and some acrylics fit into the solvent-release group. The reactive finishes are drying oils, such as tung and boiled linseed, and polymerizing varnishes, such as alkyd resin and polyurethane. For conservation purposes—the touch-up of finish losses on period pieces, for example—solvent-release finishes are preferred because they retain solubility and are therefore reversible. This reversibility is important in restoration work, since due to inevitable degradation, further repair may later be necessary. Chemically reactive finishes polymerize, making them difficult to remove.

In addition to these various finish formulas, many cleaners and polishes have been devised over the years to keep furniture glowing—everything from linseed oil and beeswax to a whole range of commercial polishes and waxes. Finishes still degrade, however. In fact, polishes that don't provide a good moisture barrier or that chemically bond to the finish can even accelerate degradation.

Finish identification—With such a variety of possible surface films, the first step in restoration is to determine the type of finish on the piece, since this will limit what cleaners can be used. I begin with a visual inspection, looking obliquely at the surface in good light to detect scratches, variations in color, and changes in gloss

Photos: Herbert Crossan, courtesy of the Henry Francis du Pont Winterthur Museum indicating worn areas. For the dressing table, examining the broken film under the microscope (a 15X hand lens works fine, too) gave me an idea of the thickness of the film and the extent of the crazing. The pattern of the cracks can give clues, too. The regular fissures in the table's finish suggested a spirit varnish. Lacquer, on the other hand, breaks down in irregular fissures or long, rectangular checks; shellac, in an island configuration. I also found an earlier finish (later identified as an oil varnish) on the drawer lips, indicating that the thick spirit varnish had been applied well after the table was built. In addition, I knew that the piece had been polished yearly with linseed oil during its first eight years at Winterthur.

At Winterthur, we sometimes have our analytical laboratory test samples of an unknown finish by infrared spectrometry or other related techniques. On this piece, the accumulation of varnish, oil, dirt and cleaning solvents, coupled with ultraviolet disintegration, made lab analysis difficult. Despite these problems, Dr. George Reilly, head of Winterthur's analytical lab, compared the finish with known samples and determined that it contained a damar or mastic resin, commonly used in varnish for oil paintings.

Even if you don't have access to a lab, you can still do some simple testing to identify a finish. The strategy I often find most helpful is to test a small, inconspicuous area of the finish with progressively stronger solvents. This may reveal more about the class of finish, and can also tell you what solvents are safe to use in cleaning (safe for the finish, not for you—be sure to wear gloves and a vapor mask). On the table, I began with a cotton swab dampened with reagent ethyl alcohol. Gentle rubbing succeeded in softening the film, confirming that it was a spirit varnish. A weak hydrocarbon such as mineral spirits will soften or dissolve many turpentine- or petroleum-distillate-based finishes such as fresh damar, wax and some oil finishes. Lacquer thinner will dissolve a nitrocellulose film. Strong halogens such as methylene chloride will soften many oils, alkyd resins and polyurethanes. If you can't dissolve the film, it's likely that it is an extremely oxidized, chemically reactive film.

Obviously, if your goal is to completely strip a finish, this solvent-testing will tell you what will work. And if you're debating whether to completely refinish or not, you might first want to try either of two processes some restorers have experimented with: reapplication or amalgamation. In reapplication, the piece is washed down with the weakest solvent that will remove the finish, and the solution is collected and then reapplied. In amalgamation, a badly crazed finish is softened with the appropriate solvent, then moved around with a pad or brush to level the film. The trouble with both methods is that you succeed only in "turning over" the finish, introducing contaminants to the wood and disturbing the patina. Because not all the solvent evaporates, you're also liable to end up with a softer finish. In addition, you'll still have a chemically degraded film. I've rarely seen either procedure done satisfactorily, even on inexpensive furniture, and I certainly wouldn't try either on a valuable piece.

Cleaning—Once you've identified the degraded finish, the next step is to clean it. This is a four-part process: touch-up of areas that have lost finish entirely, removal of dirt, reduction of the crazed portion, and rubout of the remaining finish.

To protect bare wood from the water and solvents used later on, scratches or nicks in the finish must be sealed. Because they're reversible, shellac and nitrocellulose lacquer are commonly used for touchup. For period pieces, I prefer shellac, as it closely approximates a spirit-varnish finish; on a contemporary piece, I'll often use brushing lacquer instead. I touched up scratches on the dressing table with a thin coat of 2-lb.-cut clear shellac applied with a fine-tip artists' brush. Often a repaired scratch will appear too light after the entire surface has been cleaned and polished with wax. When this happens, I remove the polish in that area and apply a second coat of shellac toned with an alcohol-soluble stain, or with artists' dry-earth pigments if opacity is desired. When matching the color, it's better to err on the dark side, as the eye will pass over such a mark more readily than over a light one.

Surface dirt can consist of dust, fibers, soot, salt, fungi and grease. Besides muddying appearance, dirt attracts moisture that will increase oxidation and mold growth. Thus for aesthetics as well as long-term preservation of the furniture, dirt must be removed. I first vacuumed the table to pick up loose particles, then lifted most of the dirt with a cotton pad dampened with a 5% solution of mild soap and water (I use Vulpex soap, available from Conservation Materials Ltd., Box 2884, 340 Freeport Blvd., Sparks, Nev. 89431). It's best to work on a small section at a time, allowing it to air-dry thoroughly.

Usually you'll need an organic solvent to soften or remove old polishes such as linseed oil and beeswax. Mineral spirits will remove most waxes and some oils, and I gave the table a thorough rubdown with Stoddard solvent, an odorless mineral spirit (also available from Conservation Materials Ltd.). A word of caution: Again, knowing the composition of the finish is important—*don't* use min-

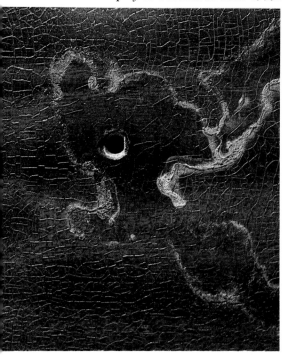

Close-up of the table's finish, before restoration. Built around 1750, the piece had been on display at Winterthur since 1959.

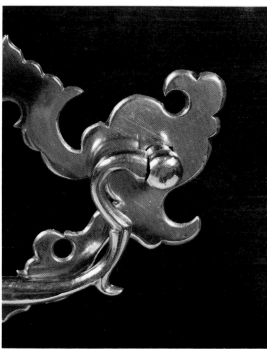

With careful cleaning, abrasion and polishing, Landrey restored the finish to period condition in less than forty hours.

eral spirits for cleaning an oil finish.

If the finish isn't badly crazed, you can skip the remaining cleaning steps and go straight to polishing. The dressing table, however, required the full treatment.

Because the crackle pattern extended only about halfway through the finish film, I could abrade off most of the degraded portion without disturbing the rest. On the flat surfaces, I used 320A- to 400A-rated wet-or-dry silicon carbide abrasive paper, dusting some fine pumice between the dry paper and the finish to reduce the paper's harshness. It takes a patient hand to keep from going through the finish, but not all the crazing needs to be removed, just enough so that the remaining finish reflects light more evenly. As you go along, look for accumulation of

sanding dust and pumice in the film's cracks: when most of the crazing has been eliminated, the dust won't have a place to collect. To prevent damage along the edges, I made a sanding block from a piece of pine with rounded corners, to which I glued 1/8-in. cotton padding. Then I rubbed down the curved areas of the legs, drawer moldings and top edges with 0000 steel wool.

To reproduce the high-gloss finish popular on such high-style pieces, I finished up by rubbing out the surface with rottenstone, a fine abrasive favored by 18th-century finishers, using mineral spirits as a lubricant. (I don't use the traditional oil lubrication for rottenstone because I prefer not to risk leaving any oil behind when restoring this type of finish.) A final rubbing with a

cotton pad dampened with mineral spirits removed the residual rottenstone.

Polishing—After cleaning, all that remains is to polish the piece to brighten the finish and to protect the rubbed-out surface. There's an assortment of commercially available polishes to pick from.

Linseed oil, though popular, is not a good choice. Even a thin film of linseed oil will darken with age and attract dust, particularly in crevices. It's not a good moisture barrier either, and it polymerizes fully, becoming extremely difficult to remove if necessary later. Lemon oil, an innocuous non-drying oil, will saturate the color of the piece but do little to protect it. It too is a dust magnet. Tung oil, although sometimes a highly desirable finish, presents some problems as a polish. Pure tung oil lacks the luster and gloss a high-style period piece should have, and like linseed oil, it will bond to the finish and become quite difficult to remove. Watco oil, which contains a significant amount of linseed oil, won't penetrate an existing finish film sufficiently to dry thoroughly to a hard, protective layer.

Carnauba and microcrystalline paste waxes are, in my opinion, the best polishes. Chemically inert, they're compatible with most finishes, and they're effective moisture barriers. Buffed to a hard, dry film, they won't trap dust. Although a wax may whiten when subjected to excessive heat or moisture, it can easily be removed with mineral spirits and a new coat applied.

I most often use brown Behlen Bros. Blue Label paste wax or Renaissance microcrystalline wax (available from Garrett Wade and Conservation Materials, respectively). Because of the relatively dark finish on this dressing table, I chose the brown wax, applying it sparingly with flannel cloths and buffing it out. Sometimes it's also necessary to use a stiff brush on some sections to work the wax into the remaining irregularities in the film. It takes a fair amount of elbow grease to get an even luster, but the wax will last, and with proper care the restored finish shouldn't need any additional cleaning or polishing for years to come. □

To protect bare wood from cleaning solvents, Landrey first touched up scratches with shellac (above left). Then he removed surface dirt with soap and water (above right), and gently abraded with silicon carbide paper, used with a padded block (below).

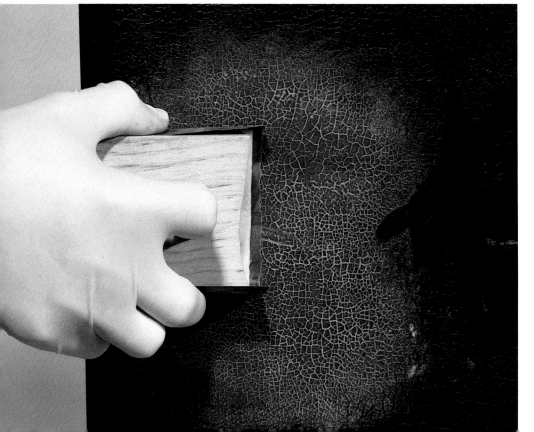

Greg Landrey is an associate furniture conservator at Winterthur Museum in Winterthur, Del. This article was prepared with the assistance of Michael Palmer, wood anatomist at Winterthur. For tips on reviving period hardware, see the article by Greg Landrey and Helen Stetina on pp. 80-81.

The viscosity of gel finishes varies from the thick, paste-like consistency of Bartley's Paste Varnish and Stain, top left, to the pourable gel of Flecto's X-3D Wood Stain, top right. Nonetheless, all have been blended with thixotropic, or thickening, agents to keep the pigments, resins and solvents from separating. Since stirring is not required and convenience for the do-it-yourselfer is one of their selling points, the brands at left package their gels in plastic squeeze bottles.

Gel Stains

Producing even color with less mess

by Jim Boesel

When I first noticed advertisements for new, improved gel stains and clear finishes, I was skeptical, but not surprised. In the last year or so, everything in my bathroom, from toothpaste to shaving cream, has "gelled," so why shouldn't this new advertising buzzword make its way into the shop? Next year, I had speculated, they'd be coming out with new, improved polyurethane *light*: covers great, less filling.

After awhile my skepticism gave way to curiosity and I tried these gelled finishes. They are available in the usual variety of wood stain colors, which can be intermixed to produce additional shades. There are also white and clear gels that can be tinted with most pigments, including Japan colors, artists' oils and universal colorants from your local paint store. White gels can also be thinned to create a limed or pickled effect. The latest entries in the gel marketplace are premixed pastel colors that subtly tint tight-grain woods and color the open grain in woods such as oak and ash.

To my surprise, these gels delivered what they promised. They were easy to apply, with little mess. They produced an even color coat without requiring you to continually stir the pigment into suspension. They were fast drying and didn't raise the grain enough to require sanding between coats. And they covered more area than a comparable portion of conventional oil-base stain. I was also surprised to learn that gel stains are not new. As Dick Fitch, finishing consultant to The Bartley Collection Ltd., pointed out, pigmented stains in paste form are at least as old as war paint, and wood finishers have been using them for centuries. Heavy-bodied wiping stains, which are thickened with additives that act something like cornstarch in gravy, have been a staple in professional finishing shops for decades. The thick consistency of these wiping stains keeps the pigment in suspension to provide predictable and repeatable results, but they have never been readily available to the weekend woodworker. Then about 20 years ago, gel stains made their appearance on the market. These new wiping stains owed their thick viscosity not to the addition of a thickening agent, as the earlier wiping stains had, but to rheology, the science of the deformation and flow of matter.

Thickness through thixotropy—Gel stains consist of basically the same ingredients as conventional oil-base stains: pigments suspended in a vehicle of alkyd resins (often alkyd-modified linseed or some other vegetable oil), driers and mineral spirits. Gels contain about twice as much pigment and resin as regular stains, but this higher solids content has little to do with their thicker consistency. So, what makes gel stains different from conventional wiping stains? The gels are thixotropic. Webster defines thixotropy as the property of various gels of becoming fluid when disturbed, as by shaking. In other words, gel stains are thick to begin with, but when disturbed, either by shaking, stirring or even just the action of applying them with a cloth, they become fluid and easy to work. When the materials are left alone again, they return to their gel state. In contrast, a conventional wiping stain will stay thick unless it's thinned with solvent.

Gels are made thixotropic by adding a polyamide-modified thixotropic alkyd resin and/or other thixotropic agents (such as bentonite clay) to the usual recipe of pigment, resin, driers and solvent. These ingredients are placed in large drums and then mixed together for about 20 minutes by a high-speed dispersion machine that looks just like a giant milk-shake mixer. The mixer blades spin at about 3,000 RPM and blend the ingredients evenly throughout the mixture. When the mixing stops, weak hydrogen bonds are formed between the thixotropic agents and the other ingredients, binding the mixture together to a uniformly thick consistency, which can be varied from a pourable gel to a thick paste. These weak hydrogen bonds break down when shear forces are applied, such as the mechanical action of applying the gel with a cloth, and then re-form shortly after the rubbing stops.

Applying gel stains—It's safe to assume that the proliferation of gel stains in the past few years is directed at the convenience or do-it-yourself market. Gels are well suited for small projects. And because they're wiped on and off almost immediately, they are especially handy where a dust-free environment for finishing is not available. Their thick viscosity makes them great for finishing in-place vertical surfaces, such as built-in cabinets or pre-hung doors. In fact, their thicker viscosity solves most of the common complaints associated with oil-base stains. They can be applied without splattering or running and, because the pigment stays evenly blended, they produce an even color coat. In addition, their higher solids content reduces their penetration into the wood, which increases the area that can be covered with a given amount of stain and makes it much easier to control the problem of splotchy color on irregular grain.

Unfortunately, even with gels, the final finish will only be as good as your surface preparation. Staining will accentuate any scratches or rough spots, so sand all wood surfaces thoroughly. Because of their high solids content, gels will help fill wood pores better than regular stains. But if you want a smooth, highly polished finish on open-grain woods, such as oak, ash or mahogany, you must still fill the pores with a paste wood filler before staining. After sanding or filling, blow the sanding dust from the wood's surface with an air compressor and then clean the entire surface with a tack cloth.

In preparation for finishing, gather a good supply of clean cloths; old T-shirts or terry cloth work well, but avoid any cloth that gives off lint. Brushes are handy for working the finish into intricate carvings or other tight spots. Have some mineral spirits on hand for lightening the color or blending lap marks when staining. As user-friendly as gel finishes are, don't forget that they contain mineral spirits or other solvents that are potentially hazardous. Rubber gloves are advisable and it's essential to provide proper ventilation, such as a window fan blowing out one end of the room and a door or window open at the other end.

Instructions for applying gel finishes are pretty much the same for all brands. Apply a small amount to a clean cloth and wipe it on the surface with the grain. If possible, cover a whole area, such as a cabinet side, at one time. On large tabletops and similar surfaces, work in logical areas—treat one leaf or one half of the table as a unit. You can blend lap marks with a little mineral spirits, although it isn't usually necessary if you work quickly. The recommended waiting time before wiping off the gel with another clean cloth varies from immediately to between two and five minutes. Again, when wiping off excess finish, work with the grain.

As with conventional stains, most common clear finishes can be used over gel stains that have dried thoroughly. The exceptions are brushing lacquer and other finishes containing high-boiling active solvents like ketones, which evaporate slowly and might re-dissolve the stain. The drying time before topcoating varies, depending on the final finish, but 24 hours seems to be the average. Up to 72 hours is recommended for spray lacquer.

What about the drawbacks of gels? For large areas such as a floor, it would be faster and easier to brush or spray on a liquid finish. And for most production situations, applying a gel is just too slow; they can't compete with a spray gun or dip tank for moving multiples out the door. Their lower solvent content, which prevents them from penetrating as deeply as conventional oil-base finishes, could be a disadvantage in some cases. However, this reduction in solvents is most likely one of the reasons for the finish industry's current interest in gels, because it will help them meet the tighter government restrictions on volatile organic compounds (VOCs) that have already been enacted in California and New Jersey and which promise to be the trend in the future.

So, in spite of my original skepticism, I have to conclude that for most small projects, the advantages of gels tend to outweigh the disadvantages. And if you dread the mess, and that feeling of uncertainty that often accompanies the finishing process, gel finishes might be just what you've been looking for. □

Jim Boesel is an Assistant Editor at FWW.

Sources of supply

The following companies manufacture gel finishes:

Bartley Collection Ltd., 3 Airpark Drive, Easton, MD 21601; *stains in wood tones (stain and topcoat in one) and clear.*

H. Behlen and Brothers, Inc., Route 30 N., Amsterdam, NY 12010; *stains in wood tones, white and clear.*

Fabulon Products, Box 1505, Buffalo, NY 14240; *stains in wood tones, white and tung-oil varnish.*

Flecto Co., Inc., 1000 45th St., Oakland, CA 94608; *stains in wood tones and clear.*

Minwax Co., 102 Chestnut Ridge Plaza, Montvale, NJ 07645; *stains in wood tones, white and pastels (stain and topcoat in one).*

Thompson and Formby, Inc., 825 Crossover Lane, Memphis, TN 38117; *stains in wood tones and tung-oil varnish.*

Wood-Kote Products, Inc., Box 17192, Portland, OR 97217; *stains in wood tones and white.*

A *professional's gel techniques*

by Gregory D. Johnson

As a professional wood finisher, I'm familiar with a large repertoire of wood finishes, from shellac and lacquer to high-tech catalyzed polyurethanes and polyesters. These finishes, which constitute the bulk of our work, are all film-type coatings that build up on the wood's surface. But now and then a piece comes through which, because of the customer's request or the style of the furniture, calls for the subtle beauty of a hand-rubbed oil finish. However, achieving a durable oil finish requires a good deal of labor, wiping each of several coats on and off. You also lose a lot of time waiting for one coat to harden before applying the next. This process can take anywhere from three or four days up to two weeks, which creates work-flow (not to mention cash-flow) and space problems for most finishing shops.

To give the customer a "close-to-the-wood" type finish without causing a backup in the shop, I've turned to paste stains and paste varnish. Compared to tung oil or Danish oil finishes or homemade oil/varnish mixtures that I've tried, paste varnish dries faster, builds faster and is more durable, while it still preserves that hand-rubbed look. Although any of the paste or gel finishes on the market will give good results, I prefer Bartley's paste stains and varnish because they contain a substantial amount of polyurethane (about 33% of vehicle solids), which increases the durability of the final finish and lets you stain and top-coat in a single step. Both the premixed stains and the clear varnish dry within four hours and can be buffed to a nice sheen after two coats.

For many pieces of furniture, such as chairs, beds and bookcases, a couple coats of paste varnish will suffice. But for a kitchen or dining room table or any piece of furniture with a flat surface that might attract an after-dinner drink or a cup of hot tea, I recommend a more durable film finish. Even with the addition of polyurethane, any finish that's wiped off almost immediately after it's applied will not build much of a film. When I want additional protection without the look of a film finish, I first brush on a sealer coat of Minwax fast-dry, semi-gloss liquid polyurethane and then top it off by rubbing on a couple of coats of paste varnish. The photos at right illustrate a test I did to see how much additional protection was gained with this sealer coat of polyurethane. The finishes looked and felt the same, but the sample that had the coat of polyurethane showed much greater resistance to water and alcohol damage.

Working with a polyurethane/gel finish: First, sand the surface well and fill or stain as needed. When the stain is dry, brush on the initial coat of polyurethane, being careful to avoid runs or drips along edges, or puddles in the corners. Often air bubbles will form right away, so without adding any more finish, brush the wet film again very lightly and with the grain to just knock the bubbles off. If there are still a few bubbles after the film begins to setup, leave them alone because further brushing will streak and damage the film. Bubbles seem to form more readily on open-grain woods, such as oak, walnut and mahogany. So when working with these woods, I first brush on a coat of polyurethane thinned 50/50 with naphtha or paint thinner to help fill the pores. Any bubbles that form with this mixture are easier to work out. I let this sealer coat dry overnight, sand it with 240-grit, 3M Trimite sandpaper (available from 3M Co., Consumer Specialties, 3M Center, Building 225-4S, St. Paul, Minn. 55144) and then apply a coat of unthinned polyurethane and let it dry overnight.

When the unthinned coat is completely dry, sand the entire surface well with 320-grit sandpaper. I prefer sandpaper because it will cut the surface flat, whereas steel wool or abrasive pads round over the dust nits or lumps in the surface. To keep paper from cutting through the film on sharp edges, I ball up used 320-grit to soften it and then flatten it out before using it. The older and more worn the paper gets, the better it is for sanding the finish on moldings and such.

If you stained the wood before applying the polyurethane and then created a large light spot by sanding too vigorously, you can repair the spot by reapplying the original paste stain. The edge of the repaired area must be carefully blended and then allowed to dry the recommended time before another coat of polyurethane is brushed over the entire surface. If there is only minor sand-through along sharp edges, which is almost inevitable on stained furniture, I touch up the area by padding with 2-lb. shellac colored with blending powder so I don't have to delay work while the repair dries. Blending touch-up powders come in a wide range of colors and are available from Mohawk Finishing Supply, Route 30 N., Amsterdam, N.Y. 12010 and Star Chemical, 360 Shore Drive, Hinsdale, Ill. 60521. Although shellac is not supposed to be compatible with polyurethane, I've used it for small touch-ups with no ill effect.

After sanding the polyurethane with 320-grit and touching up as needed, rub the surface with 0000 steel wool until it has an even matte finish. Remember, there's only one coat of polyurethane on the surface, so go easy; then blow and/or tack-rag off the dust. Now, to give the finish the sheen of hand-rubbed oil, apply two coats of paste varnish. Allow about four-hours drying time and lightly buff between coats with 0000 steel wool.

This finish is easily maintained; I give the customer a small bottle of Oz brand furniture cream polish, available from Mohawk and Star Chemical, to be used once or twice a year. The rest of the time a damp rag is all that's needed. The finish can be repaired much as you would repair an oil finish: rub with 0000 steel wool or sand first with fine-grit paper, and then apply another coat of paste varnish. □

Greg Johnson operates the finishing shop at Wendell Castle Studio in Scottsville, N.Y.

 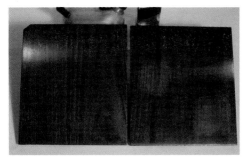

To see how much protection one sealer coat of polyurethane provides, I made up two finish samples, left. The one on the left has one coat of Bartley's paste stain, a sealer coat of Minwax fast-dry liquid polyurethane and two coats of Bartley's paste varnish. The sample on the right has the paste stain and varnish, but not the sealer coat of polyurethane. The finishes looked and felt nearly identical. Then, I poured one teaspoon of whiskey on a rag, set a glass on it and left it for 15 hours. I also poured one teaspoon of boiling water on a rag and weighted it with a cup of boiling water for 35 minutes. Right: The sealer coat of polyurethane resisted both the whiskey and the hot water.

From *Fine Woodworking* magazine (March 1990) 81:75

Photos: Greg Johnson

Opaque Lacquers
A *rainbow of colors from your spray gun*

by Gregory D. Johnson

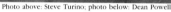
Photo above: Steve Turino; photo below: Dean Powell

The plywood cabinet above is the focal point in Jorge Cao's Manhattan apartment. Up to eight coats of lacquer were applied to some parts of the cabinet, and extensive masking preserved the details while it was being sprayed. Johnson uses this cabinet in describing the process in the text. The table at left was designed and built by Robert Kawalski of Worcester, Mass. Closed-grain woods, here maple, provide the smooth, flat surface needed to show off the table's high-gloss finish. Peter Dean of Charlestown, Mass., created the chair at right. Its mahogany frame was sprayed with a color lacquer that complements the upholstery.

Often the design of a furniture piece creates a framework for showing off exquisite woods and veneers in a pleasing fashion. Other times the wood's grain pattern visually pulls the contour of a piece in the wrong direction or otherwise detracts from the design. Designers frequently rely on solid colors to remove these distractions, to highlight the design and to allow the eye to travel uninterrupted over the form. The best color system I've found for this kind of work is opaque lacquer, which contains a variety of colored pigments suspended in clear lacquer. It provides great workability, produces a high-quality finish and gives the designer a palette of tones and shades that can be combined to play on the senses or act as a counterpoint to natural- or stained-wood components.

Adding color lacquers to your repertoire of finishes will provide you with the ability to create stronger contrasts and sharper lines than those possible with other finishing procedures. In this article, I'll tell you what you need to know to get started.

Special considerations—If you can spray clear lacquer, you already know how to work with the opaque material, so I'll concentrate here on a few new problems that usually only crop up with colors. For a refresher on basic spraying and mixing operations, see my article on clear lacquer on pp. 89-95.

When you begin working with opaque lacquer, you'll notice

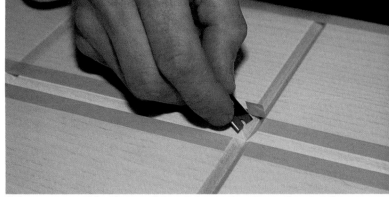

Johnson uses plastic masking tape to produce sharp, clean color edges. Here he is using a single-edge razor blade to remove the tape "bridging" the V-grooves between adjacent ash door panels. After masking the middle of the panels, the door will be ready to be sprayed with primer.

that a solid color shows flaws in the surface much more readily than a clear finish. Freed from the distractions of wood grain, the eye picks up every surface flaw. Darker colors emphasize imperfections more than lighter ones. It's difficult to get and keep large horizontal surfaces like tabletops or desks level, flat and free of imperfections, particularly if the surfaces will be subject to hard use. Fortunately, many designers are aware of how difficult it is to produce perfectly flat wooden surfaces and often prefer to use glass or marble tops instead.

As a piece ages and the wood expands and contracts, the hairline cracks that may develop around joints and gluelines will be more apparent with a color finish than with a clear finish. The type of substrate is also important: It's difficult to get a level finish with open-grain woods like oak or mahogany, because the lacquer shrinks, allowing the grain pattern to show through. For some pieces though, this tendency can be used to advantage to provide a more dramatic visual appearance.

The term "building a finish" is pretty descriptive when dealing with lacquer colors. To ensure crisp lines and maximum control of color, areas to be stained or left clear need to be sealed, clearcoated and masked prior to spraying the lacquer colors. A clear finish involves a transparent sealer coat followed by several transparent topcoats. A solid-color finish starts with a gray- or white-primer surface coat and is followed by the desired color lacquer, which in turn, is top-coated with clear lacquer for added depth and durability. The white primer is especially important with bright yellows, orange and some greens, because they have limited hiding power. The clear topcoats also will change the color values slightly, and this effect varies according to whether the topcoat is matte, semigloss or gloss. Spot repairs are almost impossible to match if you run out of a custom color and have to mix more, so be sure to mix enough for the job at hand.

Wall-mounted cabinet—Here I'll describe how I used opaque lacquers to finish the wall-mounted cabinet shown on the facing page. It was designed by architect Jorge Cao of New York, N.Y., and was built by Steve Turino of Charlestown, R.I. This piece is a particularly good example, because it has both plain and veneered doors, several large, vertical surfaces and fine details. Because of the details and number of colors involved, masking techniques are especially important here. The cabinet's four plain doors are ¾-in. birch plywood edged with ¼-in.-thick maple. These, along with the cabinet's frame, are lacquered with a medium satin gray that I've formulated to match the wall color in the room where the piece will be installed.

The corner column on the right side of the cabinet is bird's-eye maple stained a lighter satin gray. The top of the column is a burgundy lacquer with a strip of medium gray along its top edge. From the base of the column, the bird's-eye maple continues along the bottom of the cabinet, concealing a light fixture that illuminates the space beneath the cabinet.

The two larger doors flanking the corner column are birch plywood edged and veneered with ash. The V-grooves creating the grid on each door are lacquered a darker gray. To avoid exposing rough edges of plywood when the V-grooves are cut, the plywood panels are first inlaid with a grid pattern of maple strips prior to applying the ash veneer. The inside of the cabinet is lacquered with clear semigloss. The top is a solid piece of marble double-beveled and set back ¼ in. from the edge.

Surface preparation—After sanding with 150-grit paper, the cabinet is scrutinized for defects such as scratches and dents. These are easily corrected at this point, so it pays to be thorough.

But because lacquer tends to magnify the defects, you'll initially discover some you've missed as spraying proceeds. Later, I'll tell you how these can be handled.

The cabinet's interior is finished with clear lacquer. I spray two coats of sanding sealer, dry-sanding after the second coat with 240-grit silicon carbide paper. One coat of clear gloss completes the job.

The ash-veneered panels on the doors are bleached, sanded and filled with a white-paste wood filler. After sanding again, I brush on a white glazing stain. The excess is wiped off and the stain is applied with a dry brush to form a feather pattern. I finish the panels with two coats of clear lacquer.

The bird's-eye maple column is finished using a clear oil-base stain that I tint with a little bit of artist's gray pigment. When the column is dry, I apply sanding sealer and clear-gloss coats. The interior, panels and column can now be masked in preparation for spraying of the opaque lacquer.

Masking—For small areas and details, masking is done with tape alone; for openings and broad areas, tape and paper do the job. For fine lines, such as along the ash panel edges in this piece, 3M plastic masking tape preserves a virtually perfect line, because it prevents the color from "bleeding" under the tape edge—a common problem with paper tapes. Use good-quality tape: The cheaper stuff has unpredictable adhesion and can be frustrating to apply.

The cabinet's interior is masked off with a piece of cardboard cut to fit the opening snugly and held in place with plastic masking tape. I use plastic masking tape to define the edges of the ash panels, carefully pressing it into position, bridging the V-grooves as I progress from panel to panel. Then, with a single-edge razor blade, I carefully slice and remove the tape bridge at each panel corner so these areas will be exposed when sprayed. The middle of each panel is covered with nonabsorbent, 3M Scotch masking paper, which is held in place with ordinary masking tape. Once the stained and lacquered maple column is completely masked off with tape and paper in the same way, I'm ready to apply the primer.

Priming—A nitrocellulous-lacquer gray primer is available from most lacquer manufacturers. I buy my primer from Mohawk Finishing Products or Star Chemical Co. (see sources of supply on p. 69). The gray primer acts like the sanding sealer commonly used under clear coats to seal and level the surface. The primer's high-solids content (30%) allows me to achieve a heavy build with two to four coats, and the stearate sanding additives make it easy to sand (with 220-grit paper) and level the surface without clogging the sandpaper. The primer cures enough so that it can be sanded within two to three hours of application. However, it takes weeks to reach a full cure, and a small amount of shrinkage does occur during this time. This usually isn't a problem for vertical surfaces,

Plastic automotive putty is used to fill dents and scratches visible following the primer coat. The cured putty will be sanded level prior to spraying the color-lacquer and final clear-lacquer coats. Lacquer has the effect of emphasizing even small defects, but the putty is easy to apply and allows minor repairs to be made at any point during the process.

but with large, flat, horizontal surfaces like tabletops, the slightest unevenness is noticeable, and the shrinkage allows the wood grain and joint seams to "telegraph" through.

I've had good luck working with alternative materials to eliminate this problem. I've tried a catalyzed polyurethane gray primer called Polane Spray fil, made by Sherwin-Williams (see sources of supply). Heat lamps and forced hot air can be used to accelerate curing the polyurethane primer and therefore shorten the time required for full shrinkage. This catalyzed primer produces a base coat with superior adhesive properties and does not chip as easily as lacquer primer. It must, however, be mixed precisely and applied within eight hours of being mixed. It is also extremely toxic, containing isocyanates, which can cause immediate lung and eye irritations, and with prolonged usage, can have serious health implications. When using it, I wear a full face mask with an air-supplied respirator. Special filters, available for cartridge-type respirators, are necessary for protection against isocyanates.

More recently, I've been experimenting with a polyester-base primer. Like the catalyzed polyurethane, high temperatures are used for curing, but there appears to be no shrinkage at all with the polyester-base primer. The same extreme care discussed above also applies in the handling and use of this material.

With all of that said, you should keep in mind that ordinary lacquer primer works fine for most solid-color jobs, and it's a lot easier to use: You only need to dilute it with lacquer thinner and you'll be ready to spray. Also, the safety and health precautions are less stringent than required when using the catalyzed materials mentioned above. However, you should work in a well-ventilated area and wear an organic respirator. For the cabinet at hand, which has no critical horizontal wood surfaces, the lacquer primer is ideal.

The primer mixture is not critical, but I normally use it diluted 50/50 with lacquer thinner. This mixture sprays well and allows a good buildup with two to four coats. Everything except the V-grooves that separate the ash panels on the doors gets sprayed. The V-grooves were primed earlier with clear sanding sealer when the panels were finished. I use a clear sanding sealer instead of the gray primer where a solid color meets the edge of natural-finish or stained wood, because later, when I remove the ridge formed where the color meets the wood, there is no danger of sanding through to the primer's different color.

Primer dries to a matte finish due to the high content of sanding additives. Even with the low sheen, I'm amazed at how effective the gray primer is in highlighting any small imperfections. After the second coat of primer has dried for an hour or so, these small trouble spots can be repaired with a red putty such as Nitro-Stan, which is available from automotive-supply stores and Standard Coating Corp. (see sources of supply). With a plastic spatula, I apply a thin layer directly on the primer. No surface preparation is required. Deep scratches or indentations must be filled several times, and longer curing time is necessary to allow for shrinkage. If the putty is sanded too soon, before shrinkage is complete, any "dinks" will show up again later. White or light-color lacquers don't cover the red putty very well; for these, I use Acryl-blue glazing putty, available from 3M (see sources of supply).

I let the putty dry for at least an hour, then I sand the entire surface with 220-grit finishing paper, being careful to make repaired areas flat and level. On large pieces like this cabinet, I use orbital sanders and sandpaper-covered blocks. At this point, the main objective is to get a perfectly level surface, so I don't worry about sanding through the primer. If it happens, I just spot-spray with additional primer and lightly resand. This is the time to try to get a perfect, defect-free surface, but I don't spend hours on it; repairs are still possible later, after the solid-color lacquer has been applied.

Color matching and spraying – With the surface ready for the custom-color lacquer, the often tedious and sometimes frustrating job of mixing the color to match the sample begins. It is possible to find some lacquer suppliers willing to match a color sample, usually for a minimum quantity of 1 gal. I prefer to mix it myself, because all too often the customer isn't really sure of what he or she wants. Sometimes the sample is difficult to work with: Matching or complementing a color theme in a fabric sample is demanding. I've found that the quickest and easiest way to get the job done is to charge the customer my hourly rate and have them come in while I'm mixing the color. It's surprising how quickly they are able to settle on a color.

I buy my basic solid-color lacquers in 1-gal. or 5-gal. containers. I modify these with concentrated lacquer-tinting colors – raw umber, burnt sienna, chrome yellow and lithol red – which I purchase by the quart. Lithol red is the deepest, strongest red tint I've found; I used to have trouble formulating burgundy colors until I discovered it. Earth tones – umber, sienna and chrome yellow – come in handy for the more subtle tones I can't seem to get with the basic colors alone. Because I've had a lot of experience, I'm comfortable estimating the proportions by eye, but if you're just beginning, you may want to measure the quantities carefully.

I dilute the color lacquer 50/50 with lacquer thinner, making it easier to mix and spray. It's important to check customized colors with a sample by spraying a scrap piece. I let the scrap piece dry to the touch and then hold it next to the sample. I add very small quantities of the tinting color, checking often against my sample to prevent overshooting the color. A good way to see subtle changes is to drip some lacquer on a tray, and as more tint is added, let the drippings run together. There's nothing worse than spending a lot of time on a custom color and then spoiling it, so when I'm unsure of the effect a particular tint will have, I pour a small amount of my master brew into a container and begin experimenting. When I think the color is right, I get a second opinion – the customer's. I try to closely estimate the amount of lacquer I'll need so I don't end up with a gallon or more that I'll never use. Also, I save a small amount for later reference or touch-up repairs.

I spray on at least three coats with one-hour drying time in between. I keep an eye out for any imperfections I may have missed earlier. Often these glossier coats show up some flaws that the dull primer hides. I use the Nitro-Stan putty once again, taking the time to let it dry, leveling it and then spot-spraying the area again with color lacquer before going on with the next coat of color.

Final steps – I get a good feeling when I finally remove the masking materials to reveal the fine lines and contrasting colors. It's critical to remove these materials no more than a few minutes after the final color spraying is completed: Waiting too long can cause the hardened film to peel unevenly along the tape line.

I sand all the previously masked areas with 320-grit paper. Ridges formed where adjacent colors meet are sanded lightly, but I don't try to level them at this point. It is better and safer to finish leveling the lacquer ridges while building the final clear coat. Light sanding (320 grit) of the white-ash squares on the doors ensures they are good and clean before the next coat of clear lacquer goes on. I touch up here and there where necessary, using a small artist's brush to dab color on; for larger corrections, I mask off around the problem area and spray with the gun turned way down.

For the clear topcoats over solid colors, I use a prefiltered Mohawk high-solids lacquer, which has almost no amber tone. This is a durable topcoat, and its clearness makes it a good choice to cover the stained white-ash panels. If a piece is finished with a

Color-matching is an art form. As Johnson adds small amounts of tinting colors, he "puddles" the subtly different hues together to gauge his progress in matching a color sample.

single color, I finish the clear coats with what I call "clear color": a 50/50 mix of the custom color with clear-gloss lacquer. This creates good depth, because the color is continuous through the layers. This won't work for multi-color pieces, so I use untinted clear lacquer.

When everything looks clean and crisp, I spray on three to four clear-gloss coats of lacquer, allowing at least one-hour drying time between each coat. It's not necessary to sand between each coat, because the lacquer bonds to itself. But, I do sand the small lacquer ridges between colors with 320-grit paper. After three coats of gloss lacquer, ridges and surfaces should be level.

After the last coat of clear gloss, I let the piece dry overnight. Then, I sand all surfaces with 240-grit dry-lube finishing paper. Finally, I spray on two coats of semigloss lacquer, and when it's dry, I rub out the finish using the method described on pp. 94-95.

High-gloss lacquered surfaces are best cared for and protected by the frequent application of a plastic polish; for semigloss finishes, use a good-quality furniture-cream polish. □

Gregory Johnson does custom woodfinishing and antique restoration at The Johnson Co., Inc. in Newton, Mass.

Sources of supply

Lacquers, sealers, thinners:
Mohawk Finishing Products, Inc., Route 30N, Amsterdam, NY 12010
Star Chemical Co. Inc., 360 Shore Drive, Hinsdale, IL 60521
Sherwin-Williams Co., 101-T Prospect Ave., N.W., Cleveland, OH 44115
Donald M. Steinert, 800 Messinger Road, Grant's Pass, OR 97527
   (polyester finishes only)
Pratt & Lambert, Inc., 75 Tonawanda St., Box 22, Buffalo, NY 14240

Masking paper and tapes, abrasives, fillers:
3M Company, 3M Center, St. Paul, MN 55144-1000
Standard Coating Corp., 461 Broad Ave., Box 56, Ridgefield, NJ 07657

Catalyzed Lacquers
Creating a rich finish that's tough as nails

by David E. Shaw

If you want a clear wood finish that you can tap dance or iron a shirt on, try catalyzed lacquer—it's as tough and strong as baked enamel, more resilient than polyurethane, and doesn't look like plastic. Rather, it has that lovely sheen that only lacquer can produce, and it can be rubbed to a myriad of looks, from a rich gloss, to a mellow satin, or even dead flat.

Catalyzed lacquers also penetrate well and resist everything from intense cold to paint stripper. I prefer them for kitchen and bathroom cabinets, anything for a kid's room, and for tables, floors and other surfaces that are subjected to excessive moisture, temperature variations and plain old physical abuse.

Chemically, catalyzed lacquer is a nitrocellulose base blended with alkyd resins and urea formaldehyde. Hardening is induced by a phosphate ester catalyst, which reacts with the ingredients to form tough, chemical bonds. The amount of catalyst needed is critical and varies from brand to brand, so make sure that you get precise instructions. You should also heed safety warnings—any lacquer will give off fumes, but catalyzed lacquer gives off urea formaldehyde as well. I don't feel this is any more dangerous, but it does smell worse and will quickly give you a headache that can linger for days. If you do not have a good double-cone, organic-vapor respirator and can't provide fans or some other type of forced ventilation, don't use catalyzed lacquers.

There are two distinct types of catalyzed lacquers. The one I prefer produces the toughest finish because the catalyst is added to each coat, from the sealer on. Both Maclac Chemlac (available from distributors of Maclac Lacquer Co., 198 Utah St., San Francisco, Calif. 94103) and Sherwin Williams' Sherwood Super Kemvar HS (Sherwin Williams Co., 101 Prospect Ave., Cleveland, Ohio 44115, and its local distributors) fall into this category. The other lacquer is Synlac, a "bleed through" type, in which only the top coat of lacquer is catalyzed and the catalyst bleeds into the sealer and base coats (available from Industrial Finishing Products, 465 Logan St., Brooklyn, N.Y., 11208). This lacquer goes over Synlac's special barrier-coat sealer, and you can apply it over any finish that the barrier coat will adhere to, which is just about anything. If you want to refinish a lacquered or varnished table without stripping it, for example, you could reseal it with the barrier-coat, then apply bleed-through lacquer.

To use catalyzed lacquers, you must first mix the right amount of catalyst into the lacquer. Since most brands recommend two to four ounces of catalyst to every gallon of lacquer, an ordinary shot glass is an accurate measure for quart-size spray guns. Too much catalyst leaves a greasy finish that may take days to dry and

gives off a disagreeable odor for five or six months. Too little catalyst produces a relatively weak finish.

Once mixed, catalyzed lacquers spray on and dry just like ordinary lacquer, or they can be mixed with thinner and lacquer retarder—an additive which slows drying—and brushed on. Most manufacturers recommend high-grade thinner, which dries slower than inexpensive types, giving the lacquer more time to flow out smoothly and resist the whitish-blue hazing that develops in humid areas. In a pinch, you can hype-up regular thinner by making a mixture of 90% to 95% thinner (by volume) to 5% to 10% retarder. For brushing the lacquer, you can add up to 25% retarder in the thinner mixture, then spread the lacquer with a soft brush, just as you would brush on shellac. Too much retarder gives a greasy finish that can be dried only with a good deal of steel-wool buffing and lots of elbow grease.

Whether you are spraying or brushing, you first must apply at least one coat of a catalyzed sealer, let it dry, then sand lightly with 320-grit wet/dry paper. For open-pore woods, you may have to sand down two or three consecutive coats of sealer until the grain is filled, since catalyzed lacquer cannot be used over wood filler or any oil-based stain. Next apply three or four coats of lacquer, sanding between each coat with 600-grit paper. While manufacturers recommend that you wait four or five hours between coats, I have sprayed three coats in less than three hours.

Once applied, catalyzed lacquer must cure seven to 10 days to develop its full strength. The finish gives off a slight odor as it cures, but if you mixed it right, the odor will go away within a day or so. The disappearance of odor doesn't mean the finish is fully cured. Wait the full 10 days. If you rub out the cured finish with rottenstone, you can create as high a gloss as you'll get with any finish. If you rub with 00 steel wool you can kill the gloss entirely. Use 0000 steel wool for a more satiny effect.

Occasionally, when I'm in the final stages of finishing, I must alter the color of a finish to produce what my customer ordered. You can do this by adding a colored glaze between the lacquer coats or by tinting the lacquer itself. In either case, use oil-based or oil-compatible color (I use so-called Universal colors, either UTC brand, Byzantine brand or Japan colors by Ronan, available by mail order from Industrial Finishing products).

For glazing, I mix color with mineral spirits to form a very thin, weakly-colored stain that I apply with a lint-free rag, wiping with the grain and feathering the glaze at the end of each stroke until I evenly color the entire piece. Let the glaze dry about an hour until it's evenly dull before applying more lacquer. To tint the lacquer itself, add color to thinned lacquer and test until you get the shade you want. There are no tricks here, except your

From *Fine Woodworking* magazine (September 1985) 54:86-87

Shaw sprays catalyzed lacquer just like regular lacquer, with long, even, overlapping strokes, above. A double-cone, organic vapor respirator and fans or other forced ventilation are mandatory. Finishing the finish is the most time-consuming part of the job. To ensure a rich, smooth finish, each coat must be rubbed out with fine wet/dry paper. To check his work, right, Shaw examines the finish closely from a low angle where light reveals any defects.

To ensure that the lacquer is free of all dust and impurities, filter each batch through a cone filter as you fill the spray gun cup.

gun control must be perfect—an uneven coat looks horrible.

Catalyzed lacquers have many of the same problems as conventional lacquers, and the remedies are often the same. Fisheye, for example, is caused by contaminants, usually silicon, on the wood. Catalyzed lacquers will fisheye when applied over almost any contaminant, so I always assume that any refinished surface is contaminated and mix a fisheye remover into the lacquer. With new pieces, I test the sealer on some inconspicuous corner. If there is any trace of cratering, I use fisheye remover.

As with conventional lacquer, you can prevent hazing on catalyzed lacquer by adding enough retarder to slow the hardening process, giving the lacquer time to bleed off moisture before drying. The retarder also helps the lacquer flow out smoothly. To minimize air bubbles in the wet film, spray the catalyzed lacquer when the temperature is 75°F to 85°F, a much narrow range than for ordinary lacquer. If you must spray at higher or lower temperatures, add about 5% more retarder.

If something goes wrong, you can remove a catalyzed finish, but do it quickly before the lacquer cures or you're in for one miserable job. Paint stripper will remove partially-cured lacquer, but it takes an awful lot of stripper and even more elbow grease. If the finish has fully cured, straight lye (a can of Draino in a quart of water) applied over and over works eventually, but it does not do the wood any good. After using the lye, you must rinse the wood with water and vinegar and usually have to bleach it with oxalic acid before refinishing. Make sure you wear your respirator and chemical-resistant gloves, and mix the lye in a plastic bucket—the solution can react with aluminum containers to produce harmful fumes.

Clean your brushes and spray gun immediately with lacquer thinner or acetone, or you will ruin them. Manufacturers claim the lacquer mixture will be usable for about three months, but I've found it must be used within a week if you want the strongest possible coat. Old lacquer won't turn into gelatinous ooze as long as it's kept in a sealed container. You can use it, but don't expect it to be any stronger than regular lacquer. In the last four years I have applied catalyzed lacquer to hundreds of pieces of furniture and numerous kitchen and bathroom cabinets, and have yet to hear a customer complain. So, for a finish that is as tough as nails, lovely to see and simple to apply, catalyzed lacquers are the only way to fly. □

David Shaw is a writer, furniture finisher and restorer in Kelly Corners, N.Y.

Eighteen coats of clear lacquer produced the deep, glossy finish on this tray carved from sen, *an elm-like wood.*

Japanese Lacquer
Urushi, *a traditional thousand-coat finish*

by Charles Roche

When I began my apprenticeship in Japan, my teacher showed me one of his beautiful lacquered pieces. "How many coats does it take to achieve a finish like this?" I asked. When he didn't answer with a number, I thought it odd that a man who had spent most of his life doing this work couldn't, or wouldn't, directly reply to a simple question. That was not the last time I received a less than satisfactory answer. Gradually, through my own work with lacquer, I realized that part of the problem was my approach: I was trying to learn about lacquer the way I would learn about a commercial finish—by reading the can!

Lacquer, called *urushi* in Japan, must be approached differently. Craftsmen have been working for more than 2,000 years to learn how to use this viscous, brown sap produced by the Urushi tree (*Rhus vernificera*). They developed techniques to conform to its properties instead of modifying the natural substance to meet their demands, as can often be done with synthetic materials. Thus, a lacquer finish always has been as difficult to achieve as it is beautiful to admire.

Lacquer is not just a pretty finish, though. Its strength makes it perfect for frequently used bowls and trays, and for tables, chairs and cabinets. It is nontoxic and unaffected by hot liquids, food, oil, salt or mild acid. In fact, its durability is the stuff of legends. Some pieces reportedly have come through shipwrecks and months in the ocean as bright as if they were fresh from the maker's hands. I've seen a museum exhibit of ancient lacquerware bowls that had been unearthed in China—over the centuries the wood had completely rotted away, leaving only the thin red and black lacquer shell. Once I accidentally dropped a finished piece of lacquerware. The surface wasn't marred, but the wood underneath was dented, so I pierced the *urushi* film with a pin and steamed the wood back into shape with a wet cloth and hot iron. Except for the pinholes, the lacquer was unharmed.

Although lacquer finishes may be clear or colored, the materials for the opaque colored finishes are difficult to obtain outside of Japan. Also, a finish that enhances rather than covers wood grain seems to suit Western tastes best, so here I'll deal only with raw lacquer, which produces a deep brown, translucent stain. Ex-

Photos: Tsuyoshi Ito, Studio do-do

cept for the lacquer, which is sold in large tubes like toothpaste, the needed tools and materials are easy to buy or make.

I'll start with *fuki urushi,* the most complete method of lacquering and the process I used on the tray shown on the facing page. The term means "wiped lacquer" (excess lacquer is wiped off with a cloth), but it's usually translated into English as "clear lacquer" because the finish is translucent. My favorite colloquial name is *sen ben nuri,* which means "thousand-coat finish." Although this is a gross exaggeration, I've sometimes felt that I had at least approached that number before completing a piece.

I applied 18 coats of lacquer to the tray, sanding between coats with silicon carbide paper or charcoal powder. In addition, I sealed the wood pores with several coats of a paste filler made from pulverized Japanese waterstones, water and lacquer. The actual color and gloss of a finish depend on the number of coats of lacquer, the amount of sanding between coats, and the way the paste filler is used. Almost any species of wood can be lacquered. Generally the final color of a lacquered piece ranges from a dark-walnut matte to a high-gloss, translucent reddish-orange.

Before you begin working with lacquer, there are a few things to keep in mind. First of all, *be careful* (see box below). Second, because lacquer hardens by a chemical reaction, not just by the evaporation of moisture or solvents, you'll have to build a "wet box"—a sort of humid incubator that encourages this chemical change. You can fashion any type of box, but just make sure it's big enough to hold what you plan to finish. To maintain the required 80% to 85% relative humidity range, I hang towels on the box's inside walls, dampening them daily with water from a plant sprayer. On cooler days I put one or two electric lights on the box floor to keep the temperature between 25°C and 30°C (77°F to 86°F). For objects too large to fit into my regular wet box, I build a simple frame and cover it with plastic. Inside the enclosure, I bend a gooseneck lamp over a pan of water to maintain the desired temperature and humidity.

If the temperature and humidity are too low, the *urushi* may not harden; if too high, the lacquer may harden too quickly and take on a milky cast or "burn." High heat and humidity may also make a thick coat of lacquer shrink and wrinkle. Fortunately, though, the required heat and humidity ranges are quite broad and not that difficult to maintain, at least not in a humid country like Japan. *Urushi* can be fickle, though, no matter what you do. Even under perfect conditions, I've had pieces remain tacky for days.

Conditions in your workroom are important, too. It must be as free of dust as possible, especially during the final coats, which magnify even the smallest trapped particles. Oil, even the oil from your fingerprints, can be more damaging than dust—it may keep lacquer from hardening. The room must also be warm and dry to keep the lacquer fluid and easy to spread.

You begin the actual finishing process by squeezing a small amount of *urushi* onto a lacquered work table called a *joban* or onto a sheet of glass. The lacquer is then taken from the smooth

---

CAUTION: *Urushi* can cause a skin rash, which can be severe with susceptible individuals. The tree that produces *urushi* is akin to poison sumac. Some people are never affected, but others cannot even enter a room where it is being used without breaking out. It's best to assume you are allergic. Try not to get any on your skin. If you do get it on you, wash the spot immediately with alcohol. Although *urushi* has a pungent smell, it's nontoxic, so you don't have to wear a respirator.

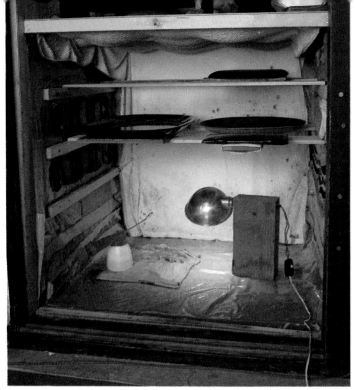

This typical wet box, shown with its door removed, is a rough container equipped with a wet/dry thermometer to monitor humidity and temperature. Towels dampened with a plant sprayer provide moisture. Lamps supply heat when the box is sealed.

Apply the urushi *with a short-bristled brush. The first, soaking coat creates a dramatic color contrast between the raw wood and the finished area. The glove keeps oily fingerprints off the wood.*

surface and applied with a short-bristled brush. Never squeeze it directly onto the workpiece. Lacquer is expensive and thus used conservatively—you don't want to expose large amounts to the danger of dust contamination or premature hardening. The *joban*'s sealed surface is easy to clean and does not absorb lacquer.

There's no formula for determining how much lacquer to squeeze out at one time, but you'll want enough to cover the piece you're doing. For the 15-in. tray used in this demonstration, a daub the size of a walnut would be enough for a generous first coat of lacquer. I use brushes made from a combination of human hair and horsehair, but any firm brush that does not shed bristles will do. Leave the first coat on for a few minutes, allowing the wood to absorb it freely. Then remove excess lacquer with a wooden spatula (called a *hera* in Japan), and thoroughly wipe the surface with a clean, dry, lint-free cotton cloth. Next place the piece on the smooth wooden slats inside the wet box until the lacquer has hardened, which may take as long as three days for the first coat. Until the stone-paste filler is applied, both sides of the piece are worked at once. After adding the filler, I

To make a wood filler, use a hera *(wooden spatula) to mix pulverized stone powder with water, then work in a small amount of lacquer until the paste can be smeared easily.*

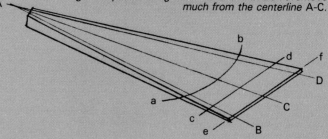

Holding one end of a nylon cloth filled with stone paste in his teeth, Roche twists the other end with one hand and uses the hera *to pick up the paste as it is filtered through the cloth. Then he uses the spatula, right, to smear stone-paste filler over the wood and into its open pores.*

Removing hardened stone paste is tedious. Wet-sand the layer to create a mud-like slurry, above, then wipe the area with a wet cloth. Wood grain is visible through the semi-transparent areas. Sandpaper is too rough for final coats, which must be polished with powdered charcoal dust and a cloth wrapped around a cotton pad, right. The polishing motion resembles that associated with French polishing.

work on one side of the piece at a time. At this point, I wrap the slats with soft paper so the finish won't be scratched.

When the first coat has hardened, wet-sand the surface with 240- to 280-grit wet-or-dry silicon carbide paper over a sanding block. Always use water as the lubricant. As you sand, you'll see the high spots become lighter in color as the lacquer is removed, while the low spots remain dark. These spots usually are so slight that you can't feel them with your fingers, but they would be obvious in the glass-like surface of the finished piece, so you must eliminate them. Don't try to remove all the irregularities in one step. After sanding with 240-grit, apply another coat of lacquer as before, allow it to dry, then wet-sand with 320-grit. Then add a third coat of lacquer and wet-sand with 360-grit paper. Be careful not to sand through the lacquer completely, or you'll damage the wood cells and they'll absorb lacquer differently than will the undamaged areas. When your sanding lightens the entire surface evenly, all the surface irregularities have been removed. Apply a final coat of lacquer to finish the smoothing process.

Next seal the surface with stone-paste filler. To make the filler, place roughly equal parts of stone powder and *urushi* on your work surface. Add a small amount of water to the powder and mix thoroughly with a sturdy spatula until you have a barely damp paste. Now gradually work the *urushi* in with a kneading, smearing motion. Before using newly prepared stone paste, mix it with some left over from a previous project. If you don't have any old stone paste, don't use the new stuff for a day or two to ensure that the ingredients have settled into one another.

You must strain the paste before using it. Put a gob of it on a piece of fine mesh nylon (used for silk-screening), then twist the nylon. With a wooden spatula, skim off the paste that squeezes through the mesh and smear a thin coat over the entire project. Press firmly to force it into the open pores and fibers of the wood. When the piece is covered, place it in the wet box until it has hardened. Usually this takes from three days to a week or more. The piece is ready to work when you can make whitish scratches by running your fingernails back and forth across the surface.

Removing the dried paste from the surface is one of the more difficult parts of lacquering. Attach 400-grit wet-or-dry paper to blocks shaped to fit the object and wet-sand until you can't see any paste on the surface. Don't remove any of the underlying coat of lacquer, or the finished piece will have an uneven color and gloss. With a wet cotton cloth, remove the thick mud created by the wet-sanding. Wash the surface with water and apply a coat of lacquer before repeating the stone-paste process and sanding with 500-grit. On the second coat, you have to apply the paste only to patches you missed on the first application—these spots will be easy to see because they'll be dull compared to the rest of the surface. Usually two coats of stone paste are sufficient, but you might need a third coat on a broad-grained wood like oak.

After you've removed all of the hardened stone paste, thoroughly wash the entire surface with fresh water. Since the wood is, or should be, completely sealed by now, there's no danger of warpage. If the stone paste washes out of the grain, however, you probably didn't put enough lacquer in the paste mixture. Make a new batch and repeat the sealing process.

Now you are ready to begin laying up coats of lacquer to achieve the depth and brilliance typical of the finest work. These coats should be extremely thin—apply just enough lacquer to moisten the surface without building up any perceptible thickness. Brush on the lacquer, then spread it over the entire surface with a soft linen cloth wrapped around a piece of absorbent cotton. Move the cloth in a circular motion at first to ensure even

application, then run down the grain in long, even strokes. For hard-to-reach places, wrap the linen over a spatula. After lacquering, put the piece in the wet box again until it has hardened.

Sand the hardened coat lightly with 600-grit paper, just enough to remove any dust that may have settled on the surface and to ensure good bite for the next coat. Apply six to eight thin coats, allowing each to harden and sanding between coats with progressively finer paper—600-, 800-, 1,000- and 1200-grits.

After the eighth coat of lacquer, even the finest wet-or-dry paper would be too rough, so you must buff the surface with charcoal powder and water on a wad of absorbent cotton. Use a tight circular motion over the entire surface, then wash off the powder with clear water. The surface should show up evenly dull.

Now apply a thin coat of lacquer, using linen wrapped over absorbent cotton instead of a brush. Let the lacquer harden as before, but do *not* buff the surface with charcoal powder. Simply apply the final coat of lacquer directly over the previous one.

If everything has gone well, the piece should have a very high-gloss finish that is durable and extremely easy to care for. If for some reason the finish is uneven or you wish to refinish a piece, you must go back to the point where 400-grit paper was used and repeat the process.

To clean up, remove excess lacquer from your brush by "prying" it out with a hard wooden spatula. Then dip the brush in vegetable oil. Work the oil into the brush and squeeze it out with a spatula. Repeat until the oil comes out clean. Leave a little oil in the brush to prevent any residual lacquer from hardening. Before using the brush, you must reverse the cleaning process, using lacquer to remove all of the oil. Work tables are also cleaned with oil, then washed with alcohol. Excess lacquer and stone paste can be saved in a bowl covered with plastic wrap.

Time is the true test of the quality of any finish. If the process I've described seems too difficult and time-consuming, take another look at the results. A good lacquer finish will not dull, and it's easy to maintain—it can be cleaned with a soft, moist cloth and polished with a dry, cotton cloth. Even if you don't want to use the complete method, don't give up on *urushi*. You can cut the work in half by omitting the stone paste, and only have to give up some gloss. You can create a dark matte finish, much like a dark walnut stain, by letting the first coat soak in, removing the excess with a cloth and allowing the lacquer to harden. I especially like the soft, semigloss sheen achieved by applying three coats. Apply a heavy first coat as previously described, let it harden, then lightly dry-sand with 400-grit. Repeat the process for the second coat, then apply a final coat.

Working with *urushi* has been a source of both satisfaction and discouragement for me. New problems arise with every piece. But among the romantic ideals my teacher, Kuroda Kenkichi, has about craftsmanship is the belief that something made from a 300-year-old tree should last for at least 300 years. Some might call that philosophy and some might call it common sense. In any case, *urushi* is a step in the right direction. □

Charles Roche operated a small furniture shop in Lexington, Ky., before going to Japan in 1978 to study woodworking and lacquering. He worked with Kuroda Kenkichi for three years before opening his own studio in Kyoto. For a price list and information on ordering urushi *and stone powder, write to the author at Kamigyo-Ku, Muromachi Dori, Kamedachiuri Sagaru, Uratsukiji-Cho 81, Kyoto 602, Japan.* Urushi *can also be obtained from Woodfinishing Enterprises, 1729 N. 68th St., Wauwatosa, Wis. 53213.*

Hydrocote: A Water-Base Lacquer

by Michael Dresdner

Although water-base lacquer has been around for years, all the brands I've tried suffer from the same generally poor finish qualities. They're characteristically soft, lack clarity and have inadequate layer-to-layer adhesion. Many wood finishers accustomed to the versatility of nitrocellulose and acrylic lacquer have given up on water-base substitutes. The need for a viable water-base lacquer is increased by the fact that the EPA Volatile Organic Components (VOC) emissions guidelines impose restrictions on the use of solvent-base finishes.

Recently, I discovered a finish called "Hydrocote" that's renewed my faith in water-base lacquers. Its impressive list of qualities sounds as if it was dreamed up by an old-time huckster selling snake oil. Because it's water-base, it is noncombustible and nonflammable; it also exceeds EPA guidelines for VOC emissions. What's surprising is that this nontoxic finish has film characteristics better than most nitrocellulose and acrylic lacquers. A dried film of Hydrocote is harder than that of typical solvent-base lacquers and surpasses them in alcohol, chemical, water and heat resistance. Even though liquid Hydrocote is milky white, a thinly-sprayed coat is as transparent as nitrocellulose and doesn't yellow with age. Hydrocote's adhesion to clean wood is excellent, as is layer-to-layer adhesion. Hydrocote can be sprayed directly over nitrocellulose lacquer, and nitrocellulose will adhere to a dried film of Hydrocote, as will most polyurethanes.

Hydrocote comes in 1-gal. and 5-gal. plastic containers as both a sanding sealer, and as gloss, satin and tabletop (extra-hard) lacquer. It's available from Hood Products, Inc., Box 163, Freehold, N.J. 07728; (800) 223-0934. Hydrocote costs a bit more than a typical nitrocellulose lacquer, but it's cheaper to use because it has more than twice the solids content of nitrocellulose—so fewer coats are needed—and it uses tap water instead of expensive solvents for thinning and cleaning the spray equipment. Hydrocote's extremely neutral color keeps blonde woods from turning amber, and it can be tinted with various water-soluble dyes and universal tints to give it a transparent or opaque color.

Hydrocote comes ready to spray from the can, but needs to be strained thoroughly as it tends to coagulate. Hood suggests spraying several thin coats in rapid succession prior to the first wet coat for better adhesion and to minimize grain raising. Hydrocote sands easily and each coat must be sanded smooth with an open-coat sandpaper before respraying. The high-solids coats build so quickly that on nonporous woods like maple, I don't use a sanding sealer at all—something I'd never do with nitrocellulose lacquer. Hydrocote sets quicker and dries almost as fast as nitrocellulose lacquer, and the final finish can be rubbed out as little as 30 minutes after spraying. It will never blush due to humidity, but spraying it on too thick will reduce finish clarity.

Spraying Hydrocote will take some getting used to for those accustomed to the "feel" of spraying a solvent-base lacquer, but the novice will appreciate its excellent flow-out characteristics that seem to compensate for poor gun technique and uneven spraying. It does, however, tend to flow out better on horizontal surfaces than on vertical ones, so it's best to spray these coats a bit lighter to avoid sags or curtaining.

Aside from a small amount of grain raising, the only problem you're likely to encounter with Hydrocote is from surface contamination. Like nitrocellulose, it develops fish-eye-like craters when exposed to oil or wax. Fortunately, Hood makes a special fish-eye-eliminating additive that alleviates the problem. Hood also publishes a guide for troubleshooting Hydrocote problems.

I've had excellent success spraying Hydrocote with conventional equipment at pressures between 25 psi and 55 psi. Hydrocote also works well in a low-pressure spray finishing system, such as the Apollo 500 sprayer. The only catch is that since Hydrocote doesn't redissolve itself, you'll have to flush out your spray gun with clean water to keep it from clogging if you let it stand for more than 15 minutes. Also, the gun must be made of stainless steel or aluminum, or lined with Teflon, otherwise contact with water will rust it. But these guns aren't prohibitively expensive, even for a small shop. Something you'll not be needing if you decide to spray only Hydrocote (or other water-base lacquers) is an explosion-proof exhaust system. Hydrocote doesn't burn, so its fumes can be expelled from your finishing room with a regular window fan. As a bonus, eliminating the spraying of flammable materials in your shop can put you in a cheaper insurance bracket.

I know of quite a few woodworkers who use Hydrocote exclusively, including both those who don't do much finishing and can't justify the expense of a spray booth and those who want to graduate from "wipe-on/wipe-off," one-step finishes. Advanced finishers may find Hydrocote somewhat less versatile than the nitrocellulose lacquers they're used to. However, with its impressive list of virtues and very few shortcomings, Hydrocote can fulfill many of the finishing needs of novices and professionals. I suggest that anyone who thinks all water-base lacquer is worthless give Hydrocote a try. □

Hydrocote's milky-white color belies the fact that it dries to be as transparent as nitrocellulose lacquer. Since Hydrocote is non-toxic, the author sprays a sample without a respirator on.

Michael Dresdner is an instrumentmaker in Zionhill, Penn.

Fixing Fish Eye

by Michael Dresdner

Fish eyes are probably the most common problem in lacquer finishing and refinishing, and one of the most difficult to remedy. In a freshly sprayed coat of lacquer, fish eyes pop up as small, randomly spaced craters in an otherwise smooth film. They're caused by silicone, a common chemical in furniture polishes, which alters the wet lacquer's surface tension, preventing it from flowing out. Silicone sinks into the wood through tiny cracks in the finish and then—when the piece is stripped—it dissolves in the stripping solution and spreads over the entire surface.

You can deal with fish eyes in one of two ways: by carefully preparing the surface before lacquering, or by using commerically available fish-eye preventers. On a wood surface that needs refinishing, I use a four-step wash to eliminate the offending silicones, as well as waxes and residues, then seal the surface with shellac before lacquering. My method might be overkill, but keep in mind that if fish eye occurs, no amount of spraying will cover it up. You'll have to strip the piece and deal with the source of the problem.

After the bulk of the stripper is scraped away, the piece is treated with (in succession): lacquer thinner, alcohol, naptha and warm water with a small amount of household-strength ammoniated detergent (not soap) added. Wearing gloves, wipe on a liberal amount of each solution and scrub down the wood, using a fresh pad of steel wool each time. Wipe the wood with a clean rag between treatments. The lacquer thinner neutralizes the stripper and removes most of its residue. The alcohol helps to remove aniline stains, oils and waxes, and what I call "shellac glaze"—that last bit of sealer that the lacquer thinner doesn't get rid of. The naptha dissolves any remaining contaminants, and can also be an early warning sign: If silicone persists, subtle but recognizable fish eyes will occur as soon as the mixture is applied. Finally, the water and ammonia solution will remove residual silicone. To avoid lifting veneers, perform this final step quickly, using liberal amounts of the solution, and wipe the piece dry immediately. Any lingering puddles cause water stains that are almost impossible to remove.

If all else fails and fish eye still occurs, the only answer is to fight fire with fire and apply fish-eye eliminator, which is simply pure silicone. Adding more of the offending material to the lacquer mix unites the random pockets of silicone to form one big silicone bubble, hence making the smaller bubbles invisible. Once used, the silicone must be added to every succeeding finishing coat.

While adding fish-eye eliminator sounds like an easy solution, it can create more problems than it solves. The silicone alters the lacquer mixture, and can change its gloss and reduce its hardness. Furthermore, silicone will insinuate itself everywhere. Some years ago, I visited a small refinishing shop that had been regularly spraying lacquer that contained fish-eye eliminator. The silicone-laden overspray was settling on bare furniture waiting to be sprayed, requiring that it, too, be sprayed with silicone additive. A vicious circle had been set up—silicone was in the guns, the lacquer reserves and the strip tanks, and was even on the workbenches and rags. If you do choose to add silicone, be certain to contain the overspray. Also, discard or store siliconed lacquers separately, and clean your guns thoroughly before using them with plain lacquer.

I recently tested two new anti-silicone materials from Hood Products, Box 163, Freehold, N.J. 07728. Purge-All is billed as a stain, silicone and soil remover that brings out the natural beauty of the wood. Hood's Fish Eye and Silicone Stop (FESS) is said to stop fish eyes caused by silicone polishes, waxes and oils.

I took some maple-veneered flakeboard, sanded it and inundated it with silicone. The board was then sprayed with a thin coat of lacquer to be sure it fish-eyed evenly (see photo), then washed off with lacquer thinner, which removed the lacquer but not the silicone. I cut the board into eight pieces, treated each sample as indicated below, then sprayed all of them with a coat of lacquer and checked for silicone contamination. Here's what I did and the results, assessed while the lacquer was still wet.

- #1: Four-step wash; very mild fish eye
- #2: Four-step wash, sealed with shellac; no fish eye apparent
- #3: Four-step wash, sealed with FESS; no fish eye apparent
- #4: Purge-All wash; severe fish eye
- #5: Purge-All wash, sealed with shellac; very mild fish eye
- #6: Purge-all wash, sealed with FESS; very mild fish eye
- #7: Sealed with shellac (no wash step); mild fish eye
- #8: Sealed with FESS (no wash step); mild fish eye

Frankly, I surprised myself. I've been using the four-step wash for years and thought the shellac step was just extra insurance. But it's clear that the sealer—FESS and shellac seem equally effective here—is just as important as the wash, and neither alone is enough. It's best to use freshly mixed shellac for the sealer coat, although vinyl sealer sprayed thin and fast is an adequate substitute. I wasn't surprised that the four-step wash was decidedly superior to the Purge-All. In past tests, other silicone washes haven't worked especially well, because they tend to dissolve the silicone and spread it around, removing only the solution that stays in the wash rag.

Although the amount of silicone I introduced was more than you'll find on an average refinishing job, I've run into similar levels of contamination. I once refinished an "oiled" walnut table. It was virtually bare wood the owner had cleaned for years with a silicone polish. The wash-and-seal process saved it, and it went out of my shop looking a lot less greasy than when it came in. □

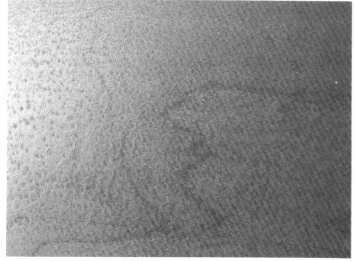

Fish-eye dimples like these often indicate silicone contamination.

Michael Dresdner is an instrumentmaker in Zionhill, Pa.

From *Fine Woodworking* magazine (November 1987) 67:80

Shading, Glazing and Toning

Three ways of using color with lacquer

by Donald M. Steinert

Shading is an effective way of neutralizing color differences. The sapwood on this walnut board, top, has been completely disguised, bottom, using a walnut-colored shading lacquer. Shading has also helped to hide the glueline.

One of the most appealing qualities of nitrocellulose lacquer is its versatility. Besides its use as a clear coating, lacquer can be mixed with various dyes and pigments to alter, enhance or entirely cover up the natural color and figure of wood. By mixing colorants with clear lacquer, three specialized techniques—shading, glazing and toning—can be used separately or in combination as an alternative to staining, as an aid to evening out color differences, and to highlight and create special effects. Used with basic lacquering skills, which I'll assume you already have, these methods will expand your wood finishing repertoire.

Before I describe the techniques in detail, I'll say a few words about wood preparation. Regardless of which coloring technique you try, the wood must be free of contaminants, such as wax or silicone, and sanded down to at least 220 grit. If staining and/or filling are required, do these steps as you would for any clear lacquer topcoats. But keep in mind that staining may or may not be necessary, since one of the techniques I'll describe may substitute. Once your sanding is done, seal the wood with a coat of clear sanding sealer. When dry, lightly sand with 400-grit paper. Once the coloring is done, as described below, you can apply a clear lacquer topcoat for the final finish. I recommend you use a nitrocellulose lacquer formulated specifically for wood. Don't use acrylic auto-finishing lacquers, which are primarily designed for metal. For more on clear lacquering, see pp. 89-95.

Shading is probably the most versatile lacquer-coloring method. In shading, clear lacquer is tinted with dye and applied between the sanding-sealer coat and the clear topcoat. Depending on the hue, the amount of color, and the number of coats, shading can highlight, alter or entirely change the wood's natural color. It can be used on an entire piece of furniture or, with careful spraying, can be selectively applied to only certain areas. Further, since shading lacquer is usually built up in a series of coats, you have a great amount of control over the color you'll end up with.

To mix a shading lacquer, start with the lacquer you'll be using for the topcoat. To this, add a small amount of transparent dye stain. It's essential to use a stain compatible with lacquer, such as Mohawk Ultra Penetrating Stain (product #520), available from Mohawk Finishing Products, Inc., Route 30, Amsterdam, N.Y. 12010). Ultra stains are universal dye stains diluted in a blend of solvents. You can mix up to one part stain with 16 parts lacquer (more than this retards the lacquer). For darker tones, apply more coats.

When mixing a shading lacquer that will serve as a stain, I use transparent dyes in various woody tones. In conjunction with these, I also use small amounts of black, yellow, green and red to adjust the shade and tone to almost any hue, as necessary. Other colors can be employed for bolder effects.

The darkness and depth of color on the wood being finished is determined by how many coats of shading are applied. The greatest degree of control is maintained by applying multiple light coats of shading lacquer, one at a time. Allow each coat to flash before applying the next. If a great deal of color change is wanted, I prefer spraying an initially darker shading lacquer, since it will require fewer coats to produce the desired shade.

One of the great advantages of coloring wood with shading lacquer is that the colored lacquer is sprayed on wood after it's been sealed. Thus you'll avoid splotching on many woods like fir, pine, oak and ash, which absorb stain unevenly. By applying several layers of lacquer, it's possible to develop a matching color gradually and precisely. This degree of color control is particularly helpful if you're trying to match the color of a reproduction to an existing piece. To blend in undesirable differences between unevenly colored boards, such as an unsightly streak of light sapwood in an otherwise satisfactory walnut tabletop, spray shading lacquer in a narrow spray pattern at low air pressure (see above photos).

Shading can also highlight wood color rather than change it. If a particular piece looks dull or flat, applying a few light coats of shading lacquer that's the same hue, but more intense, can create depth. Or if the color of the wood is unappealing, it can be "kicked" with shading lacquer. For example, a piece of walnut that looks too cool (too green in color) can be warmed by kicking it with a little red shading. Interesting effects can be produced by spraying more coats of shading on one area than another. For example, the borders of tabletops or drawer fronts can be sprayed slightly darker than the field to give some dimension to an otherwise flat piece. Playful effects, such as a transparent "candy apple" finish—great for children's furniture—are created by spraying brightly colored shading lacquer over very light wood.

Glazing is useful for highlighting carved, turned or molded details. Glazing darkens recesses while allowing raised details, a turned bead for instance, to remain lighter. Depending on the col-

From *Fine Woodworking* magazine (January 1988) 68:70-71

or and amount applied, you can create either dramatic or subtle contrasts. A glaze is made by mixing a pigment with a solvent. I use Mohawk Universal Color Concentrate (product #562) dissolved in naphtha. Proportions are not critical and will be dictated by the look you wish to create. To start, you may try one part pigment to three parts solvent. I prefer darker glazes because it's easier to wipe a little more off than to have to do a second application. Virtually any color may be used as a glaze to create an infinite variety of effects. For producing dark glazes, I often use black and earth tones, and my favorite is straight Vandyke brown, which produces a very rich-looking glaze. Light glazes usually work best on dark woods and vice versa. Metallic glazes can be prepared with Mohawk Bronzing Powder (product #380), available in numerous shades of gold, silver, copper and bronze.

Applying the glaze is not particularly difficult. This may be done with an old brush, rag or spray gun. When spraying, keep the air pressure to about 20 psi and restrict fluid flow. The entire area to be glazed is coated as if it were being painted. As soon as the glaze turns dull, wipe it off with a soft rag. As with using any lacquer products, wear gloves and a respirator. The idea is to remove most of the glaze from the details that are prominent while leaving the heaviest concentration in the recesses. There's no hurry, because even after the glaze is completely dry it can be removed with a naphtha-dampened, lint-free cloth.

Once you have achieved the desired look with the glaze, allow it to dry for about an hour. Then, spray it with a light topcoat of clear lacquer. Mastering the art of glazing takes practice and a critical eye. If you're not satisfied with the look you get on the first try, simply recoat and wipe the piece all over again.

Toning is similar to shading, but uses heavily pigmented colors–as opposed to dyes–to disguise the color of wood rather than just darken or highlight it as shading does. Of the three techniques, toning has the least application in high-quality woodworking. While a shading lacquer creates depth, toning tends to rob a piece of its transparency and depth. Because an opaque colorant is used, each additional coat of toner not only darkens the wood's color, but obscures its grain and figure. If a toner is applied heavily enough, it will become completely opaque, like paint, and the wood will not show through at all. This technique is often used by furniture factories to disguise the undesirable color and grain in low-grade or cheap wood species.

But toning isn't just for fakery. Applied selectively, it can solve some difficult finishing problems. For instance, if you have otherwise beautiful wood that has a section of unsightly grain, a toner can be sprayed over the area to completely mask the defect. Toning can save time and grief if you're refinishing a piece and can't get all the old paint off or the wood's in terrible condition. In such cases, it's undesirable to retain the wood's original color, so first cover the entire piece with toner, and then apply glaze and/or shading to add depth and contrast (see photo right).

To make a toner, mix the same type of pigments used for glazes with clear lacquer. A good proportion to start with is one part pigment to 24 parts lacquer. First, dilute the universal color with a little lacquer thinner and strain it before adding it to the lacquer. Work up to the desired toning effect gradually by spraying several light coats, using low air pressure and limited fluid flow through the spray gun. As with shading, you can speed things up by mixing a darker toner at the outset, but you'll achieve the best color control with several thin coats built up gradually. □

Donald M. Steinert restores Rolls-Royce woodwork and lives in Grants Pass, Ore. Photos by author.

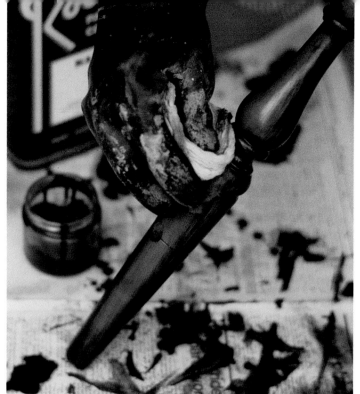

It's not critical to apply a glaze evenly, since most of it is wiped off the prominent surfaces before it dries. The pigment left in the recesses can create contrasts to highlight carved and turned details or give a piece an aged look.

These four frames illustrate several ways of using shading, glazing and toning in combination. From top to bottom, the frames are: stained light walnut; glazed with brown and clear-coated; toned with tan, glazed with brown, shaded with maple and red and clear-coated; toned with white and glazed with raw umber.

Reviving Period Hardware

Hints for restoring the gleam in the maker's eye

by Gregory Landrey and Helen Stetina

Brass hardware has been an important decorative and functional design element on American furniture since the early 1700s. Hardware catalogs of the day indicate the metal components were originally bright focal points on the furniture, not the heavily patinated antique brass sometimes envisioned today. Thus, keeping "brasses" bright, despite the effects of time, wear and pollutants, is a major concern among those working with period furniture. The 18th-century cabinetmakers and brass manufacturers used lacquer or other natural resin coatings to protect the brasses—a tradition that still is followed at The Winterthur Museum in Winterthur, Del., but with much improved materials. The Agateen 2-B cellulose-nitrate lacquer described here (available from Agate Lacquer Manufacturing Co. Inc., 11-13 43rd Road, Long Island City, N.Y. 11101), when properly applied, will help protect furniture hardware and enhance its visual qualities for at least 10 years, as long as the metal is not handled excessively.

Brass and its degradation—Most furniture brasses are alloys of copper and zinc, although they may also include lead, iron and other elements in varying mixtures. These variations are responsible for making the brass appear yellowish or reddish and also for the types and degrees of corrosion that arise, as shown in the top, left photo on the facing page.

Airborne contamination produces the familiar black tarnish on brass. "Stress corrosion cracking" (season cracking) can result when brass, stressed from being stamped out, is exposed to a mixture of water, air and ammonia (a major ingredient in most household brass polishes and perhaps hardware's greatest enemy). A green corrosion product, possibly a copper/salt mixture, is formed in this instance. Frequent polishing causes further degradation and the eventual loss of surface detail through wear. Also, in time, body salts and acids from skin appear on the hardware as etched fingerprints. Acetic acid, which is released by wood over a long period of time, is also a source of hardware deterioration.

The look of 18th-century hardware—It is rare to find an early hardware coating intact. Lacquer deteriorates as it ages and was often abraded away by polishing. The brasses were occasionally recoated, but we still have a good idea of how the originals looked. One 18th-century English catalog referred to brass hardware as "a fine burnish'd gold colour" or "burnish'd and lacquer'd." In addition to preventing tarnishing, these high-luster coatings imparted a gold-like color to the metal. In fact, the 1804 edition of *The Royal Standard English Dictionary* (published by E. Merriam & Co., Brookfield, Mass.) defines "lacker" as "yellow varnish used in brass-work." Some traditional lacquer mixtures, of such things as spirits of wine, turmeric (*Curcuma longa*) or dragon's blood (*Daemonorops draco*), were described as making brass resemble "pale French brandy," as shown in the top, right photo on the facing page.

Removing old residues—Assuming that any existing coating on the brasses is not antique, it must be removed. Soaking and scrubbing the hardware with lacquer thinner (we use Agateen Thinner #1), followed by acetone rinses ensures complete removal in most cases and degreases the metal. More tenacious, waxy deposits can be treated by swabbing them with mineral spirits or petroleum benzine (available from chemical-supply houses). Very often, incrustations of old varnishes, shellacs and polishes will accumulate on the reverse sides of escutcheons and back plates, around the bases of posts and along the ends of bails. We remove these incrustations with a fine stream of glass beads from an air-abrasion unit, which acts as a miniature sandblaster. The glass beads leave a satiny, matte finish, so this process is not recommended for the highly polished, visible surfaces of hardware. Rinsing the metal with reagent alcohol (90% ethanol, 5% methanol, 5% isopropanol) removes any abrasive residue; denatured alcohol is not recommended, because it contains too much water.

Cleaning brass—The metal should be as clean as possible before recoating, to prevent further corrosion and to provide a good bonding surface for the lacquer. Heavily tarnished brasses should first be dipped in a thiourea and acid solution (available from Fisher Scientific Co., 50 Valley Stream Parkway, Great Valley Corporate Center, Malvern, Penn. 19355). At the museum, we use a mixture of 8% (by weight) thiourea crystals, 5% (by weight) sulfuric acid and 87% (by weight) distilled water that contains 0.5% (by volume) Photo-Flo 200 wetting agent (available in photo-supply stores). Commercial preparations used for removing tarnish from silver can be used if they contain the key ingredients—thiourea (also available from Fisher Scientific) and acid (sulfuric or hydrochloric). A thorough rinsing first with water and then pure acetone should follow the dipping. Take care when handling acids and other materials like thiourea, which is a suspected carcinogen and "slightly toxic" to the skin or when ingested or inhaled. Wear latex or polyethylene gloves; if thiourea crystals are used, wear a particle mask. If the brasses still have a green, copper corrosion in crevices and in the decorative relief, swab the areas repeatedly with 10% (by weight) formic acid solution (concentrated preparations are available through chemical-supply houses), followed by thorough rinsing in warm water and drying with acetone.

Polishing—To ensure that the brasses remain "chemically" clean, polish them with pure abrasive containing no ammonia, tarnish

From *Fine Woodworking* magazine (March 1989) 75:70-71

Brasses on 18th-century furniture were bright and jewel-like, far from the heavily patinated pieces often associated with old work. That dull work, shown above left, is due more to age, wear and pollutants than to the maker's intent. However, cleaning and lacquering techniques can bring old metal back to its original state, as shown above right.

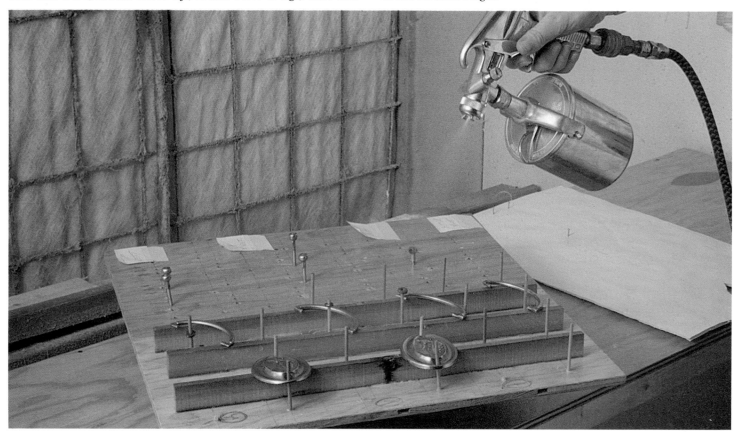

Brass hardware is sprayed on a platform equipped with various pegs and holes to accommodate the small, hard-to-handle pieces.

inhibitor or other chemicals. We apply a slurry of Buehler's (Union Carbide) 0.3u and 1.0u microaluminas (available from Buehler Ltd., 41 Waukegan Road, Lake Bluff, Ill. 60044) and reagent alcohol with soft, clean, additive-free, cotton flannel cloths or cotton diapers. Various sharpened sticks and dowels, dental picks, toothbrushes and strong, cotton thread can be used to scrape away more tenacious residues. After the alcohol in the slurry evaporates, the abrasive dust is blown away with compressed air. The brasses are then buffed to a high polish with either a soft flannel cloth or a chamois-like, 100%-cotton cloth called "Selvyt" (available through Allcraft Tool & Supply Co., 60 S. Mac-Questen Parkway, Mount Vernon, N.Y. 10550). If the hardware can't be coated immediately, it's stored temporarily in polyethylene sandwich bags; avoid potentially corrosive cling-type plastic wraps that may contain polyvinylidene chlorides.

Applying lacquer—Agateen's 2-B cellulose nitrate lacquer is clear and durable, bonds well to the metal surface, dries within seconds and flows smoothly to minimize drips and runs. Its slight yellow tint makes the brass more mellow looking. We apply two coats of a 50/50 mixture of 2-B lacquer and #1 thinner with a spray gun at approximately 40 to 50 psi in a prefabricated industrial-size spray booth. The lacquer can be easily removed with the #1 thinner by soaking or swabbing. Don Heller, Winterthur's objects conservator, who researched and instituted this metal-coatings program, has designed special boards with various pegs and holes to accommodate small, difficult-to-handle pieces, as shown in the larger photo above. □

Gregory Landrey is furniture conservator and Helen Stetina is a former metal-coatings technician at the Henry Francis du Pont Winterthur Museum in Winterthur, Del.

A compressor is a versatile tool that has a place in all woodshops, regardless of size or type of woodworking done. Whether it's hooked up to an elaborate system of air pipes or used with a simple flexible hose, a compressor can drive dozens of different air-powered devices, such as spray guns, air tools, pneumatic clamps and vacuum devices. Here, a worker uses a 2-HP portable compressor to blow chips out of a mortise being chopped by hand.

Compressed-Air Systems
Taking the pressure out of choosing and using compressors

by Michael Dresdner

One valuable tool often found in woodworking shops requires no bits, cutters or blades and never needs sharpening, yet can do more jobs than the most versatile multipurpose machine. With a few adaptations, an air compressor can accomplish a surprising range of tasks. In addition to running a spray gun for applying clear finishes or paints, a compressor system provides a ready source of clean air to blow off work surfaces and parts, and clean chips from newly cut joints. And a compressor can drive specially designed sanders, drills, routers, grinders and more; power production-oriented pneumatic clamps; and create a vacuum strong enough to run a bag-type veneer press or hang on to parts in special hold-down fixtures.

I think anyone who owns a woodshop should consider buying a compressor and the accessories to use it safely and efficiently. A basic compressed-air system isn't too expensive, and you will find more than enough uses for it to justify the cost. In this article, I'll cover the basics of compressors and accessories and what you should know before buying anything, as well as how to use compressed air in a shop. I'll also talk about how to design and install a compressed-air system. First, let's look at the anatomy of a typical compressor.

The compressor—At the heart of any air system is the compressor itself. Compressors come in all sizes, usually rated by their horsepower (HP), from small ¾-HP portables to giant 25-HP and higher industrial workhorses. Regardless of the size, though, almost all compressors consist of a motor (electric or gasoline powered) connected to an air-compression pump. Both the pump and motor are usually mounted on an air storage tank. The pump drives one or more pistons, which draw air from the room through a filter, compress it and force it into an air storage tank where it's kept until needed. A single-stage pump compresses air to full pressure with one stroke of the piston (or pistons), while a two-stage pump partially compresses air with the first piston, and then compresses it to full pressure with the second. An automatic pressure switch mounted on the air tank regulates the compressor and shuts off the motor when tank pressure reaches the desired maximum, typically 100 pounds per square inch (psi). When the air is used, the pressure drops below a user-adjustable threshold and the switch turns the compressor back on to replenish the tank. Some compressors are fitted with an unloader that controls air pressure without constantly starting and stopping the unit during heavy use.

From *Fine Woodworking* magazine (May 1990) 82:56-61

Usually the tank has a pressure gauge and a safety pressure-release valve that lets air escape if the pressure switch fails and tank pressure gets too high. When air is compressed, the moisture it carries is compressed as well, and when the air cools in the tank, the moisture condenses out. Therefore, the tank has a drain valve (also called a petcock) at the bottom (see the drawing on p. 86) to allow the water to be bled. The tank also has either feet or wheels on the bottom, depending on whether it's a stationary or portable model. Finally, the tank has an air outlet and shut-off valve where the air hose or piping is connected.

Using compressed air—A great variety of tools and devices are designed to run off a compressor—even a small-capacity model. A compressor is most commonly found in the finishing room, where it is used to drive guns that blow off sanding dust and spray guns that apply finish. Dusting guns, also known as blow guns, are available in dozens of different styles and prices; just make sure to get one that is approved by the Occupational Safety and Health Administration (OSHA). Spray guns for applying stains and finishes are available in a wide range of sizes and styles, and it is best to choose the gun with a specific use in mind (see the sidebar on p. 85).

Outside the finishing room, a compressed-air system will run sand-

ers, routers, drills, screwdrivers, nailers—virtually any hand-held electric power tool has an air-powered equivalent. Air tools often cost two or three times more than their electric counterparts, but they tend to outlast them. One of the most common and useful air-powered tools in the woodshop is the sander (see the top photo below) because, in addition to outlasting an electric model, the air sander is stronger, faster and quieter. One indisputable advantage of an air sander is wet-sanding: Final-sanding a finish using water or solvent as a lubricant. Because of a possible explosion or fire, it's foolhardy to wet-sand with an electric tool. Air sanders use no electricity, and they are standard with most professional finishers.

Probably the most novel use of compressed air is an ingenious device called a vacuum pump. Although it's called a pump, this device has no moving parts and it's deceptively small—about the size of a lipstick. Inside the vacuum pump's tube-like body is an accurately machined cone (a Venturi tube) with a small aperture. As compressed air is forced through the aperture, a vacuum is created just behind the tip of the cone. A vacuum line is connected via a threaded hole at 90° to the direction of air flow. Although there are several brands available, I've had good success with the JS-90 vacuum pump, which is available from Vaccon Co., Inc., Box 423, Norwood, Mass. 02062; (617) 762-2880.

A vacuum pump can revolutionize your shop. This ready source of suction transforms any jig into a reliable vacuum chuck or hold-down jig, like the one shown in the bottom photo below, capable of grasping complex-shaped parts during machining. Hooked up to a vinyl-bag press, the pump evacuates air, for vacuum laminating and vacuum veneering.

Other uses for compressed air are numerous. Powerful pneumatic quick-action clamps are available for many applications, and are indispensable for production work. Many new multipurpose joinery machines offer such clamps as optional accessories. On a larger scale, compressed air is necessary for operating certain large machines. The wide-belt sander, fast becoming a cabinet shop standard, uses compressed air to tension the sanding belt and, on some models, to regulate belt tracking. Pneumatic cylinders are also used on some horizontal boring machines, on which an air-operated foot switch activates both a pneumatic clamp that holds the work down and a cylinder that thrusts the bit into the work. With a little creative effort, you can use compressed air to cool machine-tool operations, such as hollow-chisel mortisers, during pro-

Practically every electric-powered hand tool has an air-powered equivalent that's stronger and faster. Here, the author sands an electric bass guitar with an air-powered orbital sander.

A small, inexpensive vacuum pump hooked to an air compressor can turn any jig or fixture into a vacuum hold-down capable of grabbing even oddly shaped work. Here, the tiny pump is built into a jig designed to hold guitar necks as the outside of the headstock is shaped.

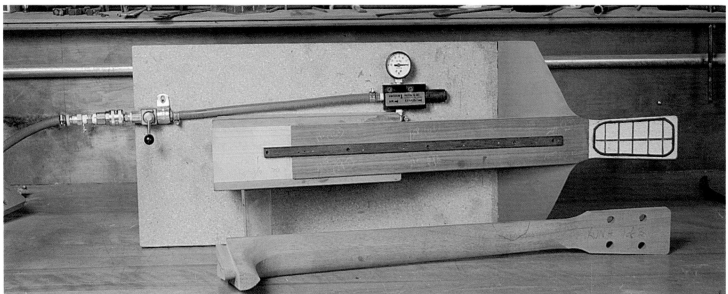

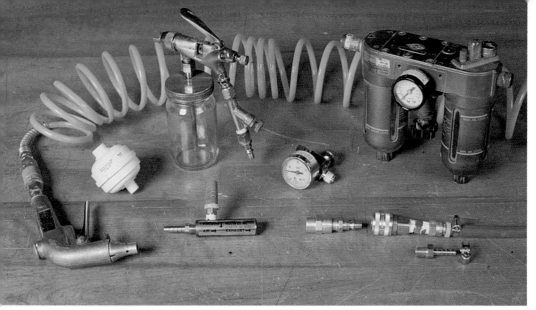

Compressed-air system accessories for cleaning and drying the air, as well as oiling and regulating it, are numerous. For instance, shown in the front row, left to right are a blow-off gun attached to a coiled air hose, for dusting work before finishing; a lipstick-size vacuum pump that is amazingly powerful; and a quick-change coupling system that allows air devices to be readily exchanged. Back row: This small, disposable air filter attaches directly to the gun or tool; a touch-up spray gun is handy for small finishing jobs; this regulator/gauge unit is made to attach at the device, to allow easy adjustment of the air flow; for air-powered tools, this combination device offers a filter, regulator, pressure gauge and oiler in one compact unit.

duction work or to blow chips away and prevent them from clogging a cut, such as when shaping with a pin router. For more demanding tool-cooling jobs, a T-shape device called a vortex tube can cool compressed air down to minus 40°F. This tube is available from Vortec, 10125 Carver Road, Cincinnati, Ohio 45242; (800) 441-7475.

System accessories—Regardless of the size or layout of your compressed-air system, there are a number of devices you can install on air lines to modify or control the air. including after coolers, dryers, filters, oilers and regulators. Aftercoolers chill the compressed air to condense and drain moisture. Dryers come in two types, mechanical and desiccant, and both prevent any further condensation of air in the system. These devices are essential to maintain high-quality air in the finishing room—especially in areas of high humidity. Filters remove oil mist, dust and particles, as well as moisture, all of which are contaminants that may ruin sprayed finishes and foul spray guns or air tools. There are two basic kinds of filters. Separators create a whirlpool effect to trap oil, water and particles, which collect in a chamber that has a "sneezer" or drain valve. Mechanical filters pass the air through either coalescing or absorbing filter material, usually in a cartridge. The cartridge must be periodically replaced when it becomes clogged with dirt and dust particles that bypass the primary air filter on the compressor pump or are products of deterioration in the air lines.

While filters clean the air, oilers add small amounts of air-tool oil to the air to lubricate air-powered tools. Though air tools require frequent lubrication, the use of an automatic-dispensing oiler makes these tools virtually maintenance free. A dial on the oiler allows you to control the number of drops per minute added to the air and a refillable reservoir holds a supply of the special oil (never substitute motor oil). Oilers are installed in a compressed-air system as close to the tool as possible, to prevent air lines from being contaminated with oil, which could ruin a finish if a spray gun were used with the same air line.

Because different air guns and tools have different air pressure requirements, air regulators are fitted to allow the user to control pressure. This is done by turning a hand knob that presses a diaphragm to either reduce the air pressure or leave it unchanged; regulators cannot increase the psi above line pressure. A regulator usually has an attached gauge, so you can monitor the outgoing pressure. With the exception of small, portable compressors that often have regulators mounted at the tank, air regulators are best positioned as close as possible to the end use, to allow the operator to change pressure as needed.

Choosing a compressor—When it comes to figuring out how big your shop compressor needs to be, there are two factors to consider: pressure, measured in psi, and volume, measured in cubic feet per minute (CFM). Pressure needs for air devices used in woodworking range from less than 30 psi to around 100 psi. Even a ½-HP single-stage compressor can generate enough pressure for most small-size shop uses, although a large air system may need the higher pressure-generating potential of a two-stage compressor, which can produce pressures above 125 psi. Generally, the most important measure of a compressor's power is its CFM output. Unfortunately, a compressor's actual output isn't always reflected by the manufacturer's claims. Just as with the horsepower rating game, where power output of a motor may be rated in either "peak-developed" or "continuous" horsepower, compressor manufacturers don't all use the same rating standards. Still, standards do exist and most high-quality compressor makers rate their units in SCFM (standard cubic feet per minute). This is the actual amount of air discharged by the compressor, measured under specified atmospheric conditions of temperature, altitude and humidity. In contrast, less-expensive compressors, rated in regular CFM, may output between 10% and 20% less than those rated in SCFM—the industry standard.

To determine your compressed air needs, add up the CFM requirements of all of the tools or devices that are likely to be running at the same time, add 25% and use that as your minimum output. If your shop is at a high altitude, say above 6,000 ft., you may also want to add another 10% or more, since the air is thinner and takes more power to compress. When computing your air-tool

Average Air Consumption of Air-Powered Devices

Device	psi	Air Consumption (in CFM)
7-in. Body grinder	90	7½-30*
Dust gun	100	2.5
⅜-in. Drill	90	6-24*
Finish sander, random orbit	90	4-16*
Jigsaw	90	7-27*
Nail gun (40, 2-in. nails/min.)	100	2.2
Router (with ¼-in. collet)	90	7-28*
Stapler (40, ¼-in. by 1½-in. staples/min.)	100	1.8
Spray gun (with general-purpose nozzle)	30-50	7.8-11.5**
Touch-up spray gun (with general-purpose nozzle)	30-50	4.2-6.9**
Vacuum pump	80	1.8

* First number indicates CFM with intermittent use. Second number is CFM with constant use.
** Range of CFM varies with pressure and different nozzle selection.

Selecting a spray gun

A spray gun for finishing is probably the most common device used with compressed air, yet woodworkers often give even less consideration to selecting a gun than they do a compressor. Most high-quality spray guns are capable of shooting a wide range of finishing materials, including stains and dyes, lacquers, varnishes, urethanes, epoxies, paints and even adhesives.

Most spray guns found in small shops are siphon feed, that is, the air pressure fed to the gun is used to create suction that pulls the finishing material from a cup attached to the underside of the gun. Practically all guns, save touch-up guns, have siphon-feed cups that will hold a quart—adequate for one or two coats on even a large cabinet or furniture piece. However, shops that do production cabinetry and need larger quantities often use a pressure pot. This is a special locking canister, resembling a pressure cooker, that holds several gallons or more of finish at a time and feeds the material to the gun via a separate hose coming from the pot.

When choosing a spray gun, the important thing to remember is that the brand, model or overall size of the gun is no indication of what finishing materials the gun is equipped to handle, or of how much air it will use. Instead, most guns allow the tip setup, consisting of the air nozzle and fluid nozzle and needle, to be changed, and various combinations of nozzles and needles accommodate finishing materials of different types and viscosity.

Various tip setups also use different quantities of compressed air measured in CFM (see main article on p. 84). A gun with a small air nozzle spraying a thin material, such as a stain, at low pressure might require as little as 2 CFM, while a large air nozzle spraying heavier material, such as varnish, will require both higher pressure and may pull more than 20 CFM. Both setups might fit the same spray gun, but the larger, more air-hungry tip setup will deliver a lot more finishing material than the smaller one in the same amount of time.

Choosing the right tip setup for your spray gun depends on the number of CFM available from your compressor and the viscosity of the finishing material you want to spray. Viscosity for finishes is usually stated as "#2 Zahn cup" seconds. This is the most common (for lab testing) of almost two dozen different viscosity-measuring systems (Ford #4, Centipoise and Sears being others) that determine how thick a liquid is by how many seconds it takes for a premeasured amount to flow through a special-size orifice. Most common wood-finishing materials range between 14 and 30 seconds (#2 Zahn cup seconds): stains, solvents and water: 14 to 16 seconds; sealers, lacquers and primers: 16 to 20 seconds; varnishes, shellacs and urethanes: 19 to 30 seconds. You can test other finishing materials by buying a viscosity cup and following its testing directions.

A spray-gun manufacturer's chart for selecting air and fluid nozzle and needle combinations usually lists tip choices in sections grouped by viscosity. The sections usually offer several tip setups, each using a different number of CFM. For a general-purpose spray gun, pick the tip setup that allows you to spray the widest variety of materials within the CFM capacity of your compressor. Although you don't have to pick the largest tip that your compressor will handle, larger aperture fluid and air nozzles will generally produce a wider-fan spray pattern, which means more material flow and faster spraying of large surfaces, such as tabletops or cabinet panels. A gun running off a pressure pot needs a different tip setup than a gun using a siphon-feed cup. If you need a gun that can use either a pot or a cup, make sure the spray gun you buy accommodates both and purchase two separate tip setups.

If you plan to spray "catalyzed" coatings, which often contain acids or water-base coatings, such as Hydrocote lacquer, you'll need to choose a gun that has stainless-steel fluid pathways. Also, I prefer guns with a fluid nozzle that mates to the gun body with a nylon gasket, rather than a gun with a metal-to-metal fit. On the latter type, even slight damage to either surface, which may occur when cleaning the gun or changing tips, can cause the gun to spit, spray intermittently or clog. Guns that have a replaceable nylon gasket below the fluid tip will outlive their all-metal counterparts. These gaskets are cheap and survive countless cleanings.

Although prices vary, a high-quality gun costs about $135 and comes with your choice of tip setup. Each additional setup costs about $55. If you're in the market for an all-purpose gun for your finishing room, try to pick a brand and model that gives you as many tip options as possible. My current favorite gun, the Binks model 2001, offers over 1,500 different setup combinations for a staggering range of materials. Also, 2001 tips are interchangeable with guns from many of the other models in the Binks line, making this gun extremely versatile.

Siphon-feed cups are sold separately, and almost all cups are interchangeable with standard guns, even cheaper imports. In addition to the standard aluminum cup, there are Teflon-lined, stainless-steel and translucent polypropylene cups. All work nicely with water-base finishes and the latter two types will handle corrosive materials, such as acid-catalyzed lacquer or paint remover, as well. If you plan to spray many different materials through one gun, it is a good idea to have several siphon-feed cups. I like to keep one cup just for clear finishes and another one for solid colors. Regardless of the brand cup you buy, make sure a replacement gasket—a neoprene, nylon or leather ring between the cup and its lid—is available from your dealer, especially if you buy an off-brand or a foreign-made cup. *—M.D.*

CFM needs, take into account that certain air tools that run at a modest CFM when run intermittently, can draw tremendous amounts of air in continuous use (see the chart on the facing page). The largest range of CFM requirements is likely to be in the finishing room: A small touch-up gun, like the one in the photo on the facing page, can draw as little as 4 CFM, while a production spray gun with a large-aperture nozzle can easily draw 20 CFM or more.

To complicate compressor selection, new as well as used models are usually rated in horsepower, not CFM. This rating applies to the size of the head, or pump, and reflects the size motor that is required to run the compressor's pump at peak efficiency. The most common compressor sizes, as rated in horsepower, are: 1, 1½, 2, 3, 5, 7½, 10, 15 and from there up in 5-HP increments. Although it's not an entirely accurate rating, a common rule of thumb is to figure an output of 4 CFM per HP. Hence, a 2-HP compressor can be expected to produce about 8 CFM, which is adequate for moderate compressed-air needs in a small-size shop. While a home hobbyist with minimal air requirements may be satisfied with even a ¾-HP compressor, most professional finishers regard a 5-HP unit as the minimum size. Smaller compressors often require only 110v AC power and can be plugged into a standard wall outlet, while motors on larger units often come in both 220v single- and three-phase models. Compressors with 5-HP or larger motors should always have magnetic starter switches.

Another factor in deciding how big a compressor you need is

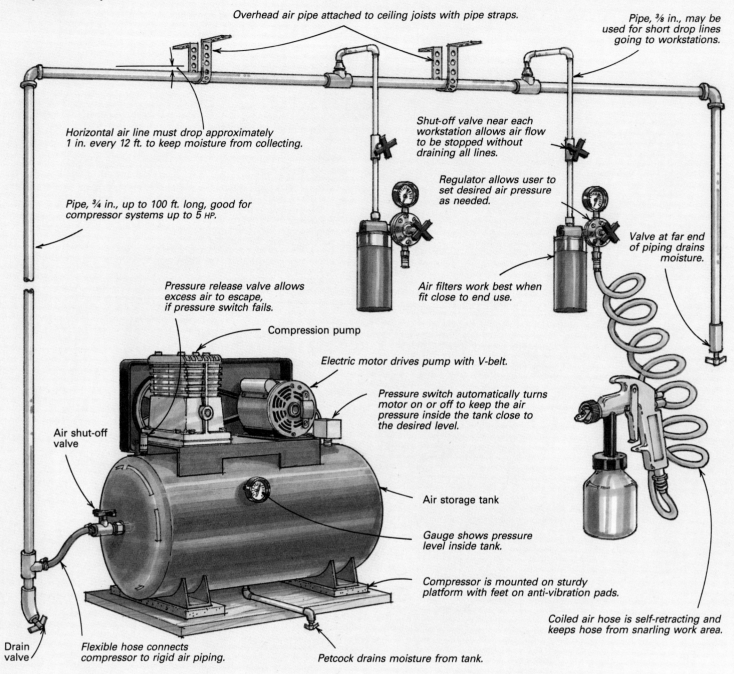

Overhead air pipe attached to ceiling joists with pipe straps.

Pipe, ⅜ in., may be used for short drop lines going to workstations.

Shut-off valve near each workstation allows air flow to be stopped without draining all lines.

Horizontal air line must drop approximately 1 in. every 12 ft. to keep moisture from collecting.

Regulator allows user to set desired air pressure as needed.

Pipe, ¾ in., up to 100 ft. long, good for compressor systems up to 5 HP.

Valve at far end of piping drains moisture.

Air filters work best when fit close to end use.

Pressure release valve allows excess air to escape, if pressure switch fails.

Compression pump

Electric motor drives pump with V-belt.

Pressure switch automatically turns motor on or off to keep the air pressure inside the tank close to the desired level.

Air shut-off valve

Air storage tank

Gauge shows pressure level inside tank.

Compressor is mounted on sturdy platform with feet on anti-vibration pads.

Coiled air hose is self-retracting and keeps hose from snarling work area.

Drain valve

Flexible hose connects compressor to rigid air piping.

Petcock drains moisture from tank.

the size of its storage tank, with capacity rated in gallons. If your air use is intermittent rather than constant, you'll want to buy a unit with a large storage tank. This is because the larger the volume of stored air you have available, the longer it will be before the compressor's motor has to go back to work to replenish the supply. If a device in your shop needs an especially high volume of air, you may wish to install a second tank nearest the end use, to provide extra air capacity. Compressor dealers sometimes have extra tanks for sale (from defunct units). Also, make sure any used or new tank you buy bears an American Society of Mechanical Engineers (ASME) certification plaque—assurance that it's safe at maximum pressure. Air piping installed in your shop (described on the facing page), can also act as a storage system, and a manifold made from larger-diameter pipe can increase your system's short-period CFM output as well.

Designing an air system—Unless you plan to use a portable compressor with a single air hose and move the unit where it's needed,

you'll want to carefully design your shop's layout of air lines and air-processing devices for best efficiency and convenience. As shown in the drawing above, a basic compressed-air system for a small- to medium-size shop consists of a compressor, air filters, regulators, accessories, air piping and hoses, and the end-use devices. The first thing to consider when designing your system is where to put the compressor. Ideally, the location should have good air circulation and lots of clean air for the compressor to draw, such as a room that's vented outdoors. Alternately, you could use flexible clothes-dryer hose to run clean air to the pump from outside. Placing the compressor near a source of sawdust will lower its efficiency and necessitate cleaning the air filter and changing the pump oil more often. Since the automatic pressure switch may start up the compressor at any time, the pulley side should be enclosed in a protective shroud or that side should face toward a wall; however, keep it at least 12 in. from the wall for unobstructed air circulation. Unless it's an explosion-proof model, the compressor shouldn't be located near the finishing area or spray booth, because a spark from

Drawing: Joel Katzowitz

its pressure switch could ignite solvent vapors. If the compressor shares the same floor as the spray room, it's a good idea to mount the compressor atop vibration-absorbing pads (cut-up pieces of old truck tires will also work nicely) to cut down on noise transmitted and/or amplified by the floor and vibration that raises dust.

When picking a spot for the compressor, try to find a location that's as close as possible to the end-use device, or, in the case of a shared shop, closest to the largest-volume air user. Because of friction inside the air lines, compressed air loses pressure (and effectively power) as it travels long distances. For example, air running through a 50-ft. length of ¼-in.-ID hose will experience a 50% drop in pressure. The same distance in a ⁵⁄₁₆-in.-ID hose will cause only a 20% drop, and in a ¾-in. line (or larger) there will be virtually no loss in pressure. If you're running fairly long lengths of pipe between the compressor and the workstation, a larger-diameter pipe will not only reduce a drop in pressure, but it will act as an air-storage manifold, as described earlier. If you're at a job site and must use a small air line, say a long, ¼-in.-ID hose on a portable compressor, you can turn up the pressure at the compressor to overcome the friction losses.

Air lines—Traditionally, threaded galvanized steel pipe has been the standard for permanent air lines in the shop. It's readily available, safe and sturdy. The connections between fittings are made airtight by using pipe thread compound or Teflon tape on the joints. But because of steel pipe's cost and weight, some shops have chosen PVC plastic pipe as an alternative. It is not only lighter, but can be cut with a regular handsaw and jointed at any point without threading hassles. A word of caution though: If you're going to use plastic, make sure it's rated to withstand the highest pressure and temperature to which it will be subjected. (Editor's note: Since this article first appeared in the May 1990 issue of *Fine Woodworking*, we have received a number of letters strongly discouraging the use of PVC pipes in compressed-air systems because of the potential for explosion. PVC pipes used in conjunction with air compressors have been shown to shatter suddenly due to the weakness of the pipes in relation to the release of decompressed gases. Therefore, we strongly recommend that they not be used.)

There are few restrictions as to how air lines should be run. Some shops have main lines crossing the ceiling with coiled hoses hovering above the bench areas; others have hard lines mounted to the workbench with hookups at workstations every few feet. A great configuration for a shop with many simultaneous air users is to have air pipes connect and form a loop around the shop. This reduces the drain that any single end user places on the system. Almost any configuration is possible, provided a few simple rules are followed. Due to moisture that condenses in the lines, all horizontal piping should be sloped away from the compressor. As you can see in the drawing, the slope of the horizontal line should be about 1 in. of drop per 12 ft. of run. At the end of each sloped line should be an elbow joint and a vertical drop leg, to collect the moisture. A petcock, or valve fitted on the end, allows the water to be drained. You should drain these lines, as well as the compressor tank, daily. On any lines that branch off, the T-fitting should point up, again preventing moisture from draining toward the tool, and also have a drain valve on the branch pipe or on the air-filter device. A typical network of air lines might have a ¾-in. main trunk running along the ceiling with ⅜-in., ⁵⁄₁₆-in. or ¼-in. branch lines dropping down wherever needed. I also like to include a shut-off valve at the head of each branch line and one at the head of the main line so that I can cut off the air to any leg of the system for repairs or alterations without having to drain all the lines. Just make certain that the system's safety pressure-release valve is closer to the compressor than any shut-off valve; mine is on the compressor tank itself.

Dresdner uses a compressed-air workstation with an air filter and regulator where they are most efficient: near the end use, preventing moisture and debris in the air lines from contaminating a finish.

Workstation air hookups—Setting up air workstations at the workbench, where clean air can be regulated and devices hooked up quickly as they're needed, makes using compressed air convenient. If you plan to use various air-powered devices around your shop and each requires different air pressure settings, you should have a separate regulator at each workstation. Air filters should also be fitted at each workstation, located just before the regulator so that the set pressure isn't affected. For air-powered tools that use both an oiler and an air filter, the filter must come first. Some air filters are small enough to mount directly at the gun or tool and, for workstations dedicated to air-tool use, there are combination control units that contain a filter, regulator, gauge and oiler all in one device (see the photo on p. 84).

I install quick-change couplings at each workstation so any hose extension, dusting gun or tool can be quickly accommodated. These handy fittings consist of two halves; the female coupling threads onto the air source, while the male stem attaches to whatever is down line (hose extension, tool, spray gun, etc.). When the couplings are joined, the air flows freely with no leakage; but when they are separated, the female end acts as an automatic shut-off valve. Unfortunately, not all couplings are interchangeable, and one brand of stem may not fit with another brand of coupling. Although there is some brand crossover, most companies design their couplings so that you must buy only their brand for your entire system.

In the spray room of my instrumentmaking shop, quick-change couplings are especially valuable because they allow me to swap spray guns at will, for applying different finishing materials. Also, using several guns on a single hose keeps the number of hoses to a minimum to prevent the spray room from becoming a snake pit. ☐

Michael Dresdner is a Contributing Editor for FWW, *an instrumentmaker and finishing consultant in Perkasie, Pa. Thanks to Randy Jenkins, woodworker and retired compressor-systems specialist from Lafayette, La., for his technical assistance.*

Improvising a spray booth

by David Shaw

While it's preferable to spray lacquer within the cozy confines of a commercial spray booth, many of us have neither the space nor the money for one. With a little ingenuity, however, and minimum expenditure, it's possible to reasonably duplicate spray booth conditions so you can spray small jobs safely inside your shop.

The three main things you need to do are to ventilate your spray area, isolate it from spark sources and exhaust the noxious and inflammable fumes. Since I can't afford a separate booth, I do all of my spraying inside my 14-ft. by 22-ft. shop. For ventilation, I installed an explosion-proof fan (mine's a Dayton 9M717) in one wall of the shop, at an opposite corner from an air vent. To keep overspray from being pumped outdoors, I installed a filter on the exhaust side of the fan, between the fan and a set of louvers that automatically open when the fan's turned on. The filters, called paint arrestors, are available from local finish supply houses. If practical, it's better to install the filter in front of the fan so overspray won't gunk up the blades.

The size of the fan (quoted in cubic feet per minute) depends on the size of the room in which you're spraying. Not too surprisingly, there are government regulations on fan size. The Occupational Safety and Health Administration recommends a minimum air flow of 100 feet per minute over the object being sprayed. To arrive at a fan size needed to move this much air, multiply the width of your spray area times the height by 100. My fan's not nearly big enough to move that much air, but by spraying as close to the fan as I can, I get good enough ventilation for short spraying sessions and also keep the overspray from settling on my tools and on other pieces.

Good lighting is critical in spray finishing. I've managed to make do with the standard fluorescent tubes in my shop, but the safest light sources are the explosion-proof fixtures enclosed in glass and wired through metal conduit to a switch outside the spray area. Similarly, the compressor should be located outside the room and preferably at a level well below the spray gun, so moisture in the air will have plenty of time to condense and gravity will pull the water back into the air tank where it can be drained.

Finally, and perhaps most important, you have to contain the buildup of fumes that will occur in your shop. Lacquer fumes are insidious and persistent and will work their way through the tiniest cracks and holes. My solution was to staple a plastic vapor barrier to the spray area walls, furr-out the wall and nail a layer of fire-code drywall over that. The combination of air pocket and vapor barrier seems to keep the fumes from wandering. Floors should have the barrier and drywall installed on the ceiling below.

Don't entirely discount spraying outside, if weather permits. This can be a pleasure or a disaster, depending on the wind, number of birds and how many flies in your neighborhood enjoy doing headers into fresh lacquer. In any case, don't forget to wear your respirator. Despite what you think, that gentle breeze will not waft away those harmful fumes. □

David Shaw is a professional wood finisher in Kelly Corners, N.Y.

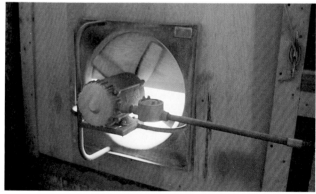

In this western Massachusetts furniture shop, a corner of the old fabric mill the shop is housed in has been converted into a spray booth. The explosion-proof fan (Dayton 6K734M, ¼ HP) is mounted in a frame fitted with a sliding door so the booth can be sealed up during cold weather. Incandescent lamps are enclosed in explosion-proof fixtures and wired through metal conduit. Furnace filters installed in the double doors leading into the booth filter dust from incoming air, allowing spraying while normal shop operations are underway. A fire extinguisher and a combustible-waste can are located just outside the booth doors. The hardware shown here is available through local industrial supply houses or from McKilligan Industrial and Supply Corp., 435 Main St., Johnson City, N.Y. 13790.

From *Fine Woodworking* magazine (January 1987) 62:72

Spray Finishing

Mastering clear lacquer

by Gregory Johnson

Sprayed nitrocellulose lacquer, though more involved to apply than a padded oil or brushed varnish, is worth the extra effort. As author Johnson explains, it's among the most workable and practical of finishes for small-shop furnituremakers.

I once heard a story about an old man in a brass foundry who had been tirelessly polishing a huge brass door for hours on end. Another man, having watched him work for awhile, finally spoke up. "That door is just beautiful. How do you know when it's done?" Still polishing, the old man answered, "It's never done. They just come and take it away."

You could say the same thing about a hand-rubbed lacquer furniture finish. The more you rub, the better it gets. But long before they come to take it away, you'll have achieved a splendid finish that protects wood against abrasion, heat, alcohol, dirt and water much better than an oil finish. True, a sprayed lacquer finish is more difficult to apply than oil or brushed varnish, but it's among the most workable, practical finishes for the small shop. It's fast drying and you can see results quickly. Lacquer alone brings out the beauty of natural wood in its lightest tone. Most problems in a lacquer finish are evident within five minutes after spraying. If it doesn't blister, pinhole, craze

or look like a lunar landscape within that time, chances are very good that it won't fail later on. And if, for some reason, you don't like the results, you can usually strip it off with thinner and start again.

In this article, I'll describe spray lacquer basics using a desk made by my nephew, Paul Johnson, as an example. The desk presents most of the problems you'll face in lacquering a piece of furniture, including spraying inside corners and finishing both sides of a flat panel that will be exposed to heavy wear. Since the desk is made of maple and purpleheart, two nicely contrasting woods, no masking or staining was required, making this a straightforward, clear lacquer job. It's possible to mix stains and glazes with lacquers or to color wood by spraying opaque lacquers, but these techniques are the subject of another article.

Getting started—Before going into the specifics of spraying, I should say a bit about safety. Spraying lacquer is extremely haz-

A good lacquer finish begins with a meticulously prepared surface. Above, Johnson repairs a minute flaw with a hot knife and a burn-in stick. Patches will later be matched with blending-powder stains.

ardous. The fumes are toxic and explosive and the lacquer itself highly flammable, as is the overspray. Consequently, I do all of my spraying inside a commercial-quality spray booth equipped with a high-volume fan that rapidly clears fumes and removes overspray from the exhausted air with a series of paper filters. The fan itself and the lighting fixtures inside the booth are wired with explosion-proof fixtures.

Obviously not everyone has access to a spray booth, but I strongly recommend that you buy one used or new or build your own, using the explosion-proof hardware available from wholesale electrical supply houses. On warm, windless days, it may be possible to spray small jobs outdoors in a sheltered area, but if you plan to do a lot of lacquering, a booth is a must. Before buying or building a booth, check with the local fire department to find out if zoning or safety laws prohibit spraying in your neighborhood. In California, where air-quality laws are strict, you should check with environmental authorities before setting up. Whether you spray inside a booth or outdoors, *always* wear a respirator designed to protect against vapors from organic solvents.

Before finishing can begin, the furniture must be completely assembled with everything fitted to perfection. There's nothing worse than rushing a piece through finishing only to discover that a door or drawer still needs a pass with a plane to achieve a perfect fit. It's sometimes difficult to know how much of a piece should be assembled before finishing. You might assume, for example, that the pigeonholes in the desk should be left in pieces, then assembled after finishing. In fact, it's not difficult to angle the spray pattern into each compartment. If finished as small parts, they'd be blown all over the place, take twice as long to spray and be bothersome to handle. Follow this general rule: assemble glued-up parts before finishing, but disassemble parts fastened with screws, hinges or bolts after they've been fitted and spray them separately.

I begin by meticulously sanding the wood with 100-grit garnet paper followed by 220 grit, keeping a close eye for imperfections and fixing them as I go. Sanding can be done by hand or with a pneumatic or electric orbital sander. Jumping from 100

grit to 220 grit may sound like heresy, but it works fine as long as the final sanding is thorough enough to remove any scratches left by the 100 grit. As I sand, I blow off the dust with compressed air to reveal any imperfections. Dents can be steamed out by placing a moist towel over the blemish and heating it with a household iron. If the ding remains, fill it with clear burn-in stick or five-minute epoxy mixed with a little sawdust. Later, the patch will need to be blended in.

Tight-grained woods, like the maple and purpleheart in the desk, don't need to be filled before sealing, but open-pored woods should be filled with paste filler. I use Star paste wood filler (available from Star Chemical Co., 360 Shore Drive, Hinsdale, Ill. 60521), which comes in pre-mixed colors and natural. To keep the filler from darkening the wood too much, spray a light coat of lacquer sanding sealer, then sand with 320-grit wet-or-dry paper before filling. After the filler has cured overnight, scuff-sand it with 320 grit before applying any more coats. At this point, you can begin thinking about a spray schedule.

Lacquer is a very versatile material and, depending on how you apply it, a tremendous number of finishing effects are possible, ranging from a subdued, low-gloss film hardly distinguishable from oil to a hard, mirror-like gloss. In any case, applying lacquer is a multi-step process that takes place over a few days or a week. I usually plan the schedule in my mind but it's helpful to note it on paper, especially for a beginner.

It's sometimes difficult to decide what degree of gloss a piece of furniture ought to have. I've found that in most cases, a dark piece looks good with a higher gloss. A satin finish on dark mahogany, for example, sometimes appears muddy, but a higher sheen brings out the depth. In most cases, any sheen looks good on light-colored pieces, but they're usually best treated with a satin or semi-gloss.

Lacquer manufacturers sell a range of glosses typically going from flat, satin, semi-gloss to gloss. To keep things simple, you can simply buy a gloss lacquer then add a flatting agent if you want a flatter sheen. Just mix up an experimental batch and spray it on a test piece.

The main disadvantage of flatting agents (and flat lacquers) is that they produce a softer, less resilient film. For vertical surfaces or unexposed areas that won't get much wear, this isn't a problem. Table and desk tops, however, need the added protection of a gloss. If glossy doesn't suit your tabletop, you can flatten the sheen, without giving up hardness, by rubbing with steel wool or pumice. It's perfectly acceptable, and often desirable, to use different gloss ranges on the same piece. Regardless of the final sheen I want, I use gloss for the base lacquer coats because it shows up defects that need fixing before applying the final coats.

Here's the spray schedule I came up with for the desk: Two coats of sealer, sand well with 320 grit; one coat gloss, touch-up any light colored patches; two coats gloss, do burn-ins, check for any remaining touch-ups; two coats gloss, sand well with 220 grit; two coats semi-gloss on base, drawer, knobs, bottom side of writing lid, sides and bottom of pigeonholes; two coats gloss on top of writing surface and top of pigeonholes. Allowing for drying times and rub out and assembly, this finish was accomplished over seven working days.

Counting the two sealer coats, there are nine coats of lacquer altogether. That may sound like a lot of finish, but lacquer has a relatively low solids content. After thinning the lacquer for spraying, it contains only about 10% solids. So, 90% of what you spray evaporates. Most lacquers are thinned 50/50 for spraying

Selecting spray equipment

The type of spray equipment you choose depends on how your shop is equipped and how much money you want to spend. If you already own an air compressor, you'll need to begin with a spray gun. These are available in two types: pressure feed and siphon or suction feed. In a pressure-feed gun, the fluid is forced through the spray nozzle by pressure introduced into a large container holding the finish. This type of gun is best suited for viscous finishes or production spray schedules. Siphon-feed guns work by drawing the material out of a small cup via a slight vacuum created by compressed air streaming through an orifice in the air cap. Siphon feeds are usually the best choice for small jobs involving light-bodied lacquers.

I like the DeVilbiss model JGA-502, a siphon-feed cup gun that costs about $120. Other manufacturers make similar guns, so you may want to shop around. The JGA-502 gun can be fitted with any number of needle, nozzle and air cap combinations, depending on the type of material being sprayed. For lacquer work, the Ex .070 fluid tip with a #80 cap seems to work best. A different cap and tip combination may be required for heavier or lighter liquids or in instances where compressor air output is limited.

In our shop, we have a 5-HP compressor that's more than capable of operating a spray gun and an air tool or two, all at the same time. Some people insist that you need a big compressor to run a spray gun but I disagree. Before we got the big compressor, I managed pretty well with a 1½-HP Sears Craftsman compressor. As long as your compressor is able to deliver about 5 to 7 cubic feet per minute at 30 to 38 psi, any siphon-feed gun should work fine. I operate my gun at 38 psi with the material-adjusting screw wide open (unscrew until you see the first thread) and the fan pattern adjusted to its full extent. This will give you a 6-in.-wide spray pattern at about 6 in. to 8 in. away, ideal for furniture.

Whatever the compressor, you need clean,

How a siphon-feed gun works

Air cap · Fluid tip · Fluid needle · Air cap · Fluid tip · Pattern adjusting valve · Material valve · Vent hole

The cup can be fitted with a plastic diaphragm to keep liquid from spilling out the vent hole when the gun is tipped.

As compressed air flows past the fluid tip, it creates a slight vacuum, siphoning the liquid from the cup through the fluid tube. The air cap can be adjusted to rotate the spray pattern. Air cap types, fluid tips and needle sizes can be varied to suit different liquids or to produce different patterns.

dry air. Water in the air supply is bad news. If there's enough, it can cause the lacquer to cloud over or blush. Oil blown past the compressor's pistons is equally troublesome. To avoid problems, pipe the compressor's output through traps designed to remove oil and water, and drain these traps regularly. We pipe air around our shop through ½-in. galvanized pipes. We've installed a trap right at the compressor's output and also at each air station in the shop. If you have only one trap, install it as far away from the compressor as possible to allow the air to cool and the water to condense. The compressor should be downhill from the air outlets so condensed water will run back into the compressor's tank where it can be drained. Our air system is charged at 120 psi. Regulators at each outlet adjust pressure downward, as required.

Recently, I discovered another type of gun that operates on low-pressure air delivered at high volume by a turbine pump instead of a compressor. These guns have been popular in Europe for about 20 years but are just catching on in this country. The system I use is made by Apollo Sprayers International Inc., but similar set-ups, all of which operate on the same principle, are available from several other manufacturers (see p. 95 for more). Where a conventional gun atomizes the material at about 35 to 50 psi at 5 to 7 cubic feet per minute of air flow, a low-pressure gun atomizes at 3 to 5 psi at 45 cfm. As a result, the gun doesn't blast the lacquer onto the surface but lays it down more gently, allowing more control with much less overspray and, ultimately, less waste. With less overspray, I can operate the booth fan at half-speed, which cuts noise and reduces my winter fuel bills. While these guns aren't cheap, they're less expensive and involved than buying and setting up a compressor system. —G.J.

---

unless stated otherwise by the manufacturer. I've learned to thin lacquer pretty much by eye, but if you want to be more scientific about it, you can buy a device called a viscosity cup. By timing how long it takes your thinned lacquer to drain through the cup, you can measure viscosity accurately. Cups come in different sizes but most lacquer manufacturers quote times for the No. 2 Zahn cup. The proper viscosity is important since it affects how well the lacquer sprays. If the lacquer is too thick it won't atomize properly, resulting in a spotty surface. If it's too thin, it's likely to run or be over atomized and produce a rough, gritty surface.

Much of the sealer and lacquer I use comes from a local company, Eastern Chem-lac (1080 Eastern Ave., Malden, Mass. 02148). For tabletops I use a higher-quality, more expensive sealer and lacquer from Mohawk (Perth Rd., Amsterdam, N.Y. 12010).

Setting up the booth—With the desk sanded and ready, I moved it into the spray booth, planning in my mind the most efficient way to spray it. I placed the pigeonhole assemblies on drying racks along the wall. A pair of sawhorses, bridged by two 8-ft. 2x4s, supported the writing lid, drawer and drawer bottom. For the writing lid, which must be finished extra carefully on both sides, I taped clean drawing paper around the 2x4s for padding. The drawer pulls were mounted on a stick so they could be

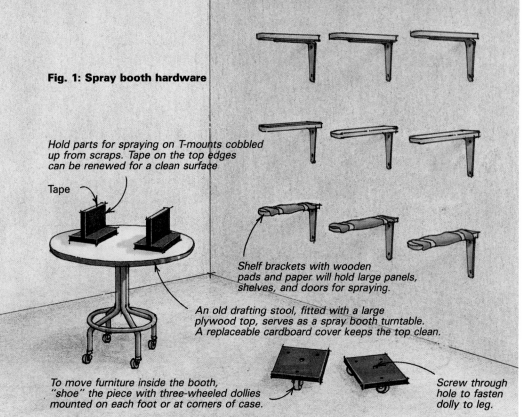

Fig. 1: Spray booth hardware

Hold parts for spraying on T-mounts cobbled up from scraps. Tape on the top edges can be renewed for a clean surface

Tape

Shelf brackets with wooden pads and paper will hold large panels, shelves, and doors for spraying.

An old drafting stool, fitted with a large plywood top, serves as a spray booth turntable. A replaceable cardboard cover keeps the top clean.

To move furniture inside the booth, "shoe" the piece with three-wheeled dollies mounted on each foot or at corners of case.

Screw through hole to fasten dolly to leg.

Spraying techniques

Parts to be sprayed are first positioned conveniently in the booth using fixtures shown in the drawing above. Small items like drawer pulls (upper right) are mounted on a scrap and sprayed separately.

With short, tight bursts and quick sweeps, it's possible to spray inside pigeonholes without getting a face full of overspray (right).

The gun's distance and rate of movement control the fullness of each coat, a technique best learned on horizontal surfaces.

Johnson sprays the insides of enclosed structures, like the drawer shown at lower right, before moving to the outside surfaces. The drawer bottom is propped up on T-mounts and sprayed separately.

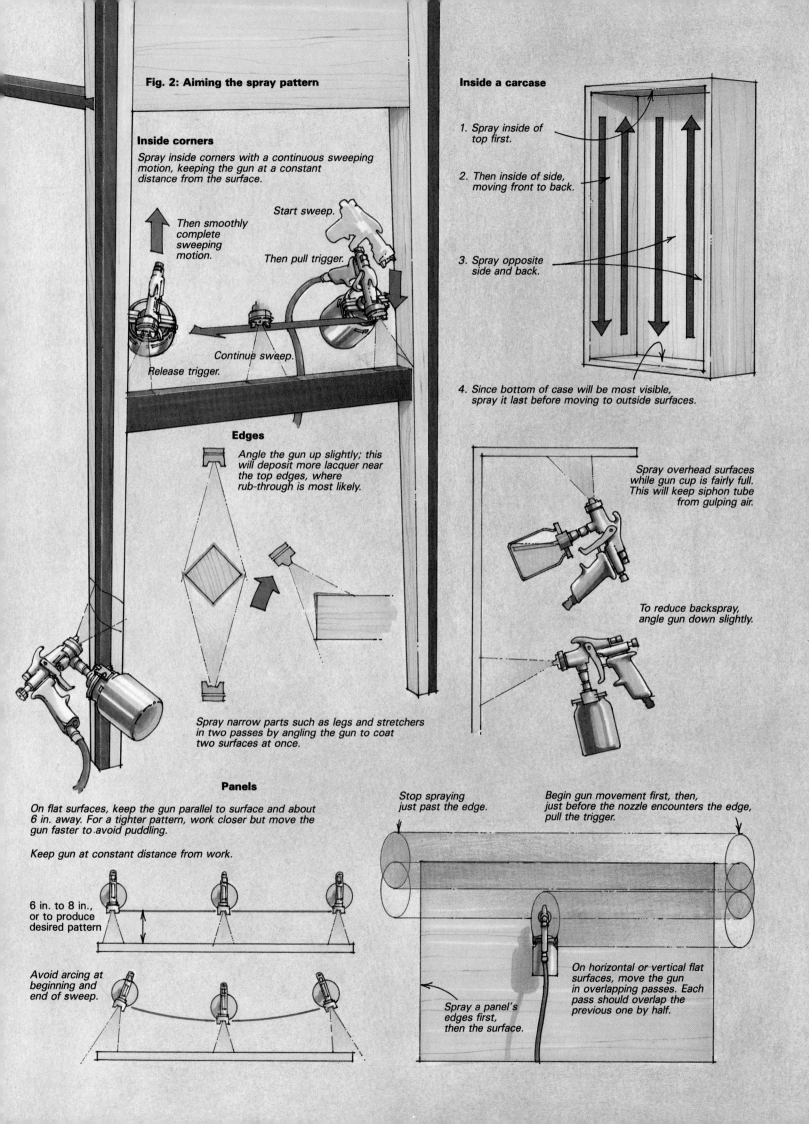

Fig. 2: Aiming the spray pattern

Inside corners

Spray inside corners with a continuous sweeping motion, keeping the gun at a constant distance from the surface.

Then smoothly complete sweeping motion.

Start sweep.

Then pull trigger.

Continue sweep.

Release trigger.

Edges

Angle the gun up slightly; this will deposit more lacquer near the top edges, where rub-through is most likely.

Spray narrow parts such as legs and stretchers in two passes by angling the gun to coat two surfaces at once.

Inside a carcase

1. Spray inside of top first.

2. Then inside of side, moving front to back.

3. Spray opposite side and back.

4. Since bottom of case will be most visible, spray it last before moving to outside surfaces.

Spray overhead surfaces while gun cup is fairly full. This will keep siphon tube from gulping air.

To reduce backspray, angle gun down slightly.

Panels

On flat surfaces, keep the gun parallel to surface and about 6 in. away. For a tighter pattern, work closer but move the gun faster to avoid puddling.

Keep gun at constant distance from work.

6 in. to 8 in., or to produce desired pattern

Avoid arcing at beginning and end of sweep.

Stop spraying just past the edge.

Begin gun movement first, then, just before the nozzle encounters the edge, pull the trigger.

On horizontal or vertical flat surfaces, move the gun in overlapping passes. Each pass should overlap the previous one by half.

Spray a panel's edges first, then the surface.

held up with one hand and sprayed from all angles. Each leg of the desk was screwed to a three-wheeled dolly, making it easy for one person to move it around.

Sometimes, if a piece seems particularly complicated to spray, I'll run through the motions of spraying without pulling the trigger. My objective is to formulate a pattern so I can coat the piece evenly without forgetting where I've already sprayed. It's important to learn to see the lacquer going on. This is best learned on flat, horizontal surfaces because it's easier to position yourself at the proper angle to a light source. I move the gun at a distance and speed that puts the lacquer down in one full, wet coat, producing a shiny, evenly wet film. Moving the gun too fast will leave a spotty, thin coat. Go too slow and you risk runs and sags, especially on vertical surfaces. Always start moving the gun before you start spraying, otherwise the lacquer will puddle.

I began the desk-spraying schedule by applying the first coat of sealer. Sanding sealer is a high-solids-content lacquer loaded with stearates which give it a dense, milky appearance. Sanding sealer serves several purposes. It contains additives that raise the grain slightly, creating a firm bond and good adhesion. The high solids content of the sealer helps fill the small pores and the stearates make it very easy to sand.

In spraying, the order of events is less important than gun position. The drawing on p. 93 gives some tips on how to position the gun. As a general rule, though, I begin with the more difficult, small surfaces and work toward the larger, flat surfaces. I try to do the vertical surfaces first, then the horizontal and if the piece has inside corners—a drawer, for example—I start there first, progressing toward the outside.

Closed structures, like the desk's pigeonholes or the inside of a cabinet, present special problems because the atomized spray tends to rebound, creating a blinding fog. To avoid this, I spray a quick burst with a slight sweeping motion in each compartment. With the inside coated, I work my way around to the outside taking care not to get too much lacquer on the front edges, which were partially coated when I sprayed the inside.

With double-sided pieces, like the desk lid, spray all four edges and then the top. Once the film has dried to the touch, flip the lid over and spray the back side. Be sure to spray both sides on the same day, otherwise you risk the wood warping from uneven moisture exchange. Spray the last coat on the surface that will show in the finished piece. Usually, applying two coats of sealer is sufficient.

Allow each coat of sealer to dry no less than an hour before spraying the next coat. On unimportant surfaces like backs and bottoms, you can "speed dry" the sealer by blowing it with air from the gun and second coating right away. An hour after spraying the second sealer coat, I sand the wood with 220-grit dry silicon-carbide finishing paper. If the sealer coat brings out an area that should have been sanded better, sand down to the bare wood, then spot spray the area with sealer. I blow the white powder left from sanding off with compressed air. Don't worry if a small amount of the powder remains, it will melt into the next coat.

After you've sanded the second coat of sealer, you can spray the first coat of lacquer, employing the same routine as for the sealer. I let the first lacquer coat cure overnight then tackle touch-ups the next morning. The first coat of lacquer will show up any light patches in the wood. These can be touched-up with blending-powder stains mixed in a paper cup with 2-lb.-cut shellac and padded or brushed on. Blending-powder stains are made especially for spot touch-ups and come in a very wide range of colors. I have a small touch-up kit from Mohawk that contains 21 one-ounce jars of blending powders. It has black, white, red, yellow and blue with many other assorted wood tones that can be mixed to match any tone I need.

With all the touching-up done and only clear lacquer to spray, I keep an eye out for any surface defects I missed. Everything gets two good coats of clear gloss lacquer, with at least an hour drying time between and no sanding. Burn-ins are done at this point, then two more coats. When this last coat is dry, about an hour, I do any burn-ins I missed earlier. With three coats of gloss on the surface, I feel safe leveling a burn-in without sanding through to the wood. Then the sixth and seventh coats are sprayed on and allowed to dry overnight before sanding everything with 220-grit wet-or-dry finishing paper. Sanding can be done by hand or with an electric or pneumatic orbital sander. After a quick dusting, the piece is ready for the final coats. By the time you spray the final coats, you will have acquired some experience with your gun (and the piece) so these coats should be your best.

In spraying the final coats, and perhaps even the base coats, you may encounter some problems. One of the most common is orange peel, a finished surface that looks slightly bumpy with the surface texture of an orange. Orange peel occurs when the lacquer is too thick or if it dries too fast, before it has a chance to flow out. To prevent it, make sure the previous coats are sanded well so the surface is level, then make sure the next coat is a full, wet one. If orange peel is severe, adding a drying retarder to the lacquer will slow the drying time and help the lacquer to flow out. On humid days, retarder will also allow moisture from the atmosphere or your compressor to escape before the finish dries, preventing a milky film called blushing, another common lacquer problem.

If you are refinishing an old piece of furniture, the lacquer may form small craters called fish eyes. Fish eyes are usually caused when traces of silicone from old furniture polish prevent the lacquer from adhering to the wood. Tools that have been sprayed with a silicone lubricant can transfer the stuff to new wood with the same miserable results. A few drops of an additive called fish-eye preventer usually clears up the problem. Once fish eyes have occurred, the best way to seal in the silicone is to mist on three very light coats of lacquer, followed by regular wet coats again.

Rubbing out the film—Once the final coat has dried overnight, you can begin rubbing out the finish. I first sand everything (except high-wear surfaces, which are treated differently) lightly with 600-grit wet-or-dry paper lubricated with water to which a small amount of dishwashing soap has been added. The purpose of this sanding is to level off any dust specks that may be caught in the lacquer. But if the surface feels smooth already, I go directly to rubbing with 4/0 steel wool lubricated with water and steel-wool lubricant. Mohawk calls its steel-wool lubricant Flat Lube, while Star sells one called Steel Wol-Wax. To use either type, dip the wool in the can, getting a small amount of lubricant on the pad. Squirt some water on the pad and start rubbing the surface in broad, long strokes with the grain. I start out rubbing lightly on an area, wiping the surface dry now and then to see how it looks. Usually, brisk medium pressure is all that's needed. If there's a small amount of orange peel in the lacquer, the rubbing will smooth it over. After rubbing, wipe everything down with a rag and clean water, then

A careful rubdown with wet-or-dry sandpaper, lubricated with soapy water, dislodges dust nits and levels the lacquer film. Johnson completes the job with 4/0 steel wool lubricated with a commercial steel wool lubricant.

Even a multi-coat lacquer finish is only a few thousandths of an inch thick so rub-throughs are inevitable. They're repaired by spot touch-ups with aerosol lacquer. Johnson has masked the desk's pencil trap (middle), and he uses thin cardboard to mask the aerosol's spray pattern (above).

immediately dry the surface with clean, soft rags.

The tops of tables, desks and chests require more attention because their surfaces are closely scrutinized. I sand these with 400-grit wet-or-dry finishing paper on a pneumatic straight-line sander lubricated with soapy water. Don't try this with an electric orbital sander, the shock hazard is too great. Hand sanding is fine. In either case, the final sanding with 400 grit should be done by hand. With the top sanded to my satisfaction, I dry it off with a rag and start rubbing with dry 4/0 steel wool. The beauty of dry 4/0 wool is that you can see exactly what's happening so you can achieve a nice even pattern. I rub the entire surface briskly, concentrating a few short strokes on the edge and then continuing the long strokes, always in one direction. The dry-wooling has brought the sheen up considerably from the 400-grit sanding, but it still appears a bit hazy. Satisfied that the sheen looks even, I add wool wax to a new piece of 4/0 steel wool, along with water, and continue with brisk rubbing.

This step goes very quickly. I check the sheen now and then by brushing some of the sudsy rubbing sludge aside with my thumb. When the sheen looks right, clean it up with water and clean, dry rags. A semi-gloss sheen is produced by thousands of minute scratches in the surface, so if you want a higher gloss you have to keep rubbing, making ever-finer scratches. Sometimes on dark woods, I rub the lacquer with rottenstone and water on a rag, bringing up a higher gloss. It's important to remember that if you didn't get an even scratch pattern with one of the coarser abrasives earlier, it will show up more as the gloss increases. For super-glossy finishes, I sand with 1,200 grit or finer instead of 400 grit, following up with automotive buffing compound.

When I had completed rubbing the desk, I noticed that I'd rubbed through the lacquer around the pencil trap on the lid. To fix this, I taped off the surrounding area then sprayed the trap with semi-gloss from an aerosol can. It's important to pull off the masking while the new lacquer is fresh, otherwise you risk tearing the film later. I also found minor rub-throughs near a couple of edges and touched them up by masking the aerosol spray pattern with a piece of thin cardboard. After the touch-ups had dried for an hour, I rubbed them lightly with steel wool and Flat Lube to blend them in. Rub-throughs that are too difficult to spray can be fixed with thinned lacquer applied with the side of a small touch-up brush or a small piece of dense felt.

One last dusting with a soft rag and the piece looks beautiful. Ship it.   □

Greg Johnson is a professional finisher and woodworker. He lives in Newton, Mass. Photos by author.

Sources of supply

Lacquers, sealers, thinners:
Grand Rapids Wood Finishing Co., 61 Grandville Ave. S.W., Grand Rapids, MI 49503.
Randolph Products Co., Park Place East, Carlstadt, NJ 07072.
H. Behlen & Bros., Inc., Route 30 North, Amsterdam, NY 12010.
Lee Valley Tools, Ltd., P.O. Box 6295, Station J, Ottawa, Ontario K2A 1T4.

Spray guns and pneumatic equipment (write for the location of the nearest distributor):
Binks Mfg. Co., 9201 W. Belmont Ave., Franklin Park, IL 60131.
The DeVilbiss Co., P.O. Box 913, Toledo, OH 43692.
W.W. Grainger, Inc., 5959 W. Howard St., Chicago, IL 60648.

Clearing the Air
A low-tech way to ventilate the small shop

by David W. Carnell

Airborne wood dust and toxic finishing vapors are less visible shop hazards than the snarling machines that can devour a finger. These substances are easily overlooked, yet they pose an equally serious health risk. They're dangerous to breathe, but it often takes years for the damage to show. If conditions are wrong, they might also cause an explosion.

Shop ventilation is the obvious solution to the dust and vapor problem. A good system should change the air often enough to dilute airborne-contamination concentrations to safe levels, leave as few stagnant areas as possible, and carry contaminated air away from workers to an exhaust fan. This kind of ventilation system, if set up effectively, minimizes the need for uncomfortable respirators.

The ideal air-cleaning system is actually several systems: local collection at each dust-producing machine, local exhaust fans in finishing and sanding areas, and a general exhaust setup to remove the dust and vapors that elude the other systems. The expense of the ideal system, however, forces most of us to compromise.

In a small shop where operations vary throughout the day, a general exhaust system is a good all-purpose solution. You don't need to spend a fortune on fancy equipment to get an effective general exhaust system. It can be as simple as an exhaust fan at one end of the shop and an air intake at the other.

Fans are rated by how much air they move, in cubic feet per minute (CFM). Here's how to find the size fan you'll need: Divide the shop volume (length times width times height equals volume in cubic feet) by 6 to find the fan rating in CFM required for 10 changes per hour; divide by 3 for 20 changes. For example, a shop with a volume of 1200 cu. ft. needs a fan rated at 200 CFM for 10 changes per hour, at 400 CFM for 20 changes per hour.

You can buy a commercially made industrial-size exhaust fan. Or you can hold down cost by using a window fan or a bathroom or kitchen exhaust fan instead. Since these are powered by shaded-pole motors that don't have brushes or internal switches, they don't produce sparks that could ignite fumes.

Window fans are good if they exhaust directly to the outside and move enough air to provide 10 to 20 air changes per hour for your shop. Bathroom and kitchen exhaust fans can feed into ducts to the outside that are up to 10 ft. long, but if you must use a longer duct, you'll need a centrifugal blower that develops enough power to overcome the pressure drop in the duct. These centrifugal blowers are often available from mail-order surplus houses at less than the retail price. A duct should be at least as large as the discharge opening on the blower. The duct should also be as straight as possible, since every bend will increase the pressure drop, and reduce the efficiency of the blower. The blower from a hot-air furnace or a central air conditioner (typically, 750-CFM to 1,000-CFM) can ventilate larger shops. Check heating and ventilation contractors for low-cost blowers from junked equipment.

Another requisite is an air intake large enough to supply the air that the exhaust fan is supposed to move. In its simplest form, this can be a hole in the wall, covered with a furnace or air-conditioner filter to keep outside dust from entering the shop. In most climates, though, incoming air must be heated in the winter. An electric space heater placed in the intake airstream will help some. Commercial air makeup units are available, but they're expensive: $500 to $700 for shops under 1,000 cu. ft. These draw outside air over a self-contained heating element before blowing it into the room. The type most practical for a small shop has electric-resistance heat, but gas- or oil-fired units are also made. If your shop is connected to a house that has steam or hot-water heat, you could place a radiator or a convector over the air intake. If you don't want to buy a heater, you can reduce the amount of heat you lose by running the exhaust fan only occasionally, when you're actually producing dust or vapors.

For thorough ventilation, it's best to make the air flow through the long dimension of the shop, so place the exhaust fan and the air intake at opposite ends of the shop, or at opposite corners of the long diagonal, as shown in figure 1. The exhaust fan should be located high in the shop wall; the air intake, low.

Check your ventilation system with a homemade smoke generator: Put two small plastic or paper cups side by side in a holder that can be moved around the shop without spilling, like the one shown in figure 2. Put two tablespoons of household ammonia in one cup, and the same amount of concentrated hydrochloric acid in the other. Swimming-pool supply houses and chemical supply houses sell concentrated hydrochloric acid (36% to 38%). Be careful, though. This acid is dangerous to handle, and eye protection is a must. Don't allow the ammonia and the acid to come in contact with one another, or they will react violently. The fumes coming from the two cups, however, will react to form voluminous white clouds of ammonium chloride that will show you how the air is flowing. Testing the airflow produced by your ventilation system is the only real check of how well it performs, so run the shop equipment and move about to simulate working in the shop. You may have to relocate your dust- and vapor-producing operations so that the contaminated air will be drawn away from the worker, toward the exhaust fan. When you're done testing, dispose of the ammonia and the acid separately, before they have a chance to spill or to eat through the cups. I suggest that you flush them separately down the toilet, or pour them separately down the drain, running lots of water after disposing of each.

Flammable dusts and vapors can, and do, create potentially explosive atmospheres in industrial operations. But it's unlikely that home workshops or small woodworking shops could develop the conditions required for such large-scale, room-sized explosions—you'd be driven out by the irritation

From *Fine Woodworking* magazine (July 1984) 47:60-61

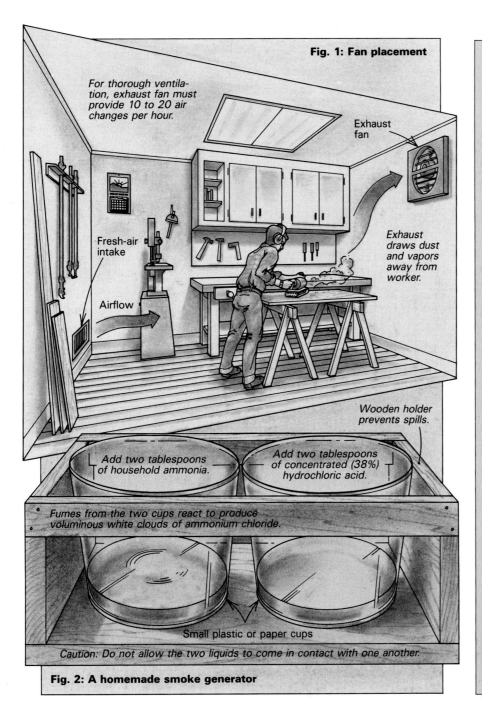

Fig. 1: Fan placement

For thorough ventilation, exhaust fan must provide 10 to 20 air changes per hour.

Exhaust fan

Fresh-air intake

Exhaust draws dust and vapors away from worker.

Airflow

Wooden holder prevents spills.

Add two tablespoons of household ammonia.

Add two tablespoons of concentrated (38%) hydrochloric acid.

Fumes from the two cups react to produce voluminous white clouds of ammonium chloride.

Small plastic or paper cups

Caution: Do not allow the two liquids to come in contact with one another.

Fig. 2: A homemade smoke generator

Sources of supply

Exhaust fans: McKilligan Industrial & Supply Corp., 435 Main St., Johnson City, N.Y. 13790; and Brodhead-Garrett Co., 4560 E. 71st St., Cleveland, Ohio 44105.

Centrifugal blowers and electronic cooling fans: Surplus Center, 1000-1015 West "O" St., PO Box 82209, Lincoln, Neb. 68501.

Flexible hose for ducts: Abbeon Cal, Inc., 123 Gray Ave., Santa Barbara, Calif. 93101.

Electric, gas-, or oil-fired air makeup units: Air Economy Corp., PO Box 29, Flemington, N.J. 08822.

Electronic air cleaners: There are two general types of units. *Electrostatic precipitators* contain a blower that draws dust-laden air over a high-voltage grid, where dust particles receive an electrical charge. When the charged particles pass over a collection plate with the opposite charge, they stick fast. Clean air blows out the other end of the unit. Units that are large enough for woodshop applications cost $2,000 and up. These are available from United Air Specialists, 4440 Creek Rd., Cincinnati, Ohio 45242; and Paxton/Patterson, 5719 W. 65th St., Chicago, Ill. 60638.

Negative-ion generators disperse negative ions into the air. The ions impart a negative charge to airborne dust particles, and the charged particles fall to the floor, where they can be swept up. ESI/APSEE units cost $595 and up, and are available from Electron Sciences, Inc., 3916 Riley St., San Diego, Calif. 92110.

before concentrations got that high. Flammable concentrations of vapors are 20 to 100 times higher (depending on the chemical) than the permissible exposure limits set by OSHA. The really fine dust from sanding operations is the only shop dust capable of forming an explosive mixture in air, but it has to be present at a concentration of 1 gram per cubic foot. It would take almost 2 gallons of airborne dust to reach that concentration in a 10-ft. by 20-ft. by 8-ft. shop.

It is possible, however, to have localized explosions. The many fires caused by solvent-based adhesives (such as contact cement), flammable finishes, or gasoline used indoors for cleaning (which is extremely dangerous) are examples of localized flammable vapor concentrations. Because the vapors are heavier than air, they collect near the floor, and they can be ignited by any spark or flame. Most gas-fired furnaces and water heaters have pilot lights that burn continuously, and these are especially likely ignition sources because the small draft through them draws the flammable mixture along the floor and ignites it. These pilots are also out of sight and easy

to overlook. Frequently, the vapors flash back to the solvent container and set it afire, too. Oil burners, sparking electric motors, lit cigarettes, even static electricity can ignite the vapors. Tool and machinery motors are all spark producers, as are most switches, except the mercury type. But none of these presents any hazard in a shop with good housekeeping and adequate ventilation.

Dust accumulation on shop motors that is dislodged when the motor is sparking can ignite and flash, so it's a good idea to regularly vacuum motors. If you dispose of sawdust by tossing it into a shop stove, you're inviting a violent combustion. It's better to put the sawdust in the trash can, or use it to mulch the garden. □

David W. Carnell is a chemical engineer, now retired, and an amateur woodworker. He lives in Wilmington, North Carolina. For information on ventilating a spray area, see the article "Improvising a spray booth" by David Shaw on p. 88.

Marbleizing Wood
Trick the eye with paints and glazes

by Beau Belajonas

The textured edge of a feather is a perfect paint applicator for duplicating the irregular veins and fissures of real marble. To achieve a realistic look, avoid symmetry in simulating the random patterns of line and color nature took millions of years to produce.

Not long ago, I walked into the United Methodist Church in Searsport, Maine, to hear a choir recital. The building's huge walls and trim were decorated with beautiful marble. I was immediately fascinated. I had to go over and touch the stone to see if it was real. It wasn't, of course; it was an excellent fake, created with paint on wood. But it was that moment of indecision—the mystery of not knowing if the stone was real or not—that got me hooked on faux ("false") marble and other decorative finishes.

Since the artist who painted the church had died long ago, I went to the nearest bookstore in search of information on false finishes. There, I found *The Art of the Painted Finish*, by Isabel O'Neil. Reading the book, I hadn't the slightest idea what O'Neil was talking about—three-color distressing, negative and positive space, casein paints and so on. By the time I finished the book, however, I'd made up my mind to find someone who could teach me how to marbleize wood—a decision that eventually led me to a two-week seminar at The Day Studio in New York City (see p. 100).

The techniques I'll discuss here are based on my experiences at the school and the marbleizing I've done since. Basically, a marbleized finish is created by applying layers of translucent and opaque paint, then blending them together with sponges, brushes, feathers, tissue paper and cloth to create patterns, the illusion of depth and a stone-like texture. The hard part is composing patterns that duplicate the subtle randomness and delicate colors that evolve in real metamorphic rock over millions of years.

This sense of composition is one of the most valuable things I learned from JoAnne Day, founder of the school that bears her name. While some practitioners feel that any finish that "kind of" makes you think of marble is adequate for faux fantasy, Day believes in creating real-looking marble. And the more marble I make, the more I'm convinced that Day is right—faux marble *should* look real. Even someone who has never created marble can instinctively separate the good from the second-rate, although they probably won't be able to say how they make the distinction.

Once I started studying real marble, I found that the differences in color and pattern—even within individual slabs—were amazing. I

From *Fine Woodworking* magazine (July 1987) 65:46-49

began collecting pictures and sketches of pieces I liked. During my stay in New York, I once stopped in the middle of the sidewalk in front of a bank on 34th Street to sketch a particularly beautiful serpentine marble slab. You'll need to do this kind of research before you begin your first marble. Get a piece of the real thing—or at least a good color photograph of a slab—to study and copy. Once you've done a lot of marbleizing, you'll have your own ideas. But, in the beginning, follow nature until you master composition.

As JoAnne Day described it, the best way to understand marble is to picture what Earth looks like to an astronaut orbiting the planet. Visualize the continents' shapes—North America, South America, Africa—and how they extend over the globe in a generally diagonal pattern. Marble is like the surface of the planet, but instead of continents, it has clouds of colors called "drifts" which extend diagonally across the slab, creating a feeling of mild movement. These clouds are punctuated with small cracks called veins, and larger cracks called fissures (see figure 1). It took millions of years of oxidation and geological change to create these patterns, but a skilled finisher can create the illusion of real stone with paint in just a few hours. In this article, I'll describe techniques for making a simple white Italian marble finish (see below) and a more intricate serpentine marble slab (see next page).

White Italian marble

A good way to learn marbleizing's basics is to create a slab of white Italian marble. You'll need white latex- or oil-based paint for the base coat, a few sticks of soft artists' charcoal (sold in art supply shops), mineral spirits and McCloskey glaze coat (McCloskey Varnish Co., 7600 State Road, Philadelphia, Penn. 19136 and local McCloskey distributors). For practice, start with a 2-ft. by 3-ft. sheet of plywood or Masonite and apply two or three coats of white paint as a base. Allow each coat to dry before applying the next. When the base is dry, you're ready to start creating drifts, veins and fissures.

When you draw the veins and fissures, forget that you've been trained all your life to think in terms of square, triangular and other symmetrical figures. To look real, faux marble can't be symmetrical. The only helpful pattern is the oval eye track shown in figure 1—an effort to make drifts, veins and fissures suggest an oval that draws in the viewer's eye. Drifts should be asymmetrical and reminiscent of continental shapes. Veins and fissures should be of different lengths and widths, suggesting the nonsymmetric pattern of a torn, twisted fishing net.

I use a slab of real marble as a model for inspiration. After applying charcoal veins, smudge parts of the veins with your hands and fingers, as shown in the near right photo. Since it mimics the cloud-like drifts of marble and blends the veins into the background, smudging will begin to make the faux look real. About 20% of the veins should be left unsmudged—to imitate the crisp surface cracks of real marble. At this point, the veins appear to be lying right on the surface but, later, the glaze coat will visually "bury" them in stone.

Next, apply the translucent white glaze. I use one part glaze coat, one part white paint and two parts mineral spirits, mixed in an aluminum-foil tray. Dip a section of a natural sponge into the glaze and dab it quickly over the veins (see photo, far right). Further passes with the glaze-laden sponge "sink" the veins, and the honeycomb of the sponge adds a subtle texture. The charcoal will blend with the glaze, creating depth and cutting the contrast between the veins and the undercoat.

Let the paint dry overnight, then bring the whole thing together by brushing on five coats of water-based varnish (available from Benjamin Moore & Co., 51 Chestnut Ridge Rd., Montvale, N.J. 07645 and its local distributors) in the direction of the drifts. The varnish will usually smooth any roughness in your finish, but, if you like, you can rub-out between coats with a piece of brown shopping bag. The paper is abrasive enough to eliminate minor rough spots, but not so aggressive as to rub through the finish. Don't worry about little pit marks; real marble is grainy and rocky, too. For the final finish, rub the varnish with 1500-grit wet/dry paper (available from auto-supply stores) lubricated with water, then buff with 0000 steel wool or 4F pumice stone and water. Polish the surface with automotive compound. I start with Meguiar's Mirror Glaze compound #3, followed by compound #20 (Meguiar's Mirror Bright Polish Co., Inc., 17,275 Daimler Ave., Irvine, Calif. 92710). The more gloss or finish you apply and the better you rub it down, the more lifelike the marble will appear.

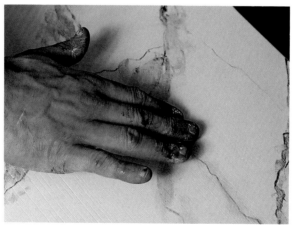

For realistic-looking marble, smudge the charcoal veins as shown above, left, to cut the contrast between the dark lines and the white base coat. Then, sponge a translucent glaze over the veins, above right, so they appear to sink into the ground coat.

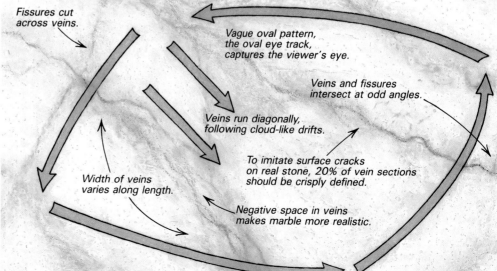

Figure 1: Trapping the viewer's eye

Fissures cut across veins.

Vague oval pattern, the oval eye track, captures the viewer's eye.

Veins and fissures intersect at odd angles.

Veins run diagonally, following cloud-like drifts.

Width of veins varies along length.

To imitate surface cracks on real stone, 20% of vein sections should be crisply defined.

Negative space in veins makes marble more realistic.

White paint—sponged on in cloudy, diagonal patterns called drifts—is applied to create the feeling of movement across the stone (above, left). A dry brush blends the drift with the green undercoat (above, right) to make the marble look more realistic.

Serpentine marble

After making a few white Italian marble slabs, you're ready to try a more elaborate faux marble. In serpentine marble, the basic techniques are the same, but you'll be working with more layers of paint and manipulating the glazes more.

Serpentine marble gets its name from the serpent-scale pattern embedded in the stone. I simulated the effect here by applying a black glaze over the drift, then smudging the glaze with a crinkled-up sheet of tissue paper (left photo, facing page) to form a scale pattern in the wet glaze. This smudging removes enough of the glaze for the white drift to show

through, heightening realism. (Always move from dark to light, or light to dark, in blending glazes. It helps soften contrast, creating a more realistic effect.)

Removing a glaze to cut contrast or reveal more of an undercoat is as important as applying paint. Finishers refer to a process as either "positive" or "negative." Applying paint is a positive application; taking paint off, or leaving an area untouched, creates negative space. At times, the distinction between the two methods blurs. When you start blending wet paint with a dry brush, it's a negative tool—the brush picks paint up. But as the

brush loads up, it begins applying paint and becomes a positive tool.

To create serpentine marble, begin by applying several coats of a dark-green paint as a ground. Use either latex- or oil-based paint for this process. Latex dries quickly—right on the sponge or brush on a warm day—so you might want to use an oil-based paint (I use Benjamin Moore GR110) until you master the techniques and can work quickly. If you use oil paints, let each layer dry overnight to ensure that top coats won't disturb your previous work.

When the base coat is dry, sponge on white paint (far left photo) to create drifts and to convey movement in the stone. The "drift" is made with a glaze concocted from one part oil-based paint, one part McCloskey Mirror Glaze and two to three parts mineral spirits. As you dab on the drift, remember the continents. The green base is the planet. The drift is like North America, thinning down into Central America, then expanding into South America. Across the Atlantic, create Europe drifting into Asia. After the continents are made, blend the wet paint into the dry green base with a dry sponge, brush (near left photo) or piece of towel or diaper. In some places, you'll want to remove all the white from a section of drift to create a green negative space. Work in a diagonal direction with rapid, piston-like hand movements. A fluid motion will help blend the colors, soften the drift and cut contrast. If you work too slowly, you'll start thinking about what you're doing and the work will become too precise. Remember, you're creating an abstract painting, so let your movements flow.

Two schools teach faux finishing

Clair Rubinroit of the Isabel O'Neil Studio-Workshop in New York City painted this Art Deco chest to look like straw marquetry.

Painted faux finishes were first recognized as art forms around the 16th century, when European artisans used paint to imitate such costly materials as marble and tortoiseshell. Since then, false finishes have lapsed in and out of fashion in both architecture and furniture. Over the past 30 years, however, the techniques have enjoyed an enormous revival, due largely to the efforts of Isabel O'Neil.

O'Neil, who became fascinated with the painted finish in the 1920s and 1930s, spent years in Europe researching techniques. In addition to duplicating Renaissance finishes, she experimented with contemporary materials and applications. Faced with declining health (she was stricken with amyotrophic lateral sclerosis—Lou Gehrig's disease) and a desire to share her skill, O'Neil opened her namesake school in 1955. She died in 1981.

I visited the Isabel O'Neil Studio-Workshop on New York's upper East Side in the Spring of 1986. The school is structured like a guild: students (amateurs and professionals alike) enter as apprentices and progress gradually to journeyman and then master status. Classes are small—three instructors, eight students—and hands-on. Students begin with a seven-week basic course covering surface preparation, striping, antiquing and color matching. A prescribed series of ten 14-week courses follows. Courses required to become a journeyman

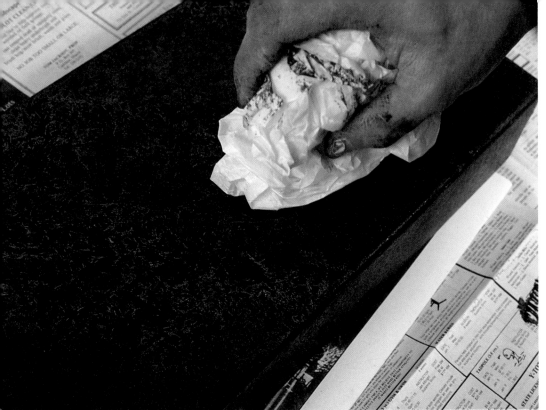

The scale-like pattern of serpentine marble can be created by working wet black glaze with crumpled tissue paper, left. The paper's crinkled facets pattern the glaze and allow the white undercoat to show through. A black/green glaze coat applied with a cloth, above, embeds the white veins in the stone.

Let the piece dry overnight before trying to create the serpentine texture. Sponge a black overglaze (one part black paint, one part glaze coat, one part mineral spirits) over the drift, then press the finish with a large sheet of crinkled tissue paper. The paper's crumpled facets are what creates the serpentine pattern. Dab the tissue paper into the paint, as shown in the photo above, until the green base coat and white drifts penetrate the glaze. You may have to go over the area several times.

Now, draw on white veins with a feather dipped in a solution of 20% white enamel paint and 80% mineral spirits. Turkey feathers (Cinderella's, 60 West 38th St., New York, N.Y. 10018) like the one you see in the photo on p. 98 make great applicators. You can paint with their edge or tip, and change the width of the line by varying the amount of pressure you use and the angle at which you hold the feather. You can draw very fine lines, then blend them while the paint is still wet. Since a box is a 3-D object, you'll need to carry veins down along its sides. I usually try to tie the sides into the top's pattern, but if that looks unnatural, I treat the sides as separate entities and give them serpentine patterns of their own.

Let the veins dry overnight, then apply another coat of overglaze (10% black, 10% green, 80% mineral spirits). This coat sinks the veins into the marble, as shown in the photo above. Once blended, this glaze coat also lowers contrast, increasing the illusion of depth. If the contrast between the veins and drift still seems too sharp, let the overglaze dry overnight, then glaze again. Finally, apply five coats of varnish and finish the box as discussed under "White Italian marble." □

Beau Belajonas is a wood finisher in Camden, Maine.

---

are gilding and leafing, casein, glazing and distressing, lacquer, marble, advanced gilding, inlay marble, color and varnishing, tortoise and, finally, lapis, porphyry and bamboo. Masters must also complete studies in malachite, *faux bois* ("false wood"), advanced lacquer, minerals and burnishing over another five-year period. In 1986, the seven-week basic course cost $350; 14-week courses ran $650 each.

The school also offers two-week-long accelerated summer workshops. The first of these covers the fundamental techniques of 18th-century painted finishes, including leafing, gilding and patination, and provides an introduction to decorative design. The second workshop covers glazing, simple and complex distressing, casein application, *gouache* shading tints and decorative design. The cost is $1,200 for the first two-week session and $1,300 for the second. For further information on these accelerated workshops, write the Isabel O'Neil Studio-Workshop, 177 East 87th St., New York, N.Y. 10128.

Since O'Neil's accelerated course didn't cover marbleizing, I looked around until I found a two-week-long workshop on stone and marble offered by the Day Studio in New York City and San Francisco. JoAnne C. Day—a design and color consultant, as well as former O'Neil journeyman and instructor—set up her school in 1974.

The Day Studio has three methods of teaching: seminars, workshops and videotapes. In a rented 12th-floor studio overlooking the Hudson River, the 20 or so other students and I involved in the two-week workshop were instructed by Day and an assistant in marbleizing techniques applicable to both architecture and furniture. We also had intense critiques.

I also attended a weekend seminar on metallic finishes—one of several Day offered in New York, Los Angeles, San Francisco and Atlanta last year at a cost of $400. In the same Manhattan studio, Day lectured while two assistants demonstrated the techniques. TV monitors offered around 100 students a clear, unobstructed view. Coupled with a lively give-and-take of questions and a comprehensive, step-by-step specification booklet, this format provided all the same information as a longer workshop—only the hands-on experience was lacking.

The Day Studio offers one-week or two-week workshops in New York and San Francisco. Topics include stone and marble glazing, gilding and metallics, wall glazing, *trompe l'oeil/* casein, color, wood graining, historical/architectural stenciling and a project workshop. Two-week workshops cost $1,500; one-week versions range between $750 and $850. The instructional videotapes cover wall glazing, marbleizing walls, stone and marble, semi-precious stones, tortoise and inlays. For information, write The Day Studio Workshop, 1504 Bryant St., San Francisco, Calif. 94103. —B.B.

Ebonized finishes created with chemical stains can blacken mahogany and other woods without obliterating the natural grain patterns. Here the author stains a piece of wood with a mixture of iron (from steel wool) and vinegar, then protects the finish with lacquer.

Ebonizing Wood
Home brew lets the grain glow through

by John McAlevey

I first started using ebonized or black finishes several years ago when I needed a dramatic touch for a special piece of furniture I was designing. Inspired after seeing the exhibit "The Art That Is Life: The Arts-and-Crafts Movement in America 1875-1920" at the Museum of Fine Arts in Boston, Mass., I returned to my studio eager to sit down and draw the multitude of lines, shapes and forms racing through my mind. I wanted to build something very special, something I would one day look back at and call a personal milestone in the way I approach my work.

The design I came up with was for a mahogany settee. I continued to refine the details of the piece in my mind as I worked on other furniture pieces that were already commissioned. Even after I began working on the settee—cutting joints, carving and modeling the top rail to flow into the side pieces and deciding on the spacing of the back slats—I continued to mull over ways to refine my design, especially how I would finish it. The settee was turning out to have a dramatic presence; the finish should be equally special.

While scraping and sanding away, my thoughts wandered back to a recent meeting of the League of New Hampshire Craftsmen's

wood jury: I'm one of the jurors who screens prospective members. Ruth Burt, director of standards at the League, had mentioned an ebonizing process where a precipitate, formed by mixing iron and vinegar, turned wood black. Since ebonized finishes were in vogue during the Arts-and-Crafts period, I though a black finish might be appropriate for my settee.

Taking a break from sanding, I hurried out to a nearby convenience store and purchased a bottle of cider vinegar. Since I didn't have any rusted iron nails around, I found some rusted pieces of steel behind the shop and put them into a plastic container with the vinegar. After an hour or so, expecting instant gratification, I dipped some mahogany scraps into the solution. Nothing happened. The following morning again nothing happened. Impatient, I tore up a piece of steel wool and threw it into the vinegar. I then left the solution to "cook" all day. Before leaving the shop that evening, I again dipped a scrap of mahogany in the solution. It quickly turned black. I next tried dipping a piece of red oak in the solution, and it also turned black.

The following morning, I sanded another piece of mahogany

From *Fine Woodworking* magazine (May 1989) 76:47-49

A strip of mahogany, above, illustrates how each coat of stain darkens the wood. The left side is plain; the center has one coat of the steel wool/vinegar mixture; and the right, three coats. Each coat is sanded with fine paper before the next coat is applied. Applying a coat of aniline dye on top of the stain darkens the wood even further (see p. 22 for more on aniline dyes).

Deft spray lacquer makes a good finish. Just make gentle overlapping passes with the spray, as shown, then sand lightly between coats.

and then brushed on my mix of steel wool and vinegar. As I applied the solution, the mahogany blackened. After the panel dried, the grain had raised, so I sanded the panel before reapplying the solution. I later experimented with white and red oak, walnut and cherry, and each of the woods darkened. The mixture didn't do much to improve poplar, but that's understandable. From my research and what others have told me, I've concluded that the mixture is most effective on woods containing tannin or other acids that react with the steel wool/vinegar mixture.

I've ebonized quite a few pieces since my first experiments, but my method remains pretty simple. I cut off the top of a ½-gal. milk container to create a plastic bucket. I rip up a pad of steel wool and add it to the container, to which I add 1 in. or so of ordinary vinegar, available from any supermarket. Then I let the mess sit for four or five days. You could use other kinds of iron, such as nails, but steel wool seems to work the fastest, and it just about dissolves in the vinegar, so you don't have much residue to worry about.

The stain will be strong enough after sitting overnight to turn most woods black, but the extra aging time just richens the color. I usually apply at least three coats, but after that additional coats are kind of overkill, giving the color a reddish cast. The greatest advantage of my mixture is that in addition to producing an even coat of color, the three coats don't obliterate the natural wood grain the way some commercial products do.

You can strain the mixture through a paper coffee filter, but I don't usually bother. The small amount of steel-wool residue that might end up on the wood is easily blown off with compressed air once the wood dries. I apply the stain with inexpensive throw-away foam brushes, available at any hardware store. Brush strokes aren't a problem here: The coats blend together very nicely and everything evens out. This even blending makes the mixture ideal for large pieces, such as a tabletop, as well as for smaller pieces, where you want to use color to accent the lines of the piece, such as the coffee table shown on p. 104.

I leave each coat on for 30 minutes, during which time it will soak in pretty well, depending on the heat and humidity. I then wipe off the excess and allow the wood to dry completely before sanding. Because vinegar is largely water, the stain will raise the grain of most woods, especially on the first coat. I usually sand the wood with 220-grit silicon-carbide paper. For subsequent coats, 400 grit is ample. You might be worried about the strong vinegar odor on the wood, but leave the piece overnight and the odor will dissipate.

One problem with chemical stains like this is that they don't penetrate very deeply. You can sand through the stain, especially near edges. To avoid any major problems, always do all your shaping and other edge treatments before applying the stain. In cases where I've sanded through, I touch-up with a black felt-tip pen.

If I want a black that's darker than the color produced by three coats of stain, I'll apply a coat of Solar-Lux nongrain-raising stain (Jet Black B503-1A46), available from H. Behlen & Bros. Inc., Route 30 N., Amsterdam, N.Y. 12010; (518) 843-1380. It's also available by mail from Woodcraft Supply, Dept. FW98, 41 Atlantic Ave., Box 4000, Woburn, Mass. 01888; (800) 225-1153 or (617) 935-5860 in Massachusetts, or from Garrett Wade Co. Inc., 161 Ave. of the Americas, New York, N.Y. 10013; (800) 221-2942 or (212) 807-1757 in New York. This stain also doesn't seem to obliterate the grain. I don't like using the stain by itself, though, because it doesn't produce the same sense of richness and depth I get with the three coats of the steel wool/vinegar mixture.

Lacquer finishes work well over the stains; I generally use an Apollo low-pressure spray system (Apollo Sprayers International Inc., 11577 Slater Ave., Unit H, Fountain Valley, Calif. 92708; 714-546-3100). You can also get good results from an ordinary can of Deft Semigloss Clear Wood finish, available at most hardware and department stores. The key here is to relax. If you get uptight, you'll make a mess, just as you would if you panicked during a glue-up. Just make gentle overlapping passes, as shown in the photo above, right. Sand between coats with 400-grit paper, then spray again. You can spray up to three coats with no problems, and the finish will be pretty durable.

To rub out the lacquer, I use 0000 steel wool, lubricated with water and ordinary grocery-store yellow soap. Always work with the grain; once the suds get going, the soap will work like rubbing compound. Rinse off the piece, dry it and then finish with a coat of paste wax, such as Minwax. □

John McAlevey designs and builds furniture in Warner, N.H.

Black finishes for dramatic accents

Small tables can be attractive and functional accents in any home. And for the small-shop woodworker, they can provide a satisfying and profitable introduction to production runs on a modest scale. The table shown here is a fairly simple design, but it is striking, especially with the strong lines created by the ebonized components.

Mahogany is used throughout. I plane all the stock and cut it to the dimensions shown in the drawings at right; the legs are the only tricky part. I rough-cut them on the tablesaw, then refine their outer edges to the curve, as shown in figure 1A, with a block plane, spokeshave, scraper and pad sander. Before shaping these 1⅞-in.-thick pieces, I cut all the joints.

I cut all the mortises with a plunge router, using a simple box jig to hold the stock and guide the tool. The jig looks like a miter box but with end stops to set the length of the mortise and a reference surface for the router's fence. You can clamp the workpiece to the box and rout the mortises easily and accurately. You can also chop the mortises by hand.

For the legs, I first cut the mortise for the lower cross brace while the stock is still rectangular, to make it easier to clamp the piece to the mortising jig. The next step entails ripping the corners of the outside edge of the leg, as shown in figure 1A. This eliminates much of the waste, making the final shaping much quicker. Finally, I rip both inside corners at a 45° angle to mate with the tenoned rails that will support the top frame. One advantage of this miter box is that you can use shaped blocks to hold irregularly shaped pieces at any angle while they are being mortised.

After shaping the legs as described above, I cut the tenons on the apron pieces and cross braces, and the lap joints on the braces. Again, use your favorite technique: router, tablesaw or handsaw and chisel. The corners of the top frame are simple butt joints reinforced with a plate joiner and small biscuits. Screws that run up through the apron, as shown in figure 1, secure the legs. Before assembling the frame, rabbet its inner edge with a straight router bit or dado blade to accept the ¼-in.-thick tempered glass top.

After all the pieces are glued up, I let the joints dry overnight and then finish-sand the table with a pad sander. Finally, I ebonize the wood as described in the main article. —J.M.

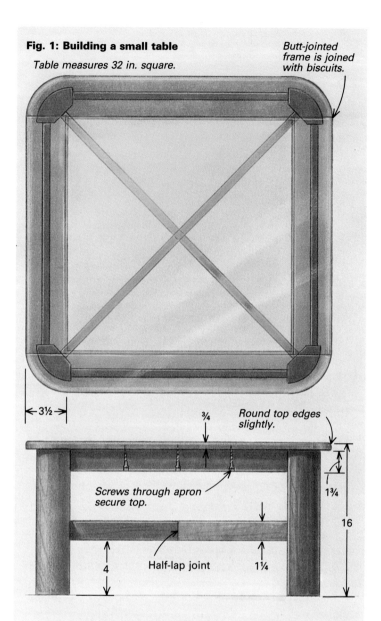

Fig. 1: Building a small table

Table measures 32 in. square.

Butt-jointed frame is joined with biscuits.

←3½→

¾

Round top edges slightly.

Screws through apron secure top.

1¾

16

Half-lap joint

4

1¼

Fig. 1A: Full-size corner

Step 1: Cut lower mortise while leg is square.

Step 2: Rip off wedge at each corner to facilitate final shaping.

Step 3: Rip 45° bevel and rout mortise.

Black ebonized finishes create a dramatic accent and highlight the lines of small pieces like the table above. The distinctive curved legs are first roughed out on a tablesaw, then refined with a block plane, spokeshave, scraper and pad sander.

Photo this page: Timothy Savard, Photoworks; drawing: Bob La Pointe

Stenciling a Boston Rocker
Color with powdered metals

by Beau Belajonas

Few early-American classics can compare with the function, comfort and beauty of the Boston rocker, with its graceful, smooth-flowing lines and colorful painted finish. Chairmakers in the early 1800s built the chairs from whatever hard or soft woods they had, rubbed on layers of red and black paint to make the chair look like mahogany or rosewood, then decorated this painted finish with colorful striping and stenciling. Many chairs were stenciled by sprinkling metallic powders on a tacky varnish base, which is the technique I'll describe here.

Most of the chairs I see as a finisher and restorer in Camden, Me., are basket cases, faded and worn and just hinting of the brilliance of their original finish. Antique buffs or museum curators wouldn't think of restoring these pieces. Their antiquity, and value, is obvious. But if you're more concerned with enjoying the original beauty of the chair, or if you'd like to try stenciling on your own work, the process isn't hard to learn.

In restoration, the first step is to clean the chair, trace the original stencils, and make notes and sketches about everything you want to re-create in the repaired chair—color, measurements, graining, and so on. As a memory check, take a few color photos. Repair structural problems, then strip away the old finish and repaint the chair before reapplying the stenciling and other decorative touches.

Water and paper towels will take off enough dirt and grime to let you clearly see the artwork. You can also use mineral spirits, but be careful not to remove the worn stencil. Set the chair on its back under a bright lamp. Place a piece of Supersee Acetate (available from most large art supply shops), matte side up, over the stenciling and trace it. You may not be able to see all of the stencil clearly, but work with whatever you have. Most patterns are symmetrical, so you can take segments from both sides of the centerline to come up with one complete half-pattern. If you can only make out half a melon, sketch in the other half. Don't be afraid to add your own creative touch—the stencil doesn't have to be an exact copy. After tracing one half of the stencil, fold the acetate in half and trace the pattern onto the blank half. When you unfold the acetate, you will have a complete pattern. If you don't have an original, you can scale-up the patterns shown on p. 109, which I used for the chair shown at right.

Stripping is the messiest part of restoration. Spread newspaper on the floor, wear rubber gloves, and make sure you have good ventilation. Stripper fumes can be hazardous. Cover the chair with a semi-paste remover (I use Zip Strip Paint and Varnish remover made by Star Bronze Co., Alliance, Oh.) and let it set for 10 minutes. Then, dip a half-pad of 0 steel wool into a bowl of lacquer thinner and scrub the softened finish. Wipe the chair clean with

A subtle interplay of red and black paints, brilliant yellow striping, golden turnings, and an ornate vine-and-fruit arrangement stenciled onto the crest rail with metallic powders, enhances the comfort and graceful lines of this traditional Boston rocker. Stenciling requires careful preparation and a steady hand, but isn't a difficult process to learn.

Photos: Kip Brundage

paper towels, then go over it again with paper towels dipped in clean lacquer thinner. Finally, sand with 180-grit paper.

Now you're ready to paint. The trick is to streak on several thin layers of different colors, so that the interplay of colors creates the impression of grain, wear or age. For an undercoat, I like oil paint because of its toughness, and I prefer the deep earth-tone reds used on the original chairs. The color is important because the undercoat will show through on parts of the chair. I've had good results with the brick-red "Old Village" enamels (Salem Brick or the New England Red). You can also tint any red paint with raw umber and yellow ochre artists' oil colors.

Thin the paint with mineral spirits so it'll brush on easily and be a little streaky. I sometimes leave a little wood showing, or rub off color with steel wool, especially on the arms, back spindles and other heavy-wear areas. If you like the aged feeling created by this light coat, apply a coat of black. If you want more red, then apply another thin coat after the first coat dries.

I put a fairly opaque coat of black on the crest rail to set off the gold stencil, but I streak it over the red on the chair rungs and legs to make tiger-striped grain patterns. After thinning two parts flat black paint (I like Benjamin Moore's Flat Black Satin Impervo Enamel) with one part mineral spirits, I begin at the bottom of the chair, with a 2-in.-wide brush, and work my way up. By the time I get to seat level, my technique is in high gear.

Before you begin painting the rockers, legs and rungs, make a graining comb, as shown on the facing page, top right, by cutting notches in a stiff piece of belt leather. After painting the undercarriage, remove the paint from your brush with paper towels. Then, dry-brush the pieces you've just painted to give the paint a thin, worn look. Dry your brush often. As the paint begins to set, drag the notched graining comb up-and-down on the runners, and back-and-forth on the legs, as shown on the facing page, center right. If your graining runs, you have not dry-brushed the black paint enough.

Instead of graining the back spindles, crest, arms and seat, I dry-brush these parts without revealing too much red. The arms and the middles of the back spindles can be rubbed with paper towels or crumpled newspapers to give the illusion of wear. Another variation is to wait until the paint dries a little and scratch it with steel wool. Periodically stand back and look at your work. If you think more red would look better, rub off more black. If too much red shows, add some black. When you're satisfied, let the graining dry overnight before sealing it with 3-lb. shellac cut 1-to-1 with alcohol. Finally, apply a coat of satin varnish over the dry shellac to protect your work. Don't varnish before sealing the chair—the varnish will pull off some of the black paint.

To duplicate the yellow seats traditionally found on Boston rockers, draw in the seat with a white China marker (sometimes called a grease pencil). An ordinary yardstick, which is about an inch wide, is a good guide. Place the yardstick along the inner edge of the arm spindles and draw a line along the stick's inside edge. You can just paint over the line—the China marker doesn't interfere with paint adhesion. Many of the seats are scooped, so you can follow the curved line along the back without a yardstick. Generally, the line is ½ in. to 1 in. behind the last arm spindle. The front edge should be 2 in. (the width of two yardsticks) before the front arm spindles.

After drawing in the seat, mix some flat yellow paint (I like Benjamin Moore) with white oil color to make a straw yellow. Thin this soft yellow with mineral spirits and paint in the seat. You'll probably need two coats. With a 1-in. brush, carefully paint along the line, working a section at a time using your other

hand as a guide (facing page, bottom left). If you go over the line, wipe the paint toward the seat with your little finger. The edge isn't critical because you will be putting a stripe around it later. If you don't want to risk doing the job freehand, block out the seat with masking tape. Brush away from the tape to avoid forcing paint under it. If paint seeps under the tape, scrape it away with an X-acto blade. If you scratch through the black to the red, it'll just add to the "aging." After the yellow has dried, seal it with white shellac cut 1-to-1 with alcohol.

In about an hour, make a glaze of yellow ochre and raw or burnt umber, mixed with a solution of equal parts varnish and mineral spirits, and brush it over the yellow seat. Streak the glaze with a paper towel or dry brush (facing page, bottom right). Let the glaze dry overnight, then seal it with satin varnish.

Next, take your acetate tracing of the old stenciling and recopy it onto tracing paper. It's better to work from tracings because you must make individual stencils for various parts and colors of the design and don't want to destroy the original. Besides, I think my patterns get better each time I trace them. Tracing is easier on a light table, which you can make by mounting two fluorescent bulbs in a frame supporting a piece of translucent white Plexiglas.

You'll need the five separate stencils shown in figure 1, a master stencil for the end scrolls and grapes, which provides a layout guide for the other stencils, and stencils of the two leaves with veins (left and right), melons (left and right), pineapple and basket lattice work. You'll also need an outline tracing of the basket, which will be painted red. To help you align the small stencils with the master, look for places where you can put in keys or reference marks. On the basket, for example, I used a couple of grapes, as shown. You can line up the leaves, melons and pineapple by eye, so no keys are needed.

After transferring the tracings onto stencil paper (available from art supply shops), cut out each design with a #11 X-acto knife. A piece of glass, 18 in. by 24 in., placed on a light table makes a good roomy work surface. The extra light will help you see better and cut much finer details. Cutting a stencil is a two-handed job. If you're right-handed and cutting a circle, for example, hold the knife with your right hand and slowly turn the stencil paper with your left hand. If you're left-handed, turn the paper with your right. This motion will give you a smooth, accurate cut. Cut the master stencil first, just the grapes and the end scrolls. Next cut the basket lattice and trace the basket outline onto another piece of paper. Then cut the remaining stencils.

Once all the stencils are cut, tape the basket outline to the center of the crest rail. Using white carbon paper, trace the outline onto the rail. Paint the basket red and let it dry. The next day varnish the crest rail and the roll at the front edge of the seat. The varnish acts as an adhesive for the metallic powders, non-precious metals in a range of colors (see p. 109 for sources of supply). Just lay on a thin coat, lightly pulling it out in one direction.

While the varnish is drying, tap about a half-teaspoon of each metallic powder you plan to use onto small pieces of velvet. Silver or copper powders can be used along with the gold. For example, grapes done in silver, flowers in copper, leaves in gold. Use clean pieces of velvet for each color. After 20 to 30 minutes, check the varnish by lightly touching it with your fingertip. When the varnish feels tacky, but you don't leave fingerprints, you can stick the master stencil on it, centered, as shown on p. 108, bottom left.

Wrap a clean strip of velvet around your fingers to make an applicator for spreading the powder. I do the lighter colors first, then apply golds and other darker colors. Use the nap of the velvet to pick up some powder from the piles you previously laid

From *Fine Woodworking* magazine (January 1986) 56:43-47

Belajonas paints a thin, brick-red undercoat on the chair, above, which has already had its old finish stripped off. Before adding a coat of black paint, he makes a graining comb by cutting different-sized notches into the edge of a 3-in. long piece of belt leather, above right. By gently dragging the comb up-and-down through the still-wet black paint on the rungs, right, he removes enough of the black to let the red show through as a tiger-stripe grain pattern.

Belajonas uses his hand as a brace, above, to support his brush as he paints the center part of the seat yellow. For a mellow, aged effect, he adds a brownish-yellow glaze over the yellow, then streaks it across the width of the yellow seat with a crushed paper towel, right. He lets the glaze dry overnight, then seals it with satin varnish.

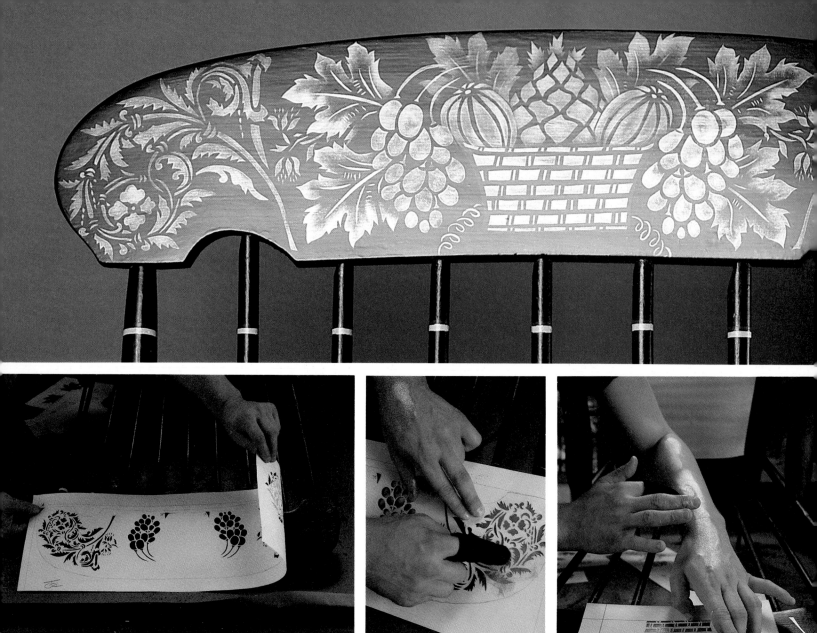

Five stencils are used to apply the metallic powders to create this traditional floral scene on the black crest rail. After applying varnish as an adhesive for the powders, Belajonas locates the master stencil by holding the pattern at the end of the rail, above left, as he centers it over the painted basket. To apply the powders, he wraps velvet around his fingers to make an applicator and dabs the powders onto the tacky varnish under the stencil, above center. A light touch is needed to shade in the powder for a lifelike three-dimensional look. After picking up powder with his applicator, right, he removes the excess from the velvet by tapping it on his arm. He stripes the spindles freehand, far right, by using one hand as a steady rest.

out on the velvet pieces, then rub the velvet applicator on the back of your hand or forearm, to remove the excess. Start rubbing lightly over the stencil to gradually shade on the powder. Work in from the edges so the powder won't get underneath the stencil. It's okay to let a little black show through. If you are doing a leaf, make the tips strong, then fade them out toward the middle. Similarly, a peach or melon should have dense edges that fade in the middle. The black showing through creates a nice soft, three-dimensional look—delicate and aged.

After applying the powder, take a soft cloth and very gently wipe any excess powder before lifting one end of the stencil and carefully peeling it away. If you don't like the result, immediately wipe off the gold powder and tack varnish with mineral spirits and try again. If it looks good, let it dry a day, then gently wash the stenciled areas with water to remove any excess powder. Powder stuck in the wrong place can be rubbed off with 000 steel wool. Finally, varnish over your work and let it dry. Repeat the process for the roll of the seat.

The final decorative touch is to add horizontal stripes around the back and arm spindles, where you feel a touch of color is needed. To stripe the back spindles, measure 1½ in. to 2 in. down from the rail and mark with a China marker. Pour some yellow paint in a little tin (clean cat food cans are great) and thin with turpentine, which makes a smoother mixture for striping than mineral spirits. Soften the yellow with white and raw umber, if you wish. Apply an opaque stripe with a #2 quill brush. Two coats are usually needed, but you can dab on the second coat 15 minutes after the first. After the yellow has dried, put a green stripe next to it. You can soften the green enamel with raw umber.

Now put a stripe around the yellow seat. The seat outline is usually guide enough, but you can mark it out with a China marker. This time add raw sienna to your thinned yellow to make a brown yellow. Run a stripe along the edge of the yellow seat with a 0 or 00 sword-striper brush. Use long strokes—the quicker the stroke, the straighter your line. Wipe off mistakes with your finger.

You may want to put gold on the ball-like turnings of the chair.

Stencil patterns

Crest rail

Trace basket outline, then paint red.

Master stencil is also layout guide for locating remaining stencils.

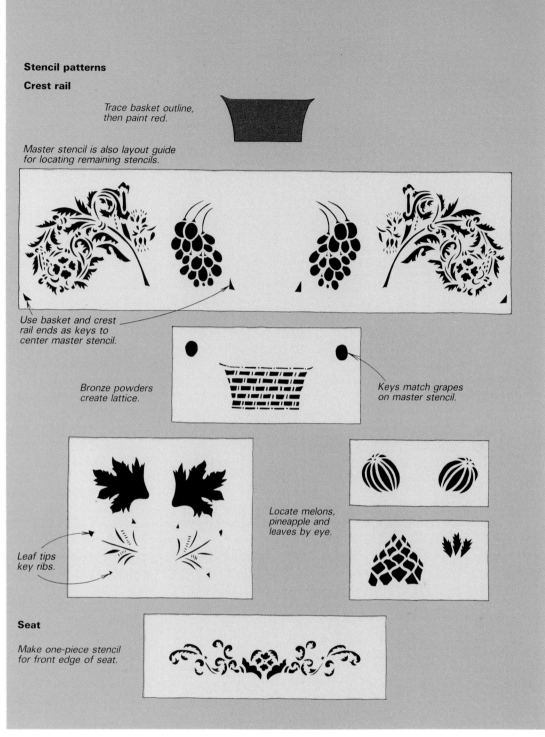

Use basket and crest rail ends as keys to center master stencil.

Bronze powders create lattice.

Keys match grapes on master stencil.

Leaf tips key ribs.

Locate melons, pineapple and leaves by eye.

Seat

Make one-piece stencil for front edge of seat.

The easiest way is to paint on Decorator's Enamel Antique Gold Paint, but the color won't exactly match your stenciling. You also can mix varnish, turpentine and just enough chrome yellow to make a semi-opaque color. Apply this with a #12 flat brush or #6 quill. When tacky, apply gold powder with velvet or a soft brush. You may also want to put a green or yellow stripe on the chair rungs. After the stripes and gold paint have dried, I protect the entire chair with a coat of satin varnish, which I usually tone down with raw umber, then wax the chair.

When American artists did these chairs 100 years ago, they added their own personality and style to their work. Don't be afraid to continue the tradition by expressing yourself a little, unless you are trying to do an exact reproduction. As art continues to move into new eras, it keeps many of the old techniques, but the personalities of the new artists can create new traditions. □

Beau Belajonas is a stenciler, grainer and furniture restorer in Camden, Maine.

Sources of supply

Metallic powders are available by mail order from Lambert Company, 920 Commonwealth Avenue, Boston, Mass. 02215, and Woodfinishing Enterprises, 1729 North 68th Street, Wauwatosa, Wis. 53213.

Finishing supplies are available from Behlen, Route 30 North, Amsterdam, N.Y. 12010.

Beaute Satin Creme Furniture Wax may be ordered from Roger A. Reed Inc., 165 Pleasant Street, PO Box 508, Reading, Mass. 01867

Stenciling supplies are available from Crafts Manufacturing Company, 72 Massachusetts Avenue, Lunenburg, Mass. 01462, and S. Sleeper Company, Route 107-A, East Kingston, N.H. 03827

Driftwood Finishes

Weathered wood in an hour or two

by Jim Cummins

hen I got into the picture-framing business 19 years ago, most framers could dash off a variety of wood finishes. One of the most popular was the barnwood or driftwood finish, usually applied to common pine. Fresh from the lumberyard, kiln-dried pine can be textured and colored in an hour or two to imitate wood that has gracefully weathered 20 years. I've seen the same finish used on trim moldings and on rustic indoor furniture, on hardwoods and softwoods both.

If you're framing a picture, the first step is to make a suitable molding for the frame. I make my moldings on the tablesaw. The next step, for a driftwood finish, is to texture the wood. Then you add layers of contrasting stain and paint so that the darker color ends up in the low spots, the lighter on the high. You can vary the look quite a bit, so the final result may be dark or light, warm or cool.

Most framers today buy pre-finished driftwood moldings, and many of these don't look like wood at all. Some are garish, others dismal. I believe this happens because manufacturers try to imitate each other's successful products instead of imitating wood, and each imitation gets further from the truth. Yet a good driftwood finish isn't difficult. All you have to do is mimic nature's own weathering.

Texture—Wood has hard grain and soft grain in alternating layers. When wood ages, the soft grain on the surface breaks down and disappears, leaving a craggy texture. Finishers duplicate the process by removing the soft grain with a wire brush. I have a 6-in. dia. wire brush mounted on the shaft of a bulky, old ⅙-HP motor. When I have a lot of frames to do, I haul the motor out and clamp it to my workbench. But for just a frame or two, I usually use a straight wire brush or chuck a

small round one in my electric drill. In addition to the brush, I sometimes use an old table fork to incise long, wandering scratches that imitate surface checking. If you want a few wormholes, try an awl. Be sure to sand any sharp edges, as these break down quickly in natural aging.

If the surface gets fuzzy, I either sand it with a coarse grit or burn off the splinters with a propane torch, depending on whether I want to keep the wood light or allow it to become darkened by charring.

Color and value—Natural wood *color* ranges from hot reddish-browns to cold bluish-grays. Any color also has *value,* the degree of lightness or darkness it would have if seen in a black-and-white photograph. The final color and value of a driftwood finish can be anywhere in the natural color and value range.

Nature's palette is broad, but it's used with discretion. One side of a weathered board may age warm and very dark, while the other side is a pale silvery gray. But you're not likely to find such extremes on any one side exposed to the same conditions. This is a guideline for a successful driftwood finish: choose similar colors and values for both the bottom coat and the top coat. Don't try to put a cold gray top coat over a hot brown base—you'll end up with a finish that's visually "jumpy." And remember that a wood surface ages dark or it ages light, not both at the same time.

My general advice is that warm pictures look best in warm frames, and light pictures look best in light frames. Avoid too much contrast. As a rule, choose warm or neutral tones rather than cool ones, except for very cold pictures. But if you're planning to hang a warm picture on a cool wall, pick frame colors that will provide a transition, or the picture may look out of place.

To my eye, the most beautiful finishes,

whether light or dark in value, occur when one color is slightly warm and the other slightly cool. If neither is extreme, the two harmonize and sparkle.

Painting—The picture framer's standby used to be casein paint sold in quarts and gallons, but I haven't been able to get any for years. Milk paint, which dries too hard, is a poor substitute. I've tried artists' casein paints in tubes, but they aren't formulated to flow well from a large brush, and I mostly use them just for tinting. So, keeping up with the times, I've turned to latex paints, poster paints and watercolors. Almost anything will work. A wide range of grays can be made by mixing white or off-white latex with raw umber and yellow ocher artists' colors, either acrylic or casein. Watch out for black, though—it's deceptive. If you use any in making a gray, the color may look warm while wet, but it will dry cold.

The sample in the color photo was made with one coat of Minwax stain, followed by latex paint tinted with artists' acrylic color. I applied the stain to the textured wood, and blended in the latex while the stain was still wet. This simultaneously lightened the dark stain undercoat and darkened the latex coat, to reduce the contrast and bring the two closer together. The wet-on-wet method is somewhat hit-or-miss and takes some practice. But there's a more methodical way that guarantees good results every time: Give the textured wood a thin toning coat of paint or stain. When that's dry, seal it with a thin coat of shellac. When this is dry, apply a top paint coat that contrasts slightly with the base coat. Remember the advice about color and value, and choose colors that won't fight with each other.

When the top coat is dry, steel-wool through it, down to the base coat. The top coat will remain in the valleys, while

Color photo: White Light

the base coat peeks through on the high spots, accentuating the grain. The shellac between the two coats will provide some luster and highlights.

That's really all there is to it, but here are some variations of the technique. After applying the base coat and the shellac sealer, lightly wax the high spots of the frame before you apply the top coat. While the top coat is still wet, use a rubber squeegee to force the paint down into the unwaxed fissures and wipe it from the waxed high spots at the same time, saving yourself the steel-wooling step. You could also use a dry-brush technique to apply the top coat: Wet the brush as usual, then spread the paint on a sheet of newspaper until the brush is nearly dry. Now lightly drag the brush over the frame so it hits just the high spots.

Fine-tuning—Now is the time to step back, compare the result with what you were aiming for, and add whatever last touches seem necessary. At the very end of the process, you can introduce a little strongly contrasting color and value to produce visual tension. If a warm brown finish looks dull, add a tiny bit of light green to the high spots. Or add orange to cool gray. But if the result draws attention to itself, it's too much. A decorative finish should sing, not shout.

If you're working on a picture frame, you can use children's crayons for the highlights. On a finish that needs more durability, you can use oil paints, barely touching the high spots. Coating the entire job with wax will make the top coat more transparent and thereby make the finish more uniform in color. Keep in mind that the finish will be seen, usually, from several feet away. □

Jim Cummins is an associate editor at FWW. His shop is in Woodstock, N.Y.

From *Fine Woodworking* magazine (January 1985) 50:64-65

A stiff wire brush can simulate the craggy texture that occurs in natural weathering. If the wood is still bland, add graining with a table fork. The sample at right shows progressive 'aging' of a molding stick, compared with a naturally aged block.

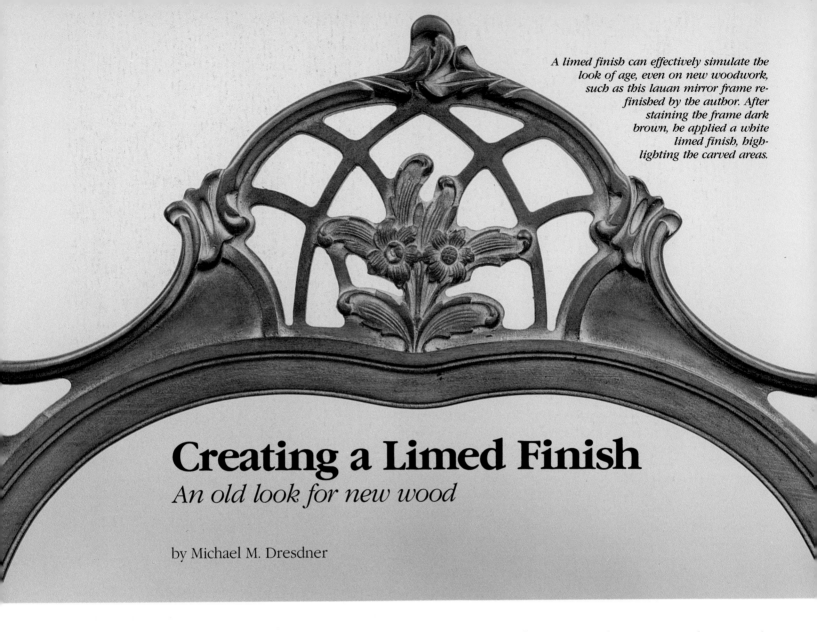

A limed finish can effectively simulate the look of age, even on new woodwork, such as this lauan mirror frame refinished by the author. After staining the frame dark brown, he applied a white limed finish, highlighting the carved areas.

Creating a Limed Finish
An old look for new wood

by Michael M. Dresdner

With its soft, ghostly white appearance, a limed finish imparts instant history to any new piece of furniture. And although it's one of the most common techniques used to create antique reproductions that mimic the appearance of aged furniture, in recent years, limed or "pickled" finishes have also become popular for new furniture, cabinets and flooring. A limed finish creates the look of a once-finished piece that was later painted over and then redeemed through an incomplete job of stripping. For the most part, it looks like a natural wood finish, but it has telltale traces of white, off-white or even colors trapped in the wood's pores or in the corners of carvings and moldings. Fortunately, a limed finish is easy to create, and the application techniques are accessible to even the neophyte wood finisher.

Traditionally, the limed finish was used to artificially age and darken oak (hence the often-used name "limed oak") to make it resemble a richer and more expensive wood, such as mahogany. The process involved soaking the wood in a mixture of lime, ammonia, lye and water until the color of the wood darkened. The name of the finish comes from the lime (calcium oxide) used in this mixture. Curiously, a modern limed finish has just the opposite appearance, with its "age" added by making the piece appear to have been painted and stripped, rather than just darkened.

In spite of its affiliation with oak, a limed finish works on almost any light-color wood. You can apply a coat of paint, usually white, and then wipe or sand off the bulk of it to allow the wood to show through. The finish can be applied to a raw, stained or sealed wood surface, depending on the desired final look. When the paint is dry, a light topcoat of satin or matte lacquer seals and protects the finish.

Selecting the paint—Because relatively little paint remains on the surface, almost any paint or pigment can be used for a limed finish—even those that are normally incompatible with the intended topcoat. Hence, you can use oil, Japan colors (available from Wood Finishing Supply Co., 100 Throop St., Palmyra, N.Y. 14522; 315-597-3743), latex, or enamel paints, pigmented white shellac or universal tints in virtually any vehicle, including lacquer. On raw wood, I prefer white latex or enamel paint, depending on what stain or dye I am using. On sealed wood, I like to use either white enamel or, for a faster-working finish, BIN, a white-pigmented shellac made by William Zinsser & Co., 39 Belmont Dr., Somerset, N.J. 08875; (201) 469-8100. BIN cannot be used over a shellac sealer, as it will redissolve it, so I generally use it on a piece sealed with a lacquer sanding seal. If you're working on a large surface and need lots of time before the paint dries, try using artists' white oil colors dissolved in mineral spirits and linseed oil.

Although white or off-white paint is most commonly used, most any light color creates a limed finish. In south Florida during the early '70s, pastel versions of limed finishes on pine became so popular that they were whimsically referred to as pickled pink pine. For convenience, I'll refer to the color as white throughout this article.

Applying the finish—After finish-sanding the wood, you must decide if you want to apply a stain, which will influence the color of

From *Fine Woodworking* magazine (December 1989) 79:82-83

the translucent white paint that will be applied over it; for example, a raw umber will give the white a grayish cast, while burnt umber or sienna will yield a warmer pinkish or orange tone. In some cases, you may need a colored stain to counter the natural tint of the wood, which itself will affect the color of the white layer. If you do not seal the wood as part of the finish (as I'll describe), make certain you avoid compatibility problems: Applying a white latex paint over a water-soluble dye or an oil-base enamel over an oil stain will cause the colors to bleed through into the white material. Sealing the wood after applying the stain will prevent these problems.

Even though most limed finishes are applied directly over raw wood, you can also use the finish on wood that's been sealed first. Each approach yields a subtly different look, but the results are equally satisfying. For a limed finish on raw wood, liberally apply the white paint to the sanded surface. If a stain has been used, make sure it has dried completely. The white paint is handled rather like a glaze: It is first applied and then selectively wiped off while it is still wet. The paint that isn't wiped off settles into the pores and crevices of the wood, creating the aged look. If you take off too much paint, you can simply apply more. If you leave too much on, wait until the paint dries and sand some of it off with 120- or 220-grit paper. Rougher sandpaper will give a more consistent, visually textured look, while finer paper will create a more patchy appearance.

The limed-finish process is virtually the same for sealed wood. Seal the piece with one thin coat of shellac, lacquer or varnish, but do not sand afterward; the roughness gives the white overcoat a little more bite. Apply the white as before, but be certain to choose a paint that won't redissolve the sealer coat. Since the sealed surface lacks wood's absorptive qualities, you'll have a bit more time to work the glaze, and you can usually leave the right amount of white in the corners and low spots of the carvings before the paint sets up. If you want to remove more paint after it is dry, you can generally do it with steel wool or an abrasive pad, as the white won't adhere to the sealed surface as well as it does to raw wood.

When you're satisfied with the dry white layer, seal it with two coats of flat or matte lacquer or varnish, and smooth it with sandpaper or steel wool between coats.

Antiquing finishes—If you would like to further age the look of your finish, mix a bit of rottenstone into some paste wax and apply it over the completed finish. Wipe off the excess, but leave some of the residue in the corners of moldings and carvings to simulate the appearance of years of collected dust and grime.

One rather attractive variation of the antique finish is called "scrubbed oak." This involves distressing the wood before finishing by dinging it up with wrenches, short lengths of chain or a wooden mallet bristling with exposed nails and screws. To impart realism, limit the damage to surfaces that would be worn with normal use. Sand the surfaces lightly to remove any raised, broken wood fibers around the distressed areas. Stain the wood a very light burnt umber color, and then lightly seal it with one thin coat of vinyl sealer or shellac. Next, brush on white enamel paint and wipe off most of it, leaving just a bit more white than you would like to have.

Highlighting details—Another method of mimicing the furniture aging process is dry-brushing, which uses a paint brush that's lightly loaded with pigment to add dark highlights. Perhaps the best way to approach dry-brushing is to think of it as glazing in reverse. When you glaze a piece of furniture, you apply a colored liquid glaze and then wipe it off, leaving paint in the pores and details. Dry-brushing, on the other hand, highlights or darkens the sharp

Although it's often referred to as a limed-oak finish, a limed finish can be applied to any type of wood. Here, a white ash sample, shown unfinished above, received a limed finish, which was applied directly to the raw wood.

edges and raised surfaces of furniture. Anyone who has handled old furniture will tell you that once the protective layer of finish wears off the sharp edges of a nicely carved maple or walnut piece, the exposed wood quickly picks up dirt and oils and gradually darkens.

Dry-brushing needs a rough surface to work on, so it's most often done either on raw wood or on chalky surfaces painted with white undercoat or BIN. On open-pore woods, such as mahogany, dry-brushing the flat surfaces will define the pores of the wood as the bristles catch on the edge of each pore and leave a tiny dark line. This allows you to intensify or even add realistic-looking grain patterns by creating thousands of small lines of color. Carvings, high spots and the sharp edges of panels and moldings pick up a color line that highlights the details. Often, a weak carving can be made to appear more crisp with careful dry-brushing.

My favorite brush for dry-brushing is black hog's hair, commonly known as China bristle. The brush should be rather springy and fit the hand comfortably, with the thumb on one side of the ferrule, the fingers on the other and the handle resting in the crook of the hand. I prefer a brush that is 2 in. wide, a full 3 in. long, and ⅝ in. thick, or what is referred to by brush makers as double thickness.

The first step is to mix the desired color by adding naptha or mineral spirits to Japan colors until you have a fairly thick but smooth liquid. With a small, stiff brush, such as a bridled glue brush, transfer a small amount of color from the can to a disposable mixing board; a scrap of wood will do. Load the brush by getting a small amount of almost-dry color on the tip by holding the brush at 90° to the surface and *lightly* scrubbing the tip in a circular motion through the dab of color until it appears dry. The brush will also appear dry, but it will be loaded with the Japan color. With light, sweeping movements, skim the tip of the brush across the surface of the wood, first on the flats and then on the carvings when the brush is slightly less loaded. The white surface will pick up color from the brush and impart a warm, translucent quality. When the brush stops transferring color, reload it with another dab from the mixing board. Each time color is added to the mixing board, give the color mixture a quick stir, since pigmented colors tend to settle rather quickly in the can. If no color transfers, load the brush a little heavier; however, if streaks show up, your brush is too heavy. When the dry-brushing is complete and the colors are dry, apply a protective topcoat as described for a regular limed finish. ☐

Michael Dresdner is a Contributing Editor for Fine Woodworking *and a finishing consultant in Zionhill, Pa.*

Left: To clean the wood's pores of impurities before filling, Frank uses a soft-steel-bristle brush, scrubbing lightly and with the grain. The brass-bristle brush on the bench can also be used. Right: After sealing the dyed wood with a thin coat of shellac, Frank mixes the filler made of powdered whiting with colored pigments and paste wax. He rubs the filler into the grain with a cheese-cloth applicator.

Creating a Decorative Filled Finish

Treating wood's pores for color and contrast

by George Frank

When I left my native Hungary and emigrated to Paris in 1924, I carried all my possessions in a small suitcase that couldn't have weighed more than 15 lbs. But I also carried a wood-finishing method in my head that was to keep me busy experimenting for many years to come. The wood-finishing process involved filling the pores of dyed open-grain woods with a contrasting-color filler to produce decorative effects. My old wood-technology teacher at the Technological Institute of Budapest, Hungary, had showed me an example of decorative filling years earlier on an oak desk that had been blackened and its pores loaded with white filler. The effect was striking! Although he told me that the piece had been made by Central-European cabinetmakers around the turn of the century, he couldn't tell me anything about the pore-filling process other than the composition of the white filler: plaster of Paris.

Three years later, I struck a bargain with the elderly owner of the rooming house where I lived: I repaired her furniture, and she gave me the key to a decent little workshop where I could experiment with decorative filled finishes. After endless research and hundreds of ruined samples—a potbellied stove helped me dispose of my errors and failures—I produced 15 pairs of master samples that helped my fledgling finishing business take a giant step forward.

Of all the finishing methods I've ever conjured up, the decorative filled finish is probably the most versatile and one of the most successful processes I've used to enhance wood furniture, cabinets, paneling and architectural interiors. A decorative filled finish is an easy, attractive way to dress up plain woods, giving them color and bringing out the grain pattern. It is accomplished by using a dye of one hue to color the surface of the wood, and a contrasting- or complementary-hue filler to color the pores. Thus, you can create a vast range of decorative effects, adding color as subtly or as boldly as you choose. I'll tell you how I produce a set of samples with my decorative filled finish, including preparing the wood, dyeing or staining, sealing, filling the grain, and finishing. With these methods and a little practice, you can produce decorative filled finishes, like the samples on the facing page, and use them to create colorful effects on your furniture and cabinets.

Preparing the wood—While the decorative filled finish will work on any open-pore wood, the finish is most stunning on ash or red oak. Close-pore woods, like birch or maple, won't work because the pores are too small to accept the filler. To prepare my original master samples, I started by cutting several dozen ¼-in.-thick boards. To make the proportions of the samples pleasing, I cut them 10 in. long by 6³⁄₁₆ in. wide, which corresponds to the "golden mean," a sophisticated and visually pleasing ratio discovered by the Greeks that occurs in nature.

After selecting the best-looking sample boards, I smooth each piece with a steel scraper blade, filed flat and freshly sharpened, and then sand with 100-, 120- and 150-grit papers. To keep the surfaces flat, I stretch the sandpaper over a hand-size block of marble. With sanding complete, I use a clean sponge to apply warm rainwater on the samples. You may substitute distilled or spring water for rainwater; the point is, use water free of chemical contaminants. After the wood has dried, I resand with 220-grit to clean up the raised grain.

From *Fine Woodworking* magazine (July 1990) 83:60-61

By staining or dyeing wood, sealing it and then packing the pores with a contrasting filler, you can create a decorative filled finish that adds color and brings out the grain pattern in any open-pore wood. From left to right, the samples are: red oak with black ani-line dye and plain white filler; red oak with red aniline dye and yellow-color filler; ash with walnut stain and peach-color filler; white oak with green aniline dye and blue-color filler; ash with logwood and potassium-dichromate dye and beige-color filler.

The sample boards are now smooth as a baby's bottom; next, the pores have to be cleaned, since the filler can't be introduced into pores filled with debris. I have a powerful air compressor in my shop and flush out most of the sawdust with a blow gun. Then, as shown in the left photo on the facing page, I use a dry, clean wire brush to scrub the wood with the grain to clean the pores of impurities. I prefer a brush with either soft-brass or fine-steel bristles. *Don't* use a brush with coarse, hardened-steel bristles.

Coloring the wood—The smooth, clean, dustless samples are now ready to be stained. For me, coloring the wood is a passion; I feel wood is alive and responds to my care with shades, hues, brilliance, depth and beauty that compensate me for all the preparatory work. To color my first sets of samples, I used mostly natural dyes, combined with some color-producing chemicals. For example, I combined brazilwood extract with varying concentrations of dichromate of potassium to create attractive reds, from crimson to pale pink. One of these colors is shown in the sample on the right. Another one of my favorite colors comes from a natural dye made from walnuts called "brou de noix." This dye changes a light-color wood to a rich brown color, as shown in the center sample. All my natural coloring ingredients are water soluble, and I use them as warm as I can handle, to get better penetration. For more on natural and chemical dyes, see my book, *Adventures in Wood Finishing* (The Taunton Press, 1981) and my article on pp. 24-27. A variety of natural and chemical dyes are available from Olde Mill Cabinet Shoppe, 1660 Camp Betty Washington Road, York, Pa. 17402.

As my Paris wood-finishing business grew during the 1920s to employ over two dozen workers (a success bolstered by my winning France's prestigious "Brevet d'Invention" award in 1928 for my finishing processes), we were faced with larger commissions requiring decorative filled finishes done by the square meter. I then reluctantly replaced my natural and chemical dyes with aniline dyes. The little lost in the sheer beauty of the natural dyes is gained back in consistency and ease of application with the anilines. I favor the German Arti brand dyes (available from Highland Hardware, 1045 N. Highland Ave., Atlanta, Ga. 30306), preparing them according to the directions on the package. To apply the dye, I saturate a small piece of scrap foam rubber and wipe it with the grain, using long, overlapping strokes. If you use a water-base aniline, you may need to lightly resand the wood with very fine paper.

Once the wood is dyed, I apply a coat of shellac using the French-polishing method. Using a tampon (but *no* lubricating oil), I rub on several breath-thin layers of shellac, so that the wood's dyed color is well protected by a transparent shield, but the pores remain open and clean. For more on this, see "French Polishing" on pp. 56-59.

Mixing and applying the filler—I filled the pores on my earliest samples with plaster of Paris, but cleaning off the hardened excess proved too time-consuming. Therefore, I improved the filler mix-ture by substituting a new basic ingredient: whiting, a powdered chalk sometimes called "gilder's whiting," (available from local hardware stores or Pearl Paint Co., Canal Street, New York, N.Y. 10013). This mixture not only fills pores well, but excess is easy to clean off. To make colored filler for a decorative finish, I combined about a cup of whiting with a couple of teaspoons of colored pigment powder (sometimes called earth colors or fresco colors, and available from Constantine, 2050 Eastchester Road, Bronx, N.Y. 10461). Mix the whiting and pigment into a paste by adding a little varnish maker's and painter's (VM&P) naphtha or mineral spirits until the filler is slightly thicker than toothpaste. Also to this mix, I add a teaspoon or so of regular paste wax (available at hardware stores or supermarkets), which acts as a binder. Don't substitute a specially formulated automotive wax, as it may contain petroleum oils or silicones that can cause finishing problems later.

To use the filler, mix it in a clean container, stirring it into a smooth, heavy paste. Then, using a piece of cheese cloth, wipe the paste on the colored wood surface, forcing it into the pores by rubbing in a swirling motion (see the photo at right on the facing page). After the pores are loaded, use a clean piece of cheese cloth and wipe off the excess filler (you don't have to wait for it to dry) *across the grain*. The filler dries completely in two to three days, depending on the thickness of the mixture and the humidity in your area.

Final finishing—With the samples sporting deep, well-defined colors, with contrasting fillers emphasizing the natural markings of the wood, the next job is to preserve and protect the colors with a topcoat of finish. While you can apply most common finishes (such as oil, varnish and shellac) over the filler, it's a good idea to seal the surface with shellac before topcoating and to check finish compatibility on a sample before doing an entire piece.

Now that I've given you the basics for preparing a decorative filled finish, experiment with different stains or dyes and color combinations. You may choose to leave the wood natural and add wild colors—maybe even metallic pigment—to the filler. Another possibility is to bleach the wood before filling and use a very light-color filler, to create a soft, weathered effect. Each of these options works well with my techniques. Just take careful notes and keep track of how you prepare each mixture, so you can duplicate it if it's a winner.

In conclusion, I'll leave you with a true story about how much a decorative filled finish can appeal to a customer. In 1935, I had my eyes on a revolutionary new car, the Citroen 6. Unfortunately, not only was it costly, it was hard to get: one could wait two or three years for delivery. So, I went to the local Citroen dealer, with samples in hand, and I told him, "I would be honored to refinish the paneling in your showroom, if you're willing to do me a little favor…" Three months later, yours truly was driving his own Citroen 6 around the streets of Paris, with a smile on his face. □

George Frank is a master wood finisher living in South Venice, Fla.

Author Hanisch renders a contemporary version of the colorful heart motif, a favorite of traditional Pennsylvania-German chestmakers.

Pennsy Painted Chests

Vivid colors brighten the basic box

by Ric Hanisch

I must confess that I don't have a ready answer when people ask me why I started making painted chests. Inspired by the colorful vitality of the old Pennsylvania chests I'd seen, I wanted to explore their potential as a contemporary mode of expression. The simple joinery, the easily worked woods and the fluency of the decoration led me to think that these chests might become an economic cornerstone of my business. I've since found the chests to be a special kind of challenge to my skills as a designer-craftsman.

The painted chests that were popular in the early 19th century in regions of Pennsylvania settled by German immigrants have directly influenced my work. The decorated-chest tradition itself dates to Renaissance Germany and Switzerland, where chests were among the earliest forms of furniture, both for sitting on and for storing household goods such as clothing and linens. In 17th-century Germany, a wealthy merchant could have afforded to commission an elaborate chest, perhaps decorated with bold carving or rich intarsia (a technique in which

pictorial designs are made by inlaying bits of colored wood). While European chests were made by professional cabinetmakers, most Pennsylvania work was probably a sideline for a farmer with diverse skills. Most likely the painting was done by the maker, a member of his family, or some competent member of the community.

The six-board chest (four sides, a bottom and a lid) was a common construction when wide lumber was readily available. The piece was dressed up with trestle, turned or bracket feet and usually a plinth or series of moldings that smoothed the transition from carcase to base. Old chests show a delightful variety of form, from crude, unadorned boxes to refined pieces sporting sophisticated architectural facades. Sizes range from 50-in. long, 24-in. high chests to diminutive boxes less than a foot long. Tulip poplar and white pine were the favored woods because they were easy to get and their mild grain, when hand-planed, provided an excellent surface for painting. Occasionally you'll see chests made of walnut, but

Photos: Ric and Mary Hanisch

these usually were treated with a clear finish, not paint.

As the drawing below shows, constructing a chest is pretty much straight-ahead woodworking. The carcase is dovetailed together and the bottom fitted into a rabbet. The architectural facade, if used, is made up in separate elements and nailed or glued onto the front. Before I assemble a carcase, I plane the inside, which will be left unfinished. I fit the hinges (fabricated to my specifications by a local blacksmith) and fasten them permanently with clinched-over wrought nails. Inside, a small lidded box called a till fits into grooves during carcase assembly. The till is handy for holding valuables and has another practical

function: when it's open, it props the main lid at a convenient angle so you can root through the chest's contents.

I like to think of the woodworking portion of making a chest as preparing a three-dimensional canvas. On this blank surface, paint brings an idea to life. The interplay between the chest's form and the paint is an important element in developing a design, so I experiment with proportion and details such as the plinth and feet. For me, this is serious business. I want each successive chest to show greater fluency in paintwork, which comes only with practice. Doors, stools, old chairs, short runs of mirror frames, small boxes, and spoon racks provide places for

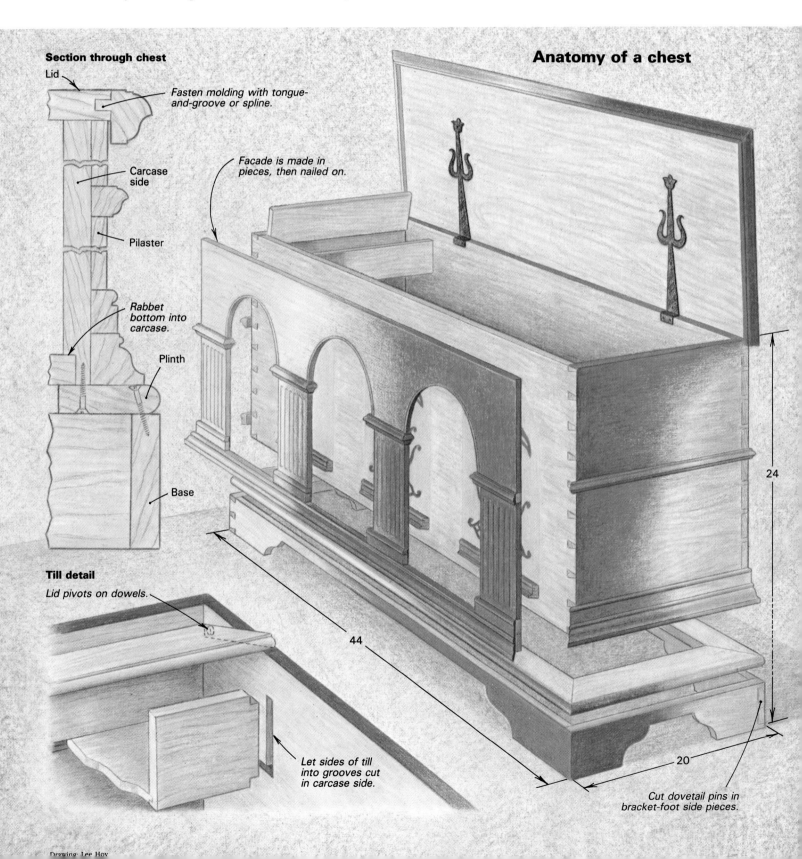

Section through chest

Lid

Fasten molding with tongue-and-groove or spline.

Carcase side

Pilaster

Rabbet bottom into carcase.

Plinth

Base

Till detail

Lid pivots on dowels.

Let sides of till into grooves cut in carcase side.

Anatomy of a chest

Facade is made in pieces, then nailed on.

24

44

20

Cut dovetail pins in bracket-foot side pieces.

Drawing: Lee Hov

me to test painting technique, study color relationships and evaluate materials, thereby broadening the limits of what's possible in a piece.

The painting on traditional chests displays a rich variety of subjects, many dealing with the symbolism and mythology of medieval Europe. Blooming flowers, fanciful birds called *distelfinks,* rearing unicorns, and bold geometric motifs—some reminiscent of the hex signs painted on Pennsylvania-German barns—are quite common. I aim for a more contemporary aesthetic, usually by choosing a strong idea and then organizing the rest of the

work to buttress this central theme. Controlling the many variables to achieve a balanced whole takes deliberate effort. As the work proceeds, I carefully review the results. How does it read at fifty feet, at ten feet and at one foot? How does it feel to the touch? Some old chests have remarkable tactile qualities, which the maker produced by manipulating thick coats of wet paint.

Creating a cohesive painted design requires discipline. I like to develop full-size drawings, exploring ideas before taking up the brush. I find that ideas come rather easily; the problem is keeping track of them before they fade from memory. I've taken to

If color is a painted chest's rhythm, texture is its harmony. A paper dauber stabbed into the wet paint stippled the orange background on the chest above. Below, an architectural facade, made separately and nailed on, dresses up a boxy chest front.

filing all my sketches. This rich mine of information provides a practical tool for future projects. And a quick leaf-through also tells me how much time I've spent on the design for a particular project—a figure I need if I expect the price of the work to reflect the effort that went into it. Design time on just the paint for the heart chest (p. 116), for example, totaled about 35 hours, including development of technique and paint tests.

Once I've designed the major elements, I scribe them onto the chest with dividers and a knife so outlines can be seen through the accumulating layers of paint. Then I'm ready to begin painting. The first step is to seal the raw wood with a wash coat of shellac. I make the wash coat from what I call my stock solution—a pound of shellac flakes dissolved in about a quart of alcohol. I filter the stock solution and dilute it by adding one part stock to four parts alcohol.

I apply undercoating next. This coat, which is the background color on which the other designs will be painted, can be a flat oil- or water-based house paint, or a tinted artists' gesso. Since I choose the color to match subsequent opaque coats, or to provide background color for transparent or textured layers, I may have to apply several undercoats on different parts of the same chest. Before working on the actual piece, I prepare sample panels so I can check the color and workability of the paints and brushstrokes I'll be using. After smoothing the undercoats with a Scotch-Brite pad, I seal the surface with shellac to ensure that subsequent coats will be absorbed evenly and to allow mistakes to be wiped off without permanently staining the surface.

For the top layers of paint, I prefer oil-based finishes, either manufactured enamels combined with a tung-oil paint base called Waterlox, or Waterlox mixed with dry pigments or artists' oil paints. Waterlox, available at most paint stores or through Waterlox Chemical and Coating Co., 9808 Meech Ave., Cleveland, Ohio 44105, is a versatile additive. It makes the paint flow more easily and dry more quickly, and the final film is a good deal tougher than that of straight enamel—an important consideration because a chest that's to be used will be subjected to a lot of wear. Another method—which probably is excellent for the beginner—is to mix pigments with shellac, thinned to the appropriate viscosity. Shellac paints are quite thin and flow easily but dry quickly, so they're unsuitable for texturing. They're "one stroke" paints. Using two strokes doubles the paint thickness and intensifies the color.

I've experimented with two kinds of dry pigments: artists' colors and bulk pigments sold as colorants for concrete. The masonry pigments, though cheaper, aren't as finely ground and they come in fewer colors. You sometimes can buy them at local hardware stores for $1.50 to $2.50 per pound. Artists' colors vary widely in cost. Earth colors and titanium dioxide (white) are at the lower end of the scale; vermilion, cadmium yellows and reds, and some blues and greens are at the upper end, costing $36 or more per pound. Pigments also vary in coloring power, ease of mixing, transparency, permanence and toxicity. Some act as catalysts to accelerate drying; some mix up to unusual consistencies (ultramarine gets stringy) or are difficult to disperse in oil. Using a muller or a mortar and pestle helps disperse the pigment in the oil medium. Ralph Mayer's *The Artist's Handbook of Materials and Techniques* (Viking Press, 1981) is a good general reference on this subject.

To mix a color, first add a little oil paint or Waterlox to a small amount of pigment, thoroughly wetting it. Once you've got a homogeneous paste, add more oil until you have the desired color and consistency. A little turpentine will thin the mix-

ture and slow drying, buying you additional time for texturing the surface. Whiting (calcium carbonate) provides bulk without changing the color value appreciably.

To make brushing easier, wipe large areas to be filled with color with a turps-dampened cloth. Brushes vary widely in kind and quality, and choosing the right one is important. When I'm aiming for a particular effect, I may try several brushes, or even modify one by trimming it. Once I've found one that performs a particular function well, I keep it in good condition with careful cleaning. Good natural-bristle brushes are made from the best materials, and even the novice will notice the difference in performance. Also, a good brush will outlast a cheaper one.

In painting a chest design, I start with the broader background colors, then progress to the finer detail. At this point, I might begin adding some texture to the still-wet paint by manipulating it with a brush, dabbing it with a sponge or my finger, or dragging a feather, corncob or perhaps a rolled-up wad of paper through the film. The possibilities are endless. On the heart chest, I textured the green heart with a feather and marbleized the yellow background by dabbing dry color into the wet paint with crumpled paper and Q-tips. Testing paints on a scrap panel is particularly important, however, since each color mixture can be textured only during a critical time period, which varies with daily conditions. If you start too soon, you may find that the paint is too wet to be worked; wait too long and the paint will be too stiff. With a fast-drying paint, I sometimes have a helper do the painting so I can concentrate on texturing.

The safest painting procedure is to allow one color area to dry, then seal it with a shellac wash coat before doing an adjacent color. Flowers, figures, borders and moldings are then painted in to connect the various details. At this point, the reflective qualities of the paints will vary from color to color, depending on the amount of whiting and turps used—both substances tend to flatten the paint surface. To even out surface sheen, richen the colors and give a protective surface film, I rub on a glaze of Waterlox mixed with a tiny bit of whatever pigment brings out the colors best.

I realize that all this will seem rather complicated to someone about to try decorative painting for the first time. In fact, if it had been explained to me this way before I felt the urge to paint, I might not have made the attempt. Confidence, born of ignorance and tempered by experience, kept alive my desire. This is a skill you can teach yourself without enduring years of frustration. Remember, the rural chest decorator of 1750 worked with no formal training and a limited palette, yet was able to achieve results that remain powerful statements of the spirit.

I grew up in a rural New Jersey house built as a church in 1880. There are still traces of the original painted adornments—stenciled fleurs-de-lis on wainscoting and cherubs holding an open Bible. During the 40 years my folks have lived there, most of the flat surfaces carpentered by my father have been enhanced with decorations painted by my mother . . . fish and anemones in the bathroom, mountain scenes down the hall, giraffes and skeletons in the closets, oriental landscapes in the stairwell. Furniture, trays, lamps—nothing was safe. It's strange but true that until a year ago I didn't make the connection that, in fact, I do come from a tradition of decorative painting. And in that way, I am indebted to the past and responsible to my own future. □

Ric Hanisch, a member of Guild X in Bucks County, Pa., has a masters degree in architecture and has worked as a builder. He designs and makes furniture in Haycock Township, Pa.

Flat, interior latex house paints tinted with artist's acrylics give the author all the leeway he needs to achieve a variety of surface effects. The cabinet hanging below the table, left, was painted and then shaded with graphite before being sealed with several clear

coats of Wood Armor for durability. On the table itself and the small stand, center, succeeding coats of paint were sanded through to reveal the color from the previous coat. At right, latex-base putty was used to texture the cabinet's doors.

Painting Furniture
Protecting brushed latex colors with a clear spray topcoat

by Douglas Redmond

Have you ever heard of a lacquer hangover? I hadn't when I started painting my furniture a few years ago. My designs demanded color, so I did some reading and discovered that the professional way to color wood was to spray lacquer. But after working with colored lacquer finishes for three years, I started to get lacquer hangovers, 24-hour headaches that just about made me blind. This is not to say that I didn't wear a respirator and take proper precautions; I did. But by the time I'd reached my early twenties, I had become sensitized or allergic to lacquer. I needed to approach furniture painting from a safer, less-toxic direction.

My choice for a colored finish was latex-base paint: interior, flat latex house paint to be exact. House paint has the characteristics I was looking for. It is safe and easy to apply, it comes in a wide variety of colors at a reasonable price ($4 to $6 per quart) and it can be found at any paint store. But latex paint had two major problems: the colors weren't robust and the painted surface was fairly fragile. A good friend and fellow woodworker showed me how to overcome the fragile nature of the paint with Wood Armor, a clear latex-base wood finish made by Deft Inc. (17451 Von Karman Ave., Irvine, Cal. 92714) and available at most paint-supply stores in gloss or satin finish. Applying a few clear coats of Wood Armor protects the painted surface and provides a hard, durable finish.

With the fragility problem solved, I began to experiment with the paint, trying to expand the range of colors. Because it took only 6 ozs. per coat for a small stand, like the one in the center photo above, I found I could easily increase my color range and intensity by

adding a few dabs of artist's acrylic paint to it. Tubes of artist's acrylics are available at art-supply stores in an array of vibrant colors. It's impractical to use them exclusively for painting large pieces of furniture because a few ounces cost as much as a quart of house paint. Besides, the vinyl in the acrylics makes them more apt to roll up or clog sandpaper when sanding between coats, just as the additives in satin or gloss paints do. In addition, their "slippery" finish causes adhesion problems for the Wood Armor. If you want a gloss finish for the final coat, simply use gloss-formula Wood Armor.

Through the years, I've experimented with different surface effects, as you can see from the pieces in the three photos above. I've painted over textured surfaces, sanded through one coat to let the previous coat show through, shaded with colored pencils and powdered graphite, and applied gold leaf, and I've locked all these coatings beneath clear coats of Wood Armor. When people ask me about the durability of this finish, I show them a set of screwdrivers, the wooden handles of which were among the first objects I painted using this method. They've been knocking around in a toolbox tray with pliers and wrenches for about seven years. Although the screwdrivers show some normal wear and some hard-won nicks, their color is still bright and the finish is still strong. I've been happy with this method for adding color to my furniture, but I'm even happier knowing I'm using a finish that's not detrimental to my health.

Construction and surface preparation—Long before starting the finishing process, and even before beginning the building

From *Fine Woodworking* magazine (September 1989) 78:51-53

process, you must consider the wood surface you'll be painting. If you want a smooth finish without having to fill the wood's pores, maple, poplar, birch and birch plywood work well. If you have to fill open pores, you may find yourself spending more time finishing the piece than building it. However, if necessary, you can fill the pores after the piece is built with a thin coat of spackling paste applied with a 4-in.- or 6-in.-wide drywall knife. Remove as much of the excess spackling as possible to cut down on the amount of sanding you'll have to do later. Of course, you could also leave the pores unfilled so they show through the paint and give the final finish a textured effect.

Contrary to popular belief, using paint as a finish does not let you cheat on your construction techniques or your surface preparation. I use traditional joinery and I don't rely on Bondo or putty to hide poor craftsmanship. Wood movement caused by seasonal changes in humidity will eventually expose any joints that were repaired with large amounts of putty. A good rule of thumb for painted furniture is to approach the finishing process the same way you would for a clear finish: The piece must be as perfect as possible.

After the piece is built, I first scrape all the surfaces that will be painted. The scraping eliminates most small defects in the surface and gives me a chance to locate any others that need to be filled. I use latex-base wood putty, such as Elmer's Wood Filler. If you prefer sanding to scraping, work up to about 120-grit. The idea here is to get the piece smooth; there's no need to overwork it. I almost always break the sharp edges by block-planing a small bevel. This has two advantages. First, a beveled edge on the finished piece is less likely to get dinged up, and second, the bevel reduces the amount of excess paint that's left on the adjacent side (rollover) when the brush is dragged over a sharp edge.

Applying the paint—Manufacturers generally recommend applying oil-base primer as a foundation for interior latex house paint. The oil-base primer is meant to penetrate the wood or wall surface to help create a better bond for subsequent coats of paint. However, I prefer to start with the water-base latex. The first coat seems to adhere well enough for my purposes and also lets me see how the piece will look in color. This is a major consideration if you have never worked with color. An unpainted birch table makes an entirely different impression than the same table painted in mixed hues of blue. I approach color intuitively; I often start with a base color that is quite different from the desired final color, steering each coat a little closer to the desired hue. It's not a question of progressing from light to dark or vice versa; in fact, I often use entirely different colors and sand through one coat to see the previous one.

The painting process is easy and straightforward. It isn't nec-

Redmond sands the first coat thoroughly to smooth any raised grain. Even the beveled edges get a once-over. You can see by the paint dust on the cabinet's top that flat latex paint can be sanded without clogging the paper.

essary to thin the paint with water unless the paint is old and thick. The best way to apply the paint is also one of the cheapest—foam brushes. They come in a number of sizes, give almost a strokeless finish and are easily cleaned. With the money saved on foam brushes, I bought a couple of expensive nylon brushes for detail work.

The paint should always be applied in the direction of the wood grain. If you brush across the grain, sooner or later the grain will stand out as running perpendicular to the brush strokes. When dealing with mitered corners and other intersections where grain direction changes, always apply the paint so it mimics the construction, as shown in figure 1 below. Miters should be painted so you're left with a mitered brush stroke. Running the brush across a miter is a mistake that will eventually show up. With mortise-and-tenon joints, or any joint that results in one surface butting into the other, the brush stroke on the mortised piece should cut off the brush stroke on the tenoned piece.

In 30 to 60 minutes, the first coat will be dry. The painted areas will have sections of raised grain and may show small imperfections that were not filled. Lightly sand all the painted areas to cut

Fig. 1: Brush strokes mimic construction

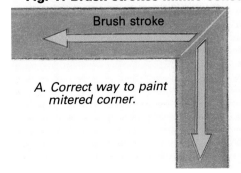

A. Correct way to paint mitered corner.

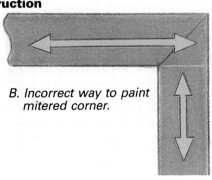

B. Incorrect way to paint mitered corner.

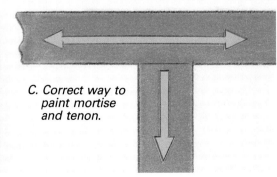

C. Correct way to paint mortise and tenon.

Drawing: Roland Wolf

Finishes and Finishing Techniques **121**

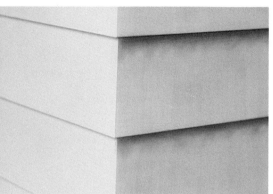

Before sealing the painted surface of this small cabinet with Wood Armor, powdered graphite is brushed on (above) to give the beveled siding a weathered look (below).

After the first three coats of Wood Armor have dried, the author uses a cabinet scraper to smooth out any dust particles. He then applies two final coats of the clear finish.

the raised grain, and then fill and sand any remaining small defects with wood filler. Use 120-grit paper throughout the painting process. Finer sanding may even retard the adhesion of the next coat; besides, with a brushed-on finish, any finer sanding is really just overkill. After the first coat dries, I sand the large, flat areas with a small orbital sander. However, for succeeding coats, I lightly hand-sand (see the photo on p. 121), partly to avoid sanding through to the color below and partly because each coat usually requires less sanding to achieve a smooth surface. Before moving on to the second coat of paint, run your hand over the entire surface to be sure you've sanded every inch, and then wipe down the piece with a damp rag to remove paint dust.

The additional coats of paint are applied with a foam brush in the same way as the first coat. If you begin each coat on the bottom of the furniture or on some other obscure area, it gives you a chance to look at the color and make adjustments before you paint the crucial areas. Three coats is the minimum to ensure good coverage, although I apply five coats on the average piece. Any more than five coats and you've probably gone beyond the point of diminishing returns; the extra buildup doesn't have any real advantage and the thick paint is more likely to chip. I don't sand the last coat of paint unless I intend to sand through to the previous coat. The painted finish is now at its most fragile stage; any scratch will cause a burnished area in the paint, which will result in discoloration when the clear coat is applied. Avoid touching the painted surface; the oils left by your fingerprints will sometimes cause dull spots in the clear coat.

Special effects and final finish—Before applying the first coat of Wood Armor, I apply colored pencil, graphite or charcoal if I want a shaded or mottled effect. The photos above, left, show how I used powdered graphite to achieve a weathered look on the small cabinet that hangs below the table in the left photo on p. 120. With the cabinet in a horizontal position, I use a brush to apply the

graphite below the overlap of each course of the beveled siding. Then, I tip the cabinet so the graphite runs across the siding, and I lightly brush off the excess, shown in the top photo above at left. When overhead light strikes the cabinet, the shading adds depth, exaggerating the actual shadow line of the siding; straight-on light fools you into thinking that the overlap is just an illusion created by the shading. In either case, the clapboard siding and the graphite shading combine to create a familiar picture of a weathered building, shown in the bottom photo above at left.

I usually let the paint dry overnight before spraying on the clear coats of Wood Armor. There's nothing tricky about doing this; follow the tips given in the article on spray finishing on pp. 89-95 and clean your spray gun with soap and water when you're done. There is no reason you can't brush on the clear coats. Although spraying gives you a slightly smoother final finish, I have used both methods. I start with three light coats of Wood Armor, and let each coat dry completely (one to two hours depending on the temperature and humidity) before applying the next coat. I then scrape the piece to remove any dust particles that may be trapped in the finish, as in the photo above, right. Caution must be used here. If you wear through the clear coat to the painted surface during scraping, the next clear coat will cause discoloration in that area. This type of wear-through problem can only be solved by repainting the whole area. Take heart though: A sharp scraper is a trusty tool to use on finishes. Apply light pressure and don't bow the scraper as you might when scraping bare wood. If the idea of scraping a clear finish makes you uneasy, you can sand with 220-grit wet/dry paper wrapped around a block of wood and lubricated with water and a little soap. After the scraping or sanding is complete, I apply two more coats of Wood Armor and rub the last coat with rottenstone and water. □

Douglas Redmond is professor of wood design at The City University of New York, Covenent Avenue at 138th Street, New York, N.Y. 10031.

Painted Carvings
Translucent color from linseed and oil paints

by John Heatwole

Several years ago, I received a commission to design and carve figures for the Christmas window display at Neiman-Marcus in Washington, D.C. I wanted my painted carvings to be colorful, yet subtle, so I began trying to duplicate the finishes on some carvings I had seen as a child at the home of a neighbor who had traveled extensively in Europe.

I was always fascinated by the way the grain of the carved wood showed through the translucent colors on her carvings. There was also a nut-brown richness underlying the finish that, through the years, I saw in almost every carving that came out of Germany, Austria or Northern Italy. I figured the colors were produced by stains, but could never duplicate them. Oil paints, acrylic art colors and watercolors didn't work, nor did the undercoatings, sprays, waxes, or dry-brush techniques I tried. The oil colors I'd been using were often so thick and opaque that you couldn't tell if the carving was wood or plaster. Diluting the colors hadn't helped; thinner coats just ran and blurred through the wood grain.

One night, just as I was dozing off, an idea came to me. I decided I'd try staining the carvings with a thin, brown undercoat before applying any colors. The next morning I put the idea to the test. I squeezed a long strand from a tube of raw sienna oil color onto a palette. The raw sienna color was pretty close to the rich brown I'd seen on the old carvings. Next, I added boiled linseed oil and blended the two until the brown mixture was nearly the consistency of the plain linseed oil. I liberally applied the brown stain to a 14-in.-tall basswood carving, and let the color soak in for a few moments before wiping off the excess with several soft paper

Heatwole's carvings reflect his love of history and storytelling. The wizard roams his medieval fantasies; the Gypsy queen enlivens an old family story.

towels. Then I mixed the colors I wanted for the details, diluting each with boiled linseed oil until it was the same consistency as the initial base stain, and applied them with an artists' brush.

This technique changed my work. Now I had colors that were simultaneously rich and subtle, and the grain of the wood showed beautifully. By using small artists' brushes, 00 or 000, I could do the most intricate details and not worry about colors diffusing or running together, not even on endgrain. The color stayed in the spot where my brush touched.

There was no scientific thought in this, just my idea that perhaps the nut-brown, antique-ivory patina of the old European carvings was due to an undercoat of brown stain. Besides coloring the wood, I believe this raw sienna/linseed oil undercoat fills the wood's hollow fibers. When I touched other colors to the wood, they stayed in place because adjoining fibers, which are normally hollow, were filled with the undercoat, which prevented bleed-over yet allowed color to be absorbed wherever the brush touched.

Eventually, I discovered that time was a crucial factor in the process. If I started staining a piece late in the day and left it partially unfinished overnight, colors applied the next day would just sit on the surface and not sink into the wood. Apparently once the raw sienna begins to harden, it won't allow the other colors to be absorbed. Now, I start my staining early in the morning and work rapidly, so I can complete the process before the oils harden.

Discovering this staining method was significant for me because I'd always used color to help convey the story behind each of my characters. I enjoy telling people about my characters and where they came from because I think that if you know the story behind the carving, you'll feel closer to it. The stories are also personally significant. My fantasy pieces come from the books of my childhood—kings and castles and wizards of the dark ages in England and Wales, where part of my family originated. The folk pieces developed from my family's Germanic heritage, and the experiences we've had since settling in Virginia's Shenandoah valley in 1760. I've been fascinated with this blend of legend and history, folklore and family, fantasy and humor as long as I can remember.

The Gypsy Queen of Ottobine is a good example of how I rely on color. Note her red comforter. It's an essential part of the character because it was given to the Gypsy by my great-great-grandmother, Elizabeth, during the dark days following the Civil War. The Gypsy came one afternoon and said, "Mrs. Heatwole, you have a coverlet that I've admired for years, and if you give it to me, I'll tell your fortune." After the offer was refused, the Gypsy revealed her fortune anyway, asking only that she be given the comforter if Elizabeth thought the information worthwhile. The fortune was: "You've got two men off because of the war. Tonight they'll both come home. One'll come a-walking and one'll come a-riding. One'll have money in his pocket; one'll have none." That night her brother-in-law, a Confederate cavalryman, rode in from Appomat-

tox broke and tired, and was soon followed by her husband, John, who had a pocket full of coins from picking apples in West Virginia. John, a potter and a hunter, had left the valley because he was wanted, dead or alive, for avoiding military service. When I carved him, I showed him with a panther slung over his shoulder, the man and his quarry staring quizzically at the world. □

Painting procedure

My painting system works best on basswood and Virginia mountain laurel, but it doesn't do very well on open-grained woods like oak. The paint goes on nicely if the carving is sanded to at least 400 grit, to break all of the extremely sharp edges. This fine sanding is crucial on the face, where even the slightest amount of fuzz can distort the colors. All colors work equally well, except for black, which seems to make everything dark and murky—instead, use burnt umber for darkening. I prefer Shiva and Grumbacher oils, available at artists' supply stores. Grumbacher's raw sienna is the best shade of brown for the undercoat; other brands seem a little too green to me.

In the photos I show how to paint the Gypsy queen, a 14-in. figure that I carved from basswood. I begin by squeezing a long strand of raw sienna oil paint directly from the tube onto a paper palette, add boiled linseed oil and whisk it briskly (1) until the mixture is translucent, no thicker than the original linseed. Thorough mixing is important; otherwise the wash leaves dark-colored streaks on the wood.

I apply the stain liberally to the entire carving (2), flooding all of the surfaces, then immediately wipe off the excess (3). It's important to get all the excess out of the cracks and crevices so it doesn't interfere with the later color coats or make them look muddy. Once the undercoat is applied, I figure I have four to five hours to complete the painting before the wash coat hardens. On large pieces, I treat a half or a quarter of the carving, then completely paint that area before adding more wash. It can be difficult to blend the colors so sections painted at different times don't clash with each other, so divide the work into logical whole units, like the head or chest, rather than doing the bottom half

1. Blend raw sienna and linseed oil on a paper palette.

2. Apply the thin brown stain liberally to the carving.

3. Let stain soak in a few minutes, then towel off excess.

From *Fine Woodworking* magazine (March 1987) 63:73-75

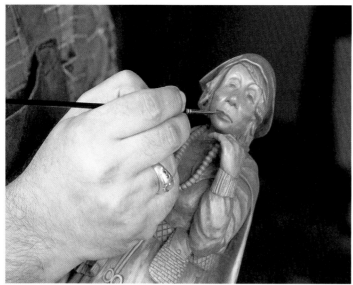

4. To make the basic fleshtones more lifelike, Heatwole adds red highlights to the cheeks and lips.

of the carving, then trying to make the top half match. You can't re-wet the areas with wash if you run out of time. If you wait too long, nothing will work.

The face is always one of the most scrutinized areas of a carving like the Gypsy queen, so I'm especially careful here and use very dilute mixtures of oil colors and boiled linseed oil. I begin by applying a fleshtone for the face, a mixture of white, red and raw sienna, then immediately, in sort of a wet-on-wet technique, a ruddy red color to highlight the cheeks and add details like the lips (4). The colors as they appear on the palette give you a pretty good idea of what the colors will dry like on the wood, although sometimes the blues and greens are a little more vibrant when dry. I generally try to do the light shades before the dark colors. This way I can use the dark colors to cover over any mistake I might make in the lighter ranges. Again, working with a wet-on-wet technique, I apply dark colors—such as burnt umber or burnt sienna—to create shadows on the carving, which makes the colors seem more realistic.

On detailed areas like the Gypsy's kerchief, I paint the area white before putting in the blocks of color. With a fine 000 brush (5), I can put down a pattern of squares or diamonds as small as $\frac{1}{16}$ in. Fine detail seems to work best when done on a slightly heavier, higher-contrast background than the rest of the carving. Many subtle accents are possible, like the white highlights applied to the carved basket pattern (6, left). Note how the color stripes and bands make the dress more interesting. Color, also, is largely responsible for visual details like the decorated beads worn by the Gypsy (6, right).

After the painted carving has dried for a couple of days, I spray it with Grumbacher's Tuffix Matte fixative, used by artists to protect charcoal and other fragile drawings. I apply several fairly heavy coats, rubbing down each coat with 0000 steel wool after the fixative dries. This spray gives each piece a very fine, satiny sheen that is pleasant to look at and makes the piece easier to clean. I have been using this system for more than seven years now, and, so far, the colors have remained translucent and have not faded.

John Heatwole is a professional woodcarver with a studio in Bridgewater, Va. His work was recently featured in an international juried exhibit of fantasy art at the Delaware Art Museum in Wilmington.

5. Heatwole paints the kerchief pattern with a fine brush.

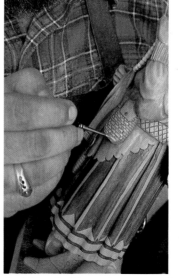

6. A bit of white paint accents basket and beads of Gypsy queen.

Index

P

Paint:
  applying, 119, 121-22
  bleed-retarding undercoat for, 123-24
  book on, cited, 119
  for carvings, 124-25
  china marker for, 106
  dipped, and moisture resistance, 19
  18th-century, classes in, 101
  fixative for, 125
  formulating, 119
  gold, 109
  latex and acrylic, applying, 110-11
  latex oversprayed, process for, 120-22
  moisture resistance of, 18-19
  Pennsylvania tradition of, 116, 118
  shellac wash-coat under, 119
  soya-tung, tested, 18-19
  supply sources for, 112
  texturing, 122
  undercoat for, 119
  See also Colors.
Paint removers:
  safe use of, 105-106
  toxicity of, 9
Penetrating-oil finishes:
  applying, 48, 49
  fire danger with, 48
  makeup of, 47
  moisture resistance of, 18-19
  oil-varnish over, 46
  with paint, technique for, 110-12
  as polish, discouraged, 62
  removing, 48
  repairing, 48
  rubbing out, 50-52
  sanding with, 46
  and shellac, 29
  tinted, 21
  See also Tung oil.
Picture frames:
  designing, 110
  driftwood finish for, 110-11
  lacquer finishes for, 79
Plaster: as filler, 28
Polishes:
  automotive rubbing compound, 51, 52
  for brass, source for, 81
  cloth for, source for, 81
  cream, source for, 65
Polyurethane: *See* Varnishes.
Potassium dichromate:
  and hardwoods, 21
  as mordant, 25, 26
Potassium permanganate: and hardwoods, 21
Pumice: for French polish, 57

R

Refinishing: supplies for, 109
Respirators:
  cartridges for, organic-vapor, 26
  source for, 39
  using, 12
  for varnish, cartridges for, 38
Rocking chairs: Boston, refinishing, 105-109
Rosin: for tack rags, 30

S

Safety sheets: reading, 13
Sanders, wide-belt: pneumatic, 83
Sanding:
  of old finishes, 62
  wax for, 62
  with blocks, Celotex, 46
Sanding sealers:
  as filler, 29
  phenolic-tung floor, tested, 18-19
  and polyurethane, 34
  soya epoxy, tested, 18-19
Sandpaper:
  discussed, 46
  for finish rubout, 50
  See also Abrasive pads.

Sapwood: coloring, 78-79
Sealers:
  polyurethane as, 65
  sanding, varnish as, 39
Shellac:
  advantages of, 42-43
  alcohol-resistant, 44
  books on, 45
  brushing, 45
  categories of, 43, 45
  for end-grain sealing, 21
  as filler, 29, 31
  and French polishing, 56-59
  hardening of, ensuring, 44
  heat damage to, repairing, 44
  history of, 42-43
  moisture resistance of, 18-19
  and other finishes, 42
  over filled wood, 115
  padding, 45
  as paint, with pigments, 119
  as paint undercoat, 110, 111, 119
  and penetrating oils, 29
  preparing, 44, 45
  rubbing out, 50-52
  seedlac, 43
  solvents for, cautions on, 44
  sources for, 43
  spraying, 44-45
  and tung oil, 29
  water damage to, repairing, 43-44
  white-pigmented, 112
Silicone:
  in lacquer, 77
  removers, commercial, 77
  removing, 77
  and varnish, dealing with, 38-39
Soap: finish-cleaning, source for, 61
Sodium carbonate: and hardwoods, 21
Solvents:
  danger from, 96-97
  organic, toxicity of, 8-12
Spray equipment:
  air consumption of, 84
  booth for, setting up, 88, 91, 94
  cleaning, 39
  explosion-proof fans for, 88
  guns for, siphon-feed, 91
  guns for, turbine-pump, 91
  lights for, explosion-proof, 88
  masking tape for use with, 67
  with polyurethane, 34
  selecting, 85, 91
  setting up, 85
  system for, designing, 86-87
  techniques for using, 92-93
  for varnish, 37-38
Stains:
  black, source for, 103
  bleed prevention for, 21
  chemical, 21
  vs. dyes, 24
  on end grain, 21
  and fillers, 21
  five-minute, 20
  gel, reviewed, 63-65
  gel, using, 64-65
  and glue, 21
  in lacquer, 21
  with limed finish, 112-13
  oil-based, 20-21, 22
  problems with, 21
  purpose of, 20
  sources for, 21
  varnish, 21
  water-based, 20-21
Stands: painted, 120
Steel wool:
  for finish rubout, 50-51
  lubricants for, 94
Stenciling:
  classes in, 101
  process of, 105-109

T

Tables: painted, 120
Tack cloths: using, 30, 37
Tortoise: faux, instruction on, 101
Trees: chemical circulation in, 27
Trompe l'oeil: classes in, 101
Tung oil:
  luster with, 31
  in oil finishes, 47, 48
  as polish, discouraged, 62
  and shellac, 29
  toxicity of, 9

V

Varnishes:
  acrylic gloss latex, tested, 18-19
  advantages of, 36-37
  aluminum-pigmented, tested, 18-19
  applying, 37
  classes in, 101
  coloring, 39
  driers for, 38
  epoxy gloss, tested, 18-19
  as filler, 29, 31
  for marbleizing, 99
  masks for, 38
  moisture resistance of, 18-19
  paper rub-down for, 99
  polyurethane,
    applying, 34-35
    exterior, 33
    as filler, 29
    glosses of, 32, 33, 35
    kinds of, tested, 32-35
    and oil mixture, 46
    over old finish, 35
    recoating of, 34
    and sanding sealers, 34
    spraying, 34-35
    two-part, tested, 18-19
  rubbing out, 50-52
  and silicone, dealing with, 38-39
  soya-alkyd phenolic-tung spar, 18-19
  stains of, 21
  water-based, applying, 40-41
  water-based, evaluated by brand, 40-41
  wax for, 39
Ventilation:
  fans for, procuring, 96
  and flash fires, 97
  heat loss from, preventing, 96
  supply sources for, 97
  systems for, designing, 96
  testing, 96
Vessels: turned burl, 49
Wall glazing: instruction in, 101

W

Walnut, black:
  dye from, 24
  filler for, 29, 30
Waterlox: as paint base, 119
Waxes:
  coloring, 39
  finish-lubricating, 51
  moisture resistance of, 17, 18, 19
  pigmented, 54
  as polish, choosing, 62
  properties of, 53-55
  as rubbing compound, 39
  solvents for, 54
  source for, 109
  using, 53-55
  for varnish, 39
Whiting: using, 115
Workshops:
  dust in, danger from, 97
  explosion-proof fixtures for, 88
  oily-rag handling in, 35, 48
  ventilating, 96-97
  See also Health hazards.